C0-ATB-111

The Maurice Case

The Maurice Case

From the Papers of
Major-General
Sir Frederick Maurice
K.C.M.G., C.B.

IIIIIIIIIIIIIIIIIIIIIIIIIIIIIIIII

Edited by
Nancy Maurice

With an Appreciation by
Major-General
Sir Edward Spears, Bart.
K.B.E., C.B., M.C.

Archon Books
1972

042874

Library of Congress Cataloging in Publication Data

Maurice, Sir Frederick Barton, 1871–1951
    The Maurice case.

    Includes bibliographical references.
    1. European War, 1914–1918—Great Britain. 2. Lloyd George,
David Lloyd George, 1st Earl, 1863–1945. I. Maurice, Nancy, ed.

II. Title.

D517.M383 1972   940.4´0942   72–3245
ISBN 0–208–00871–3

Copyright © Nancy Maurice 1972
Appreciation Copyright © Sir Edward Spears 1972
Published in Great Britain 1972
by Leo Cooper Ltd, London
and in the United States of America
as an Archon Book
by The Shoe String Press, Inc.,
Hamden, Connecticut
Printed in Great Britain

35391

Contents

0428741

Illustrations

Maps

Drawn by Patrick Leeson

35391

Acknowledgements

I have had so much and such generous help from so many that I cannot thank them as adequately as I would wish.

I owe a particular debt of gratitude to Mr F. C. Atkin of the Cabinet Office, and to Mr W. D. King, O.B.E., Chief Librarian of the Library of the Ministry of Defence.

I am also indebted to Dr Cameron Hazlehurst for the notes on General Maurice's diary, and for help in the arrangement of the material.

I am very grateful to Mr M. J. Williams, but for whose help I should not have been able to publish several of the most important documents which the book includes.

Mr D. S. Porter, Assistant to the Keeper of Western MSS at the Bodleian Library, was kind enough to read the typescript and make a number of helpful suggestions.

For permission to publish copyright material I thank the Bodleian Library, Lord Robertson of Oakridge, Mr Mark Bonham Carter, *The Spectator*, the Duke of Northumberland, Colonel N. S. G. Kirke and Earl Balfour.

My sister Peggy and her husband, Professor Eric Boyland, have given me unstinted support and encouragement.

Finally, I would like to thank Miss Nell Martindale, whose rapid and accurate typing and skill in deciphering MS letters greatly helped me.

Part I

1 An Appreciation
by Major-General Sir Edward Spears

To have been asked to write about this book is an honour. Not only is it an important contribution to history, but it gives me the opportunity of paying a tribute of respect and affection to Major-General Sir Frederick Maurice, who was my Chief in the First World War.

As the young man of under thirty I then was, I became profoundly attached to him because of the admiration he inspired in me by his thoroughness, efficiency and character; for we had nothing in common.

His detachment is well illustrated by an incident which occurred soon after the war. He had taken his daughter Nancy, the editor of this book, then nineteen years old, on a holiday to Switzerland. She, on skis for the first time, was following as best she could her father who was in animated conversation with Sir Martin Conway, both on snow shoes. Crossing a bridge of planks, our editor's skis slipped between them, leaving her hanging upside down over a torrent. Fortunately a passing ski instructor rescued her and she resumed her progress. Her father remained totally unaware of what had happened. This occasion is, to me, a vivid illustration of General Maurice: aloof, distant, unobservant of any matter he was not mentally concerned with, he no more noticed anything irrelevant to his immediate preoccupation than shadows reflected on a wall.

In writing of him and of his own Chief and mine, the Chief of the Imperial General Staff, Sir William Robertson, in *Prelude to Victory*, a book first published many years ago, I wrote:

This whale of a man (Sir William Robertson), this soldier shipwrecked on the desert island of politics, had his Man Friday. This was the Director of Military Operations, General Maurice, Freddy Maurice to the army. He

3

and his chief evoked the idea of Don Quixote and Sancho Panza reversed, if it is possible to imagine a short and portly Knight of La Mancha followed by an elongated attendant.

Maurice represented another but equally characteristic type of Englishman. As imperturbable as a fish, always unruffled, the sort of man who would eat porridge by gaslight on a foggy morning in winter, looking as if he had enjoyed a cold bath, all aglow with soap and water, just as if he were eating a peach in a sunny garden in August. A very tall, very fair man, a little bent, with a boxer's flattened-out nose, an eyeglass as flat and not much rounder than his face, and a rather abrupt manner. A little *distrait* owing to great inner concentration, he simply demolished work, never forgot anything, was quite impervious to the moods of his chief, the accurate interpreter of his grunts and groans, and his most efficient if not outwardly brilliant second. No man ever wasted fewer words or expressed himself when he spoke with greater clarity and conciseness.

An admirable character, the soul of military honour, with a deep sense of civic duty inherited from a family which placed service to the country and to the people of the country above all else, he suffered acutely from the tactics of the politicians and their too subtle methods. Mr Lloyd George in particular he came to distrust profoundly, and he finally ruined his career in the Army (though he gained the admiration of his fellow-countrymen) by defying the all-powerful Prime Minister and telling the nation the truth that was being withheld from it.

Even after this long lapse of time, I find it difficult to improve on this description.

This book is far more than the account of a tragedy in one man's life. It reveals, without solving it, the problem of Democracy at war, which will only be answered when democracies either give up being democracies or forswear war, or on the rare occasions when they throw up leaders like Abraham Lincoln, or a man possessing both character and military knowledge like Winston Churchill.

Lloyd George was not such a leader. In the Britain of 1917 there was in the first place a conflict of personalities. Lloyd George, the Prime Minister, was quick and subtle, moving from one idea to the next as lightly as a bird springs from one branch to another. In contrast, the soldiers plunged heavily from one argument to the next. Bound together, soldiers and politicians rattled against each other like the links in an iron chain.

Lloyd George, always aware of his great and growing power in the country, fresh from his victory over Asquith, but warned by his instinct of the latent power that soldiers draw from the faith of the people in their natural leaders and the massive support for them of the Conservative classes, would not tackle the Generals openly.

Straightforwardness was not the most obvious weapon in his armoury. To him the soldiers, who, it must be admitted, took little trouble to convince him, were stupid unimaginative blunderers whose outlook was that of their forebears, who had set out to war armed with stone hammers; they could conceive of no military concept beyond that of hurling men against barbed wire. On the other hand, the ideas Lloyd George put forward on military matters outraged all the teachings of military experience and history, concerning which the Prime Minister was as ignorant as he was about French poetry or the French language.

In any case he had no time to read; and if he had he would have found little guidance in the sermons in Welsh which were the only printed matter, apart from newspapers and official reports, to be found at No 10 Downing Street.

His strategic conceptions were so amateurish that the Generals, mistakenly, gave up all attempt to enlighten him. He saw little of Haig, whom he distrusted as an aristocrat of the kind he felt was instinctively opposed to his policies. Haig's shyness made him unapproachable, as did the over-strict protective layer provided by his staff to insulate him from the world. In any case, the Commander-in-Chief was tongue-tied when in the presence of the Prime Minister who found no difficulty in believing that lack of words meant lack of ideas.

Very different to Sir Douglas Haig's reaction to the Prime Minister was that of the GICS, Sir William Robertson, who was the soldier responsible for advising the Cabinet on military matters. This ex-private of Dragoons did not give the impression of having any more Celtic blood in his veins than aitches in his vocabulary. He was too English to be true, an irascible bull straight out of a Lincolnshire field. In his opinion Lloyd George's views on military matters were plain silly, too silly to argue about. So, on several occasions in Cabinet, when the Prime Minister opened an argument by saying 'CIGS, I have heard,' and then gave his fancy free rein, Wully Robertson, with a face of thunder, his eyebrows a zareba that would have kept the Zulu tribes at bay, would produce a groan that rumbled all the way up from the furthest fathom of his inside and say, 'I've 'eard different,' at the same time smacking a ruler on the table with the gesture of a governess hitting at a child's fingers showing over the edge. This was certainly hard to bear for the politician who had only to close his eyes to see immense audiences in over-crowded halls listening with bated breath to his every word, carried away by the music of his voice, hypnotised by the rhythmic melody of his sentences, which were in fact translations, perhaps unconscious, from the Welsh.

But it must be admitted that Lloyd George's interventions were exasperating to soldiers responsible for advising the Government on decisions on which depended the lives of men, perhaps the life of the nation. I need only quote an incident of which I was myself a witness.

Mr Lloyd George was in Paris, staying at the Hotel Crillon on the Place de la Concorde, and, to some suggestion of his concerning moving troops across the desert, the CIGS had objected that the plan was unworkable owing to the difficulty of getting guns over the sand.

Presently the Prime Minister saw a young officer walking across the hall whose light clothing suggested that he was probably on leave from the Middle East. The Prime Minister beckoned to him and asked him how you could move artillery across the desert. With an *aplomb* I have never forgotten, the young man, who possibly had a sense of humour and enjoyed what seemed to him a huge joke, declared that nothing was easier, you only had to wrap straw round the wheels of the guns, which would than roll across the sand as they might down Piccadilly. Whereupon Lloyd George dashed upstairs in a towering rage and summoned Wully Robertson, expatiating with flashing eyes on the stupidity of soldiers who declared a fine military coup to be impossible because the guns could not be moved across the desert; yet here was a young officer who at once gave the simple solution that had baffled the Generals. His manner and voice, even more than his words, expressed his opinion that this instance did much to explain the slaughter on the Somme.

It would, however, be unjust to lay all the blame for the mis-understandings that had become a permanent feature between soldiers and politicians on the Prime Minister. If he struggled within the prison walls his lack of understanding of the simplest facts of history and military science had built round him, it may also be advanced that the soldiers failed to realise the supreme importance of carrying with them the political leader of the nation. It was but natural, right, and proper that Lloyd George should be

6

aware of his own personal responsibilities in the conduct of the war and should endeavour to discharge them to the best of his ability.

But the soldiers did not trust him. They had completely lost faith in him and his methods as a result of the Calais Conference in February, 1917, when he had staged an ambush in agreement with the French Prime Minister, Monsieur Briand, and the new French Commander-in-Chief, General Nivelle, the object of which was to place the British Army under French Command. Lloyd George had thought out this device in order to supersede Haig and Robertson because he did not feel politically strong enough to dismiss them himself.

Personally I admired Mr Lloyd George's powers of leadership, and, save on one occasion which I have recorded elsewhere, he was kind and considerate to me.

But he was no strategist and he never accepted that strategic decisions can only be taken on the advice of military experts, and not by inspired amateurs.

The main point to remember in Mr Lloyd George's relations with the soldiers is that he has always regarded himself as a strategist. . . . For such a man strategy offers terrible temptations. It seems so simple, indeed is so simple, when considered in the abstract. With a map and an imagination one may cover the world with one's fleets and armies, deal the enemy a shrewd blow here, make an unexpected diversion there, give him an unforeseen thrust on one flank, and before he is aware what you are at hit him hard on the other flank or in the back. It is only when one comes to the application of strategy that any difficulty arises for a man who has the power of ratiocination and prides himself on being able to raise a ladder of logic from a base of fact, or, what is unfortunately not quite the same, from premises assumed to be facts. . . . Alas for himself and for the nation Mr Lloyd George forgot . . . that strategy when applied is so appallingly difficult an art that even the most carefully trained men make blunders which when they have been made, but not till then, look as if they were something that even a child should have avoided. Mr Lloyd George forgot what Cromwell told the House of Commons in his first parliamentary speech:

This I would recommend to your prudence, not to insist on any complaint or oversight of any Commander-in-Chief upon any occasion

7

whatsoever. For as I must acknowledge myself guilty of oversight, so I know they can rarely be avoided in military matters.

Lloyd George approached the problems of the war with a whole stock of untested strategical views opposition to which, or even criticism, seemed almost a crime. . . . Those who opposed him were no true friends of their country but obstacles to the winning of the war who must be removed at all costs. The fanaticism of the amateur strategist went even further than this. Not only did the men who opposed him become anathema, but even inanimate things took on a sinister hue. The whole Western front became a subject for hatred, for it was a hindrance to golden schemes that ranged from the Po to the Jordan, from Laibach to Aleppo, from Jerusalem to Trieste!*

The Prime Minister completely misread the situation in the autumn and winter of 1917. He felt certain that we were 'over-insured' on the Western front, because there was no possibility of the Germans breaking through a defensive position which had defied them, as it had us, for years. Undoubtedly he also feared, such was his distrust of the Generals, that if they were provided with the men they clamoured for, they would start a new Passchendaele. 'Blood and mud, blood and mud, that is all they can think of.'

He believed that it was sheer lack of imagination which caused the War Office to oppose so many of his brilliant schemes for winning the war elsewhere than in France.

But in fairness to the General Staff it must be said that they did not rule out 'sideshows' in principle. They had approved the Salonika operation, Allenby's campaign in Palestine and the support given to the Italians after Caporetto.

But they argued that if the Armies in France were beaten the war would be lost. They were certain, and so informed the Prime Minister, that when Russia collapsed the Germans would make their greatest effort in France, and that if the Western front was not reinforced in time, we would run a grave risk of defeat.

Unfortunately, as General Maurice's diary shows, Lloyd George would not believe them, in spite of the accumulating evidence from our Intelligence that the German divisions from the Russian front were pouring towards France. The Government refused to send the drafts from home for which the General Staff had asked, and kept

* The Amateur Strategist and the Soldiers. *Spectator*, 11 May, 1918.

8

an unnecessary number of divisions in Palestine for an offensive which in the event never took place, divisions that might well have prevented the German break-through in March, 1918. All this was heart-breaking to commanders who had to watch the Army melting away for want of reinforcements. Many a staff officer working by the light of his lamp late at night fancied he could hear the monotonous broken rumble of steel wheels on steel rails as the unending procession of trains laden with grey-clad soldiers followed each other through innumerable stations with Polish, German and finally French names.

This book exposes the fallacy of Lloyd George's claim to be 'the man who won the war'. It shows that, because he refused to heed the warnings of his military advisers in the spring of 1918, he brought us nearer to total defeat than at any other period in the war.

Defeat was averted by the fighting qualities of the troops and the skill of the Commanders; but the cost in men's lives of Lloyd George's strategic conceptions was staggering. In the four weeks from 21 March, 1918, British casualties were 70,000 more than in the fourteen weeks of the Battle of Passchendaele.

After the German attack, the reinforcements for which the Staff had pleaded were sent—over 640,000 men between 21 March and 31 August.

One of Lloyd George's strangest aberrations was his conviction that it was he who had imposed unity of command on unwilling Generals. There could be no greater distortion of the truth, and General Maurice's diary plays an important part in proving this. It shows how, from 10 January, 1918, he and Sir William Robertson made attempt after attempt to get a co-ordinated command set up before the German attack, and how, thanks to Lloyd George and General Sir Henry Wilson who, as we shall see, succeeded Robertson as CIGS, all their attempts failed.

As long as Joffre was Commander-in-Chief, the soldiers, but not the politicians, accepted the wisdom of the principle of a single strategic direction of operations. General Maurice's diary establishes that throughout this period the British Generals were in favour of unity of command and unified control of the reserves. To have put forward any other point of view would have been to admit that they were ill-versed in the rudiments of their profession. What they opposed was the method of execution put forward by Mr Lloyd George and Sir Henry Wilson, not only because it would not work but because it flouted the very principle it was intended to uphold.*

Sir William Robertson was dismissed on 16 February, and unity of command was only achieved on 26 March, five days after the German attack was launched.

The problem arose from the fact that the Allied Governments, frightened into action by the defeat of the Italians at Caporetto in November, 1917, agreed at a conference held at Rapallo to establish a Supreme War Council at Versailles, an excellent step which could and did provide a permanent organisation to deal with the hitherto rather haphazard meetings of the Conferences of allied statesmen.†

This useful and efficient committee advised the Allied Governments on military plans, but was incapable of issuing orders to the Commanders. Yet this is precisely what the politicians, led by Lloyd George, resolved that it should do. It was decided on 2 February, 1918, to add to it an Executive Board, on which Sir Henry Wilson was to be the British Representative and which was to have control of the general reserves of the Allies—French, British and Italian. In the Prime Minister's view, this plan had the enormous advantage of robbing the British military leaders, in whom he had no confidence, of effective power in favour of the inspired warriors he believed Sir Henry Wilson and the French Generals to be.

The French, although in favour of a single control of the war under French command, and fully aware of the foolish conception of the Executive Board, did not oppose it, for the simple reason that it spelt French control, since their representative, Foch, was the only member of the Board who could exercise effective control of the reserves of his own Armies. Furthermore they believed that Sir Henry Wilson would be Foch's willing tool.

The Board was to control a reserve consisting of a number of divisions provided by each of the Allied Armies. It was, in fact, control by Committee, which is contrary both to common sense and to the teachings of history, as General Maurice points out; and it

* In his diary on 20 February, 1917, General Maurice wrote when commenting on the Prime Minister's speech in the House of Commons 'Idea given is that Robertson was opposed to unified control which is quite untrue.' And on 13 March, after giving Sir Douglas Haig's reasons for refusing to contribute to the Allied General Reserve he adds, 'But that doesn't alter the necessity *for an effective Allied Command.*' (My italics.)
† John Terraine in *The Western Front* (p. 102) writes of Rapallo that Robertson told Wilson 'He thought it (the Supreme War Council) might work if Maurice was a member, but not otherwise.'

collapsed even before the first 'Huff and Wuff' of the German wolf.

On 28 January General Maurice wrote that Foch and Pétain had agreed that Robertson and Foch were the best organisation for controlling the inter-Allied Reserve. On 2 February he noted that the Prime Minister and Sir Henry Wilson had put forward a proposal putting all power into the hands of the Executive Board at Versailles.

It was particularly misleading, but very characteristic of the Prime Minister's methods, for him to imply in a speech in the House of Commons on 20 February that both Haig and Robertson had agreed to the constitution of the Executive Board. They had not expressed their dissent because, as General Maurice's entry for 1 February shows, Robertson, having on that day strongly criticised the policy advocated by the Prime Minister at the meeting of the Supreme War Council, was informed by him that having already protested in writing he had no business to disagree with him before foreigners. This outburst effectively silenced Robertson when the proposal was passed by the Council, although the CIGS told Maurice that it was absolutely unworkable.

General Maurice's diary tells how the Versailles organisation, which bore no more resemblance to an effective military staff than a stage property background would have to the Normandy landings, bickered, quarrelled, and refused to act. Sadly he notes on 15 March, 'So we finally end with no general control at all on the eve of the Boche attack' (prophetic words indeed for the Germans attacked on the 21st), and, to quote the diary for 8 March: 'So Wully (Sir William Robertson) was sacked because he did not agree with the Executive War Board, and now it commits suicide.'

Ludendorff was the real author of Unity of Command.

Five days after the German attack of 21 March, Foch was appointed 'to co-ordinate the action of the Allied Armies on the Western front'. General Maurice's last efforts at the War Office were concentrated on endeavouring to ensure that General Foch was provided with a good British Staff, his argument being that, having appointed him to the position of overall control of our forces, he should be equipped with the means of carrying out his duties efficiently. But even in this he was confronted with opposition.

Sir Henry Wilson being now CIGS, General Maurice, intent only on the efficient direction of the War, suggested that a senior

British officer should be appointed to Foch's staff. But he noted in his diary on 31 March that Wilson was inclined to demur. 'He really wants to reconstitute Versailles and is shy of giving Foch too much power.'

This is indeed a terrible condemnation of Wilson: to wish to re-establish control by Committee, the only advantage of which was that it would provide him with the opportunity for renewed intrigues and the possibility of limiting Foch's powers. This conclusion is borne out by the next entry of the diary: 'Wilson is decidedly against giving Foch more power.'

So Brigadier-General Grant, a liaison officer on Wilson's staff when the latter was Chief Liaison Officer, was appointed on 31 March; his main qualifications were amiability and good family connections.

It was not until the enemy began bombarding the Armentières front that a senior and highly qualified officer was sent to Foch. This was General Du Cane, an experienced Corps Commander, who, when he was given an adequate staff, provided the help that Foch needed.

This book throws new light on events of which I had some, but only partial, knowledge as Head of the British Military Mission to the French Government during the period it covers.

The pamphlet, *Intrigues of the War*, here published as an appendix, is of compelling interest. Although General Maurice is critical of Lloyd George's method of conducting the war and suffered much at his hands, he writes of the Prime Minister with a coolness and detachment which are not matched by Mr Lloyd George's writings about him.

General Maurice writes:

We were saved (from defeat in 1918) by Haig's cool leadership, by the stubborn valour of the British soldiery, by the fierce energy with which Foch filled the gap between the British and the French armies, and by Mr Lloyd George's power of rising to heights in an emergency . . .

Mr Lloyd George's strength as a War Minister was his faith in victory and his power of keeping the confidence of the public. His weaknesses were his belief in his military judgment, his power of deceiving himself (and) his failure to understand that opportunism, sometimes successful in peace, is highly dangerous in war.

His missed the chance of victory in 1917, and brought us nearer to defeat in the Spring of 1918 than we had ever been, while the final triumph was won by methods which he had previously opposed with all the vigour at his command.

To quote Lord Crewe's Preface, 'The pamphlet represents a technical and historical verdict.' It does more; it is a clear and balanced account of one of the greatest crises Britain has ever faced. It is a document that neither student nor interested reader can afford to ignore.

General Maurice's diary is the most important part of this book. It gives a kind of shorthand account of events and the men who influenced them at perhaps the most critical period of the war. He displays no hatred, only on occasion a cool disapproval. One might have expected more rancour, but that was not in General Maurice's character.

He had to be tried very hard to criticise anyone as he did Jack Seeley, who had been Secretary of State for War in the Liberal Administration. I have described him as 'Colonel Y' in *Liaison 1914*. I personally thought he was a type likely to bring democracy into disrepute. But he was friendly and brave, though perhaps not so brave as to have justified his recommending his chauffeur for the VC in 1914, with the citation 'he has always kept within 50 yards of me'.

General Maurice describes a scene in which Seeley declared to Mr Lloyd George, 'Burn the books, this war is different from any other war. No history or previous experience is of any value.' But even then all General Maurice wrote was, 'What an ass.'

An occasional note of exasperation is sometimes heard; as when on 7 January he writes: 'Haig told the War Cabinet that he did not think the Germans would attempt a break-through—very rash.' It was more than rash—it was disastrous. It played into the hands of Lloyd George and those Ministers who maintained that the Western front was 'over-manned' and that the demands of their military advisers for reinforcements could safely be ignored.

Two days later, on 9 January, General Maurice wrote:

Haig note on future prospects received. He regards next few months as critical and thinks Germans may attempt to force a decision. That's better.

But the harm done by Haig's statement on 7 January was irreparable. It was because of it that Curzon stated in his speech on 9 April:

There seems to have been a tendency in some quarters to suppose that, either from a reluctance to tap the available resources of man-power in this country or from a failure to appreciate military advice, the British Army in France has been allowed to decline numerically to a point that was fraught with peril. There is no foundation for such a suspicion; nor were any apprehensions of such a character either entertained or received. Our Commanders were equally satisfied with the numbers, the equipment, and the morale of their forces. Nor is it in any of those respects that fault has been found. Up to the very eve of the battle the Government continued to receive the most confident and gratifying assurances from the Allied military authorities on the spot.*

In the opinions he expresses in the diary, General Maurice has almost invariably been proved right. When he writes on 28 January that he found the Staff at Versailles working at their War Games and expecting a big German attack on the Arras/La Bassée front about May, he told them he thought Cambrai more likely, and he was not mistaken. The Germans attacked at Cambrai on 21 March. He had already, as early as 11 January, told the War Cabinet that the signs of a German offensive on the Western front were increasing but that it was not likely to take place before the end of February. But he notes in his diary that they did not believe in the offensive. They knew better. The amateur strategists were having a field day. No doubt heads were wisely shaken, small-scale maps unfolded on which fingers drew imaginary lines, and Ministers announced, with the uncanny prescience which characterised Mr Lloyd George's Cabinet, that the Germans really intended to attack Italy, unless of course Salonika was their objective.

On 18 January General Maurice was at it again: nagging, the secretariat called it. He well knew the Prime Minister would dislike the statement he put in showing further recent increases in the German strength on the Western front. In his diary on this date he notes that the Prime Minister does nothing but count heads, reckoning a Portuguese, a Belgian or an untrained American as the equivalent of a trained German soldier, and on the 25th he writes that Government attacks on Robertson and Haig are developing because both are insisting on the vital necessity of sending out more men to France and the CIGS refuses to support Lloyd George's strategic brain child, an attack on Aleppo.

On 25 January the diary states that the Versailles Committee proposed an offensive campaign against the Turks *provided the Western front is not weakened*. Maurice says he tried to explain the

* See page 120.

impossibility of this, but remarks that he was speaking to deaf ears. The Cabinet gave Lloyd George and Milner carte blanche to settle the Palestine question, which Maurice knew meant the advance on Aleppo. And his final note, on what must certainly have been a miserable day, was 'Versailles maintains that the Western front is safe'.

At Versailles on 29 January General Maurice saw the Prime Minister, who told him that he had sent Smuts on a short tour of the Western front. Smuts reported this to be safe, 'except for a little anxiety as to the Portuguese'. Maurice remarks that 'Smuts' advice is of course preferred to William Robertson's though he knows nothing of European War.' (I can confirm this judgment. One night the Prime Minister asked me to dine with him and Smuts at the Ritz in Paris. No one else. I well remember my astonishment at finding that this charming South African's well-known wisdom did not go so far as to restrain him from expressing opinions on military matters of which he had little or no knowledge.)

On 30 January the first meeting of the Supreme War Council was held in Paris, Maurice remarking that it was a great gathering to look at but useless for military decisions. At once a wrangle developed over man-power. Haig and Pétain both maintained that if the enemy attacked and inflicted heavy losses on the Allies they would have to reduce a considerable number of divisions.

No great effort of imagination is required to accept General Maurice's statement that the Prime Minister expressed amazement at such statements—he had, he asserted vehemently, provided plenty of men. But next day (Thursday, 31st) General Foch attacked Lloyd George on the question of manpower, maintaining that England had not done as much as France, which was certainly true as far as bodies were concerned; whereupon the Prime Minister at once slithered into his most eel-like impersonation.

I can see him now evoking in a cascade of words the catalogue of Britain's contributions. Waving arms conjured up British fleets sailing the oceans, while you could almost hear the din of anvils in English and Scottish shipyards as the workers—soldiers in every sense of the word—worked infinitely long hours to fill the gaps torn by the merciless submarine in the Allies' life-line, and the Prime Minister, his eyes blazing like forges, struck the table, while Clemenceau, the most cynical and the most feared of men, his thread-gloved hands folded across his stomach, fixed his wicked cruel eyes, eyes that could be kind only when thinking or speaking of France, contemptuously on Lloyd George, whom he regarded as little better than a clown.

Then the Prime Minister, with the agility of an acrobat, threw into the discussion his favourite Aleppo plan which, by knocking the Turks out of the war, was to secure victory. Clemenceau and Foch, who generally disagreed with each other, were for once of one mind and loudly voiced their opposition; but this was soon replaced by grunts of indignation and surprise when Lloyd George repeated his amazing statement that we were, and always had been, over-manned in the West.

Next morning Lloyd George secured the assent of both Clemenceau and the Italian Prime Minister Sonnino to his Palestine plan by promising them that he would not weaken the Western front. 'Not weaken it?' writes General Maurice, 'what it needs is strengthening.'

The February entries in the diary are of particular interest. That for 5 February is especially so to me. It is a simple statement that the Secretary of State for War, Lord Derby, had declared that 'he will stand by Wully Robertson and will resign if the Government insists on the Versailles proposals'. Had Derby done so, Robertson might well have been saved, but he did not.

Derby did not have the reputation of a last-ditcher. Just after Wully had been given the sack I realised why, when Derby called me me in to his room facing the great staircase at the War Office. I knew him only as a very young Brigadier-General would know the Minister who ruled the Army, and I do not suppose I shall ever understand why he brought me in to witness the extraordinary scene which followed. That he knew I was stationed in Paris and probably guessed I was devoted to Wully Robertson is hardly a sufficient reason for telling me to sit down while he walked up and down the large room, a soul driven by a tormented conscience, as he kept on repeating 'I should have resigned with Robertson. I certainly should have, I said so,' then, after a pause, 'I certainly said so but was over-persuaded'.

It was a very painful scene and completely surprising—utterly beyond my experience. It only dawned on me by degrees that what was torturing the Secretary of State was the knowledge, the intimate certainty, that were similar circumstances to arise again he would behave in exactly the same manner; he would always run out, as some horses will always shy away from an obstacle they know they cannot face. It was so unexpected to see this man, apparently so genial and so trustworthy, exposing a soul racked by regret that was not remorse, but merely a realisation that he had been guilty of the sort of conduct he would be guilty of again in similar circumstances. And somehow I remembered how when Gilles de Rais, the Bluebeard of legend, was led to the stake at Nantes, the entire population, in spite of, or perhaps because of, his terrible crimes, knelt by the road as he passed, in their mediaeval belief that here was a soul on its way to eternal damnation.

The entry in General Maurice's diary for 8 February reports the next step in Lloyd George's plan to get rid of Robertson.

Wilson recalled from Versailles to be in readiness to step into WR's place as soon as LG can get rid of him.

There was further news from Versailles. Smuts had been there, apparently with instructions to press through the Aleppo plan. And Colonel Kirke, who was on Maurice's Staff, wrote to him that 'Wilson says the Western front is safe and two or three divisions from Palestine could make no difference.' On this General Maurice expresses his indignation, a rare occurrence, but in very mild language: 'How can a soldier make such a statement!'

Maurice notes in his diary on 12 February that the Prime Minister had offered the post of CIGS to Plumer who, however, refused it on the 14th.

By 14 February Maurice was certain that a big German attack was being prepared on the Cambrai front. Evidence to that effect was accumulating, he wrote, adding, with what seems to have been an uncanny prophetic sense but was merely a sound deduction from carefully observed and weighed facts, that it was unlikely to be ready before the middle of March.

While Lloyd George's strategic blinkers still confined the Cabinet's vision to the sunny Middle East, a somewhat less occluded view was noticeable in Paris, where General Foch succeeded in obtaining that the British Cabinet should order two divisions from the Italian to the Western front.

But by the 21st the Italians were protesting loudly at the withdrawal of these divisions. On military matters, too, they tend to be a somewhat highly-strung nation. This time their objection was on procedural lines: the Versailles Executive Board had been charged with the control of reserves and the Board had not been consulted. This, they argued, was highly irregular. But fortunately, writes General Maurice on the 21st, Foch had jumped the gun, quite rightly, realising that the matter was urgent. So no wringing of hands on either side of the Alps could stop the division that was already on its way.

No one has described the scene when Sir William Robertson sang his swan song on Saturday, 16 February, at 10 Downing Street. General Maurice called it his swan song, but it was certainly the wrong definition, for we can be certain that his audience of amateur strategists were treated to no musical serenade from the rough professional they understood so little and disliked so much as he grunted out in his asthmatic and phlegm-laden voice views as often heard and as unpopular as himself. Still, they probably thought, it was bound to be over by lunchtime, so they took but did not swallow his bitter medicine. The arrangements they had made were unworkable, he declared, and he could not accept them. He would stultify himself equally if he remained as CIGS while Wilson moved troops at Versailles, or if he moved troops at Versailles while Wilson functioned as CIGS in London.

Later that day the Government announced that Sir William Robertson had resigned, which he promptly denied. Then he was offered the Eastern Command, which he accepted.

We learn from the diary that on 18 February Sir Henry Wilson took over. Robertson said good-bye at the War Office, and we witness yet another small example of skullduggery. Wilson's power to issue orders to the troops was abolished, but, as Maurice points out, this was mere camouflage, since exactly the same procedure as before was to be followed, the only difference being that telegrams were to go out in the name of the Secretary of State instead of in that of the CIGS. It is not easy to perceive what advantage the Secretary of State derived from assuming responsibility for matters he knew nothing about.

On 20 February Sir Henry Wilson informed General Maurice that he had decided to replace him by 'a man from the trenches' and that Haig had promised to give him a division. This news naturally pleased Maurice greatly. No real soldier can be anything but elated by the prospect of an active command in wartime. He confided to his diary, 'I shall be delighted to get out of the War Office where I have been for too long.'

But it was not to be.

Major-General P. de B. Radcliffe was to take his place, but owing first to the threat of the German attack and then to the attack itself he did not actually arrive at the War Office until 11 April. If Radcliffe had taken up his appointment within the normal three weeks, General Maurice would have been on leave when the Germans attacked on 21 March, he would not have gone to France as DMO on 13 April and would not have been told of the disastrous effect on the morale of the army of the Prime Minister's speech on manpower on 9 April.

There would have been no Maurice letter and no Maurice case.

On 22 February there were great rejoicings at No 10: news came that Allenby had captured Jericho. No great flight of imagination is necessary to picture Lloyd George in his elation, visualising himself as a new Joshua blowing the trumpets that brought down the walls of a town which now comprised only a few mud hovels and a third-rate hotel.

But Jericho sounded wonderful—a name that had echoed down the ages from the chapels in the Welsh valleys—and here was a son of Wales who could claim that the Armies to which he gave orders had captured a city made famous in the Bible, a city that had defied that great warrior Joshua until the trumpets blew. And the Prime Minister can certainly have found no difficulty in imagining what the response would be if he asked any large audience in any of Britain's great cities, 'And who blew the trumpets?'

General Maurice's assessment in his diary of the emotion generated in Whitehall by the news is, as one would expect from him, a very calm one. 'LG delighted since he had heard of Jericho before Passchendaele.'

I, on the other hand, the night I read this entry in the diary, dreamt I saw a band comprising Lord Curzon, Bonar Law, Balfour and Lord Milner, led by Lloyd George, marching down Whitehall blowing silver trumpets borrowed from the Life Guards, at the sound of which the War Office on one side of the road and the Admiralty on the other collapsed, while Ludendorff danced a jig in the distant background.

On Saturday 23 February, Maurice gave the War Cabinet ominous news. The German divisions were already moving up on the Western front. This, he warned them, could only mean they intended to attack.

I do not know whether General Maurice gained the impression I did when I read this entry, that he was addressing an audience of ostriches, their heads buried deep in Palestinian sand. But presently they emerged and reassumed their role of inspired Napoleons, or more probably Wellingtons, gifted with the power to see 'what lay hidden on the other side of the hill', for most of them declared that they thought the Germans would not attack the Western front 'because they said they would'. General Maurice's comment is that this was no doubt clever camouflage on the part of the Germans, particularly as they were now spreading reports of attacks on Salonika, Italy, etc, leaving all commanders on all fronts cowering behind their barbed wire, reluctant to abandon its protection however loud the squeals of alarm from their allies.

The entry for 28 February states that at the War Cabinet that morning Ministers were still disinclined to believe in an attack on the Western front. St Thomas should have been their collective patron saint. Says Maurice, 'They still believe in an attack in Italy because nothing much is heard about it.' A really profound military deduction. The Prime Minister said he wanted another review of the War. It was much as if people sitting in a chalet in the Alps had asked for the solution to a crossword puzzle, deaf to the rumble of the avalanche of which their experienced guide had given them warning. Maurice seems to have retorted somewhat tartly to this that Lloyd George had 'first better settle his policy as to Palestine which has been in abeyance for three months'.

Maurice had an answer to this request on 1 March, for Colonel Kirke, back from his visit to Palestine with Smuts, reported that 'Smuts practically told Allenby it had been decided to carry out a big offensive in Palestine and asked him what he would want.' Smuts had proceeded to suggest means of providing the necessary troops without drawing on the Western front. One of these consisted of skinning Mesopotamia below the narrowest margin of safety. General Maurice goes on to point out that the Allied General Reserve had now dwindled to 20 Divisions of which 11 were in Italy. 'What a farce!' he writes.

He then notes that the question of bringing the second British Division from Italy had been referred to Versailles. He concludes his comment for the day with one more prophecy, 'The Boche will attack before this settled.' The great German offensive that very nearly destroyed our Armies, and dissipated the effort of four years of war at a cost of several million lives, was just twenty days off.

So we arrive at 4 March, and one is left as one reads that day's entry with the impression of watching a Grand Guignol play where all the lunatics have assumed the garb of nurses and doctors. Maurice writes: 'We may expect big German attack on Cambrai front before very long now. Probably as soon as the Easter moon begins. Weather extraordinarily dry for the spring, it may break before they begin.' And he adds: 'Told CIGS (Sir Henry Wilson) I thought attack certain.'

What can General Maurice have felt when he heard General Wilson's reply that he was afraid the attack would not come? Wilson did not think that if it came, it would be on the Cambrai/St Quentin front because of the devastated areas on the Somme. General Maurice, having listened to all this wisdom, writes in his diary that *he* goes 'by the evidence of preparation', and that this front is the point of junction of the French and British Armies, always a favourite with the Germans—and the road to Paris.

The diary for Tuesday, 5 March, tells us that the 'War Cabinet are at last beginning to think attack on us likely'. It was now sixteen days off. What dread, what foreboding, can have been dire enough to cause those sleepers to stir in their slumber? Prehaps it was only the thud of the scales falling from their own eyes that startled them.

On Wednesday, 6 March, the Versailles Executive Board showed signs of exploding, hoist by its own petard. Haig declared he could not contribute to the general reserve, whereupon Foch announced that he would dissolve the Board.

Dilemma of the War Cabinet: Sack Haig, which they did not feel strong enough to do without a little further manoeuvring (for suppose, contrary to all their strategic conceptions, the Germans did attack, what would the reaction of the country be to the dismissal of the Commander-in-Chief on the eve of an offensive it would certainly be known he had foreseen?)

Or suppose, instead of sacking Haig, they disregarded the Board they had just set up? Humpty Dumpty can hardly have been more puzzled when he contemplated his broken shell, but he at least disposed of all the King's horses and all the King's men, who unfortunately under present circumstances were to a large extent dispersed in Palestine and Italy.

The face-saving device hit upon by the politicians was to summon

21

042874

the Supreme War Council to London and consider Haig's refusal to have been merely a decorous appeal to the Versailles body.

The entry in the diary for the next day, Thursday, 7 March, is not only of great factual interest but is especially revealing as to the overall strategic picture on which Maurice was brooding. He noted Allenby's orders concerning his offensive in Palestine: one division was to be sent to him from Mesopotamia instead of two and the Cavalry Brigade Smuts was proposing to endow him with. Then Maurice writes: 'Allenby will get to Haifa and will be in no better position than where he is now. So we make war.'

No more stinging comment on the amateurish, disingenuous way in which we waged war could be made. Troops desperately needed in France were sent to Allenby to justify Lloyd George's conception of how to win a war; they were not numerous enough for a successful campaign, and at best could have enabled our Army in the Middle East to occupy a town representing not a single step on the road to victory, nothing more than a further if minor strain on our resources by lengthening our lines of communication, with the blue Mediterranean stretching between them and the Amiens uplands.

Whatever General Maurice may have felt when he heard Sir Henry Wilson inform the War Cabinet on 12 March that he was anything but certain that the Germans were going to attack, he was content to confide to his diary: 'I have no doubts about it. The Germans are not piling up divisions in the West for fun.'

But why was General Wilson so persistently wrong about everything? Was it simply that he could not bear that old Wully Robertson and his man Freddy Maurice should be so consistently right? Some may think that the CIGS's attitude provided Ministers with an excuse for seeking and generally finding new red herrings to pursue. On 13 March they were hot on the scent of an attack on Salonika, and General Maurice remarked in his diary, 'Ministers still looking for attack anywhere but in the West'.

On 14 March the Supreme War Council sat in London. It cannot have been a congenial occasion. Already on the previous day Wilson had, according to Maurice, been inclined to blame Haig for refusing to contribute to the allied General Reserve. At the Council Meeting itself Foch delivered an all-out attack on Haig for not complying with the orders of the Executive Board. Astonishingly, it was parried by Clemenceau. He 'shut him up,' writes Maurice. 'He and LG evidently arrived at a compromise.'

Whatever this arrangement was, we can be certain that the milk of human kindness was not one of its ingredients, for Clemenceau distrusted Lloyd George (who at times had to lash himself into a fury to face up to the formidable old Frenchman, whom he feared as most people did), and hated Foch as a soldier who was sometimes right, and also because he was a clerical; and Foch, though he respected Clemenceau's courageous stand in ruthless opposition to political defeatism, looked upon his Prime Minister as a dangerous radical, to all intents and purposes a Communard of 1871.

It is very impressive to read, after all these years, the certainty with which Maurice foretold with such astonishing accuracy the moment and place of the German onslaught; and the strength of mind with which he pressed his conviction on a Cabinet whose blindness matched his foresight. But he must have suffered agonies and felt as would a man strapped into a car driven towards a precipice by a mad chauffeur.

On Thursday, 21 March, at 10 minutes past 5 am the Germans

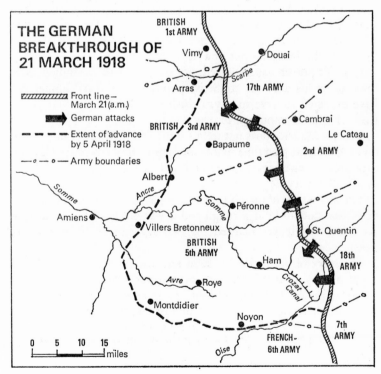

THE GERMAN
BREAKTHROUGH OF
21 MARCH 1918

Front line—
March 21 (a.m.)
German attacks
Extent of advance
by 5 April 1918
Army boundaries

attacked. 6,473 guns and 3,532 mortars opened fire at their maximum rate. This lasted for five hours until many of the guns were red hot. That morning there must have been many among the British who, grinding their teeth, muttered, 'The Devil looks after his own', for a dense fog shrouded the battlefield and garrotted our defensive system, which, owing to paucity in numbers, depended even more than usual on the cross-fire of mutually-supporting machine and Lewis guns. Our gunners could not see, and when the German infantry rushed forward, they were often almost unopposed, so that they achieved the objective—never before achieved by either side— of reaching our gun lines.

That day the Fifth Army lost 382 guns. By midnight on the 22nd the Third Army reported the loss of 150. John Terraine does not exaggerate when he writes that a disaster of the first magnitude had struck the British Army . . . 'on the second day of the battle the Germans poured through. It was no longer a question of assault: it was pursuit.'*

In London Maurice told Henry Wilson that the battle had started, but that politico-military oracle informed the Cabinet that this might be nothing more than a big raid. According to Maurice 'he wants the Boche to put in a heavy attack on us'.

Wilson's prayer was answered, but the price was certainly heavier than he or his amateur strategist pupils of the War Cabinet can have expected to have to pay. British casualties in the four weeks from 21 March amounted to over 220,000 men.

General Maurice does not tell us if the Prime Minister mentioned on 21 March his plan for a march on Aleppo, or if any other Minister expressed renewed fears for Salonika. If they did there is no record of it in the diary.

The magnitude of the disaster was not at first realised in England; news was slow to filter through and it was not until the evening of the 22nd that it was realised that we had suffered a very severe defeat indeed.

The story of the battle has been told with admirable clarity and simplicity by General Maurice in a paper written in 1918 *The Defeat of the Fifth Army*, published as an appendix to this book. It would be difficult, in my opinion impossible, to improve on it.

The diary for 23 March is sinister. On this day, General Maurice and General Macdonogh reported to the War Cabinet that the

* The Spring Offensive, *History Today*, April, 1968, p. 236.

Germans had 191 divisions to the Allies' 165, and a superiority of 117,600 in effective rifle strength.

The War Cabinet Minutes record 'that the Chief of the Imperial General Staff considered that for purposes of calculation the present forces might be reckoned as approximately equal'.

I find General Wilson's statement both staggering and incomprehensible.

Presumably he could count, and in any case could command the services of men who could both add and subtract. It seems evident and quite in character that accuracy and truth were far less important to him than to provide that dispenser of all favours and honours, the Prime Minister, with the means of avoiding his responsibility for the disaster, a responsibility lack of men was proclaiming ever more loudly.

At this meeting of the War Cabinet on 23 March General Wilson appears to have been even less accurate on the all-important matter of the forces retained in Palestine on the War Cabinet's instructions than on the numbers of the opposing forces.

The Cabinet Minutes report him as stating that 'there were three British divisions in Egypt'. This inaccuracy Lloyd George took full advantage of. He embroidered on Wilson's statement in his speech in the House of Commons on 9 April and informed the House that 'there were only three white divisions in Palestine and Egypt; the rest are either Indian or mixed with a very, very small proportion of British troops'.

It was this statement which General Maurice challenged in his letter to the press.* In the Maurice Debate, Lloyd George, having no evidence to support it, did not repeat it, but relied for his defence on General Wilson's statement about the 'three divisions', which, he inferred, had been endorsed by General Maurice.†

On 23 March, there were in fact six British infantry divisions in Palestine. A seventh contained 9 British and 4 Indian regiments, and when Lloyd George spoke on 9 April, there were five—one division having meanwhile been ordered to France.

While relating the Cabinet's panic on 23 March, General Maurice does not fail to note that in this dreadful emergency, so largely of his own making, Lloyd George showed his best side, did not panic

* See p. 97.　　　　　† See p. 130.

like the rest, and set about taking all possible steps to stop the haemorrhage.

On 27 March, orders were at last given to Allenby to adopt the defensive in Palestine and to send one division to France immediately and a second as soon as possible.

In *Intrigues of the War*, Maurice writes:

When the crisis came, Mr Lloyd George was splendid. While others wavered and began to give up hope, he never lost his faith in victory, and with rare energy he repaired in a few weeks all the errors of omission of the previous year.

but, he added:

Unfortunately, immediately the first crisis was passed, Mr Lloyd George reverted to his former methods. He had rid himself of Robertson, and he now saw a chance of ridding himself of Haig.

On 25 March General Maurice reported to the War Cabinet that the enemy was bending all his energies to separate us from the French, skimming troops from the north of our front and from the French front to the south of us, staking everything on knocking us out. Maurice's conclusion was that the situation was decidedly critical but not desperate, but the next day, Tuesday, 26 March, he had to paint an even darker picture. The Third Army and the left of the Fifth had had to fall back to the Ancre and there was a real danger of a breach on this part of the front.

He was not, however, afraid of the situation south of the Somme, as he was confident the French reserves would arrive in time to prevent anything really serious happening there.

It is clear from his diary that he had to reiterate and re-emphasise that any question of falling back on the Channel ports or of permitting a separation from the French Armies would be madness.

On the 28th the Germans were still pressing south of the Somme, but this did not worry Maurice unduly, for he was sure the French reserves would arrive in time to prevent a break-through.

When I read the entry for the 29th I saw again a picture of Amiens, where I had been less than a week earlier. Absolutely dead, grass beginning to grow in the streets, not a soul to be seen, no civilians, only an occasional soldier. The great and beautiful town through which the Germans had poured in 1914 lay prostrate and helpless like a defeated gladiator, throat bared for the blow it could do nothing to avert.

The loss of Amiens would have been a disaster.

It was a railway junction of the greatest importance, the main artery connecting the France of the French and the France defended by the British Armies. It was also the point of junction between the French and British Armies, always a neuralgic and vulnerable area. The Germans were entitled to hope that if they could break through to Amiens they could roll up one or both Armies like a carpet, calculating that each would consider that the protection of its own vital interests surpassed all other considerations, for the French Paris, for the British the Channel ports, leaving a gap through which the bulk of the German forces would pour. This was the danger General Maurice never ceased warning against.

Fortunately by Saturday, the 30th, the situation south of the Somme had improved. The enemy had been checked and the French reserves were coming up well.

On Sunday, the 31st, General Maurice was in France visiting GHQ and seeing Foch, now virtually Commander-in-Chief, at Beauvais. He was, says Maurice, in good form, but with only a rudimentary staff, 'and he hasn't got hold of things. He wants help from us and should have a good English staff.'

On Monday, 1 April, Maurice saw Haig and told him he did not think the situation south of the Somme was satisfactory and pressed him to see Foch about it, which Haig agreed to do. He was calm, looked well and said he would not 'ungum' Gough who was given too long a line to hold and whose troops were overwhelmed in the fog.

It is not my purpose to criticise or defend General Gough's conduct of the battle of 21 March. The high water mark of my admiration for him was reached before the war at the time of what was called the Curragh Mutiny. I admired and followed his lead when, as Commander of the Cavalry Brigade at the Curragh, he had announced that he would not obey orders to march against Ulster if these were given. What I had seen and heard of him as a Commander had not tended to encourage my early hero worship, but, as so often happens in life, General Gough, whose tactics may well often have been open to criticism, was defeated on 21 March because of faults others than he had committed. That he had insufficient troops to hold too long a line was the responsibility of the Government, that God blinded him with fog was a misfortune for which he bears no responsibility either. His good fortune, and it was good fortune, which all who are British can claim to share, lay in the stubborn bravery of his troops, who, weary, unrested, blinded and decimated, never broke.

The next few days were a period of intense anxiety for General Maurice, watching the Germans driving deadly thrusts with ever-fresh troops against our tired, patched-up divisions. On Friday, 5 April, they made heavy attacks north and south of the Somme. On the Albert front, however, they were completely repulsed, but they gained some ground south of the Somme. On Monday, 8 April, the enemy bombarded the Armentières front, and on 9 April they attacked. This front was held by the Portuguese and some of our tired divisions which had already fought on the Somme and had been hastily made up to strength.

We were all, in those days, hard on the Portuguese, but I have often thought since that this was unjust. After all, a man's life is something he is justified in holding on to, and what can have been the appeal to those men from a sun-drenched southern land to risk their lives in the dreadful sodden fields of Flanders for a cause most of them can hardly have understood?

This attack on the 9th was the second great wave of the German offensive, this time in the north. General Plumer was driven from Messines, and on 11 April the Germans got into Steenwerck and we had to evacuate Armentières.

Foch, not for the first time in the war, was late. Says Maurice: 'his counter-attack should have got off 3 days ago. Now it is useless and will have no effect on the situation in the north.'

On the 12th the news from France was still worse. The Germans were in Neuville and on the outskirts of Bailleul. It was on this day that Sir Douglas Haig issued his Order of the Day: 'With our backs to the wall, and believing in the justice of our cause, each one of us must fight to the end.' But on Saturday, the 13th, the news was slightly better. The enemy had not made any material progress.

It is possible to picture, though impossible to assess, the strain on General Maurice during these days when bad news came pouring in as he sat watching the map which marked the enemy's advance on so many points, while he tried to find means of reinforcing our silk-thin line. We see him trying to make General Pershing realise that it was more in the interest of the United States to prevent our collapse than to await the day when he could assemble

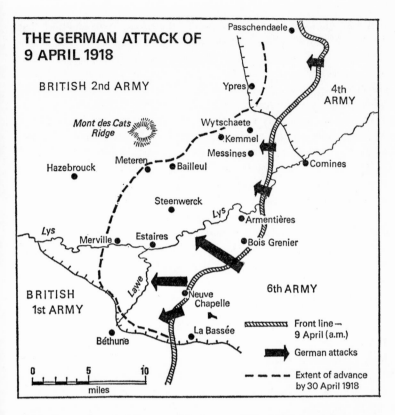

THE GERMAN ATTACK OF
9 APRIL 1918

BRITISH 2nd ARMY

Passchendaele

Ypres

4th
ARMY

Mont des Cats
Ridge

Wytschaete

Kemmel

Messines

Meteren

Bailleul

Comines

Hazebrouck

Steenwerck

Lys

Armentières

Lys

Merville

Estaires

Bois Grenier

Lawe

BRITISH
1st ARMY

Neuve
Chapelle

6th ARMY

La Bassée

Béthune

Front line —
9 April (a.m.)

German attacks

Extent of advance
by 30 April 1918

0   5   10

miles

all his forces in martial array. We know of his efforts to bring every
pressure, military and political, on General Foch, to make him
realise how close we were to defeat for lack of troops.

And at the back of it all were the politicians, so responsible yet
so irresponsible, so guilty yet so uncomprehending, panicking now
that the consequences of their mistakes were emerging too obviously
to be overlooked by even the most gullible public. Maurice observed
how in their anxiety to ensure that the blame for the present disaster
fell on other shoulders than their own, Ministers were taking obvious
steps to find carpets under which their recent failures could be swept,
and scapegoats were being sought for.

And all the time he was trying to explain the war to Ministers.
We can understand his exasperation when Lord Curzon at the War
Cabinet on 6 April became petulant 'because he cannot be told at
once the number of prisoners we lost and has to turn to the German

communiqués for this information'. One might have thought that even a child would have realised it was less difficult to count men in a cage than to find out the exact losses suffered by retreating armies, which were casualties and which were prisoners, which belonged to units momentarily out of touch with headquarters or with whom communications had been severed.

On 9 April, the day of the German attack on Armentières, Maurice notes in his diary that both the Prime Minister in the Commons and Lord Curzon in the Lords made speeches on manpower. He only read the Prime Minister's speech in the newspapers and did not realise its implications, but noted that 'although very moderate about the soldiers Lloyd George is as usual working sub rosa against Haig'. Of Curzon's speech, he wrote: 'Curzon made a number of absolutely untrue statements in the House of Lords.'

On Sunday, the 14th, General Maurice together with Lord Milner crossed over to France at 6 am in a bad storm. This visit was to play an important part in the events which were so soon to affect his life and career.

He had breakfast with Douglas Haig, whom he found tired and worried, as were Haig's Chief of Staff, General Lawrence, and his DMO, General Davidson. But General Plumer, whom he also saw, looked splendid and was more satisfied with the position; he had, however, decided to withdraw from Ypres. Then General Maurice saw Foch, whom he found in excellent form and confident of holding the enemy, but he notes in his diary that Foch 'is naturally anxious to hold his reserves but doesn't quite appreciate condition of our troops'. How could he? How could a French General assess the morale or the real condition of British troops? French liaison officers would be as uncomprehending as he was himself. He would have to rely on the statements of British Commanders, but their standards of measurement in such matters were not French and could not be compared with them. Such are the difficulties of Allies. There can be but one standard in such matters—the absolute confidence the Commanders of two Allied Armies have in each other that each will go to the extreme limit of the fighting power of his own troops in support of their common cause. Wellington and Blücher provided such a tandem. The staunchness of the two Armies may differ, but so does that between two regiments in one Army, and no one can ask for more than comradeship that is faithful unto death.

It was on this day that Maurice made a disconcerting discovery, considering his position at the heart of things in London: this was that the Army in France was more aware of and more sensitive to the speeches of Cabinet Ministers than he had been. I am convinced that this very conscientious man, who was not in the habit of hiding the truth even from himself and never sought pretexts for pushing responsibilities on to the shoulders of others, felt as would a sentry who had slept undiscovered at his post. He made no excuses for himself. He did not even contemplate what it had cost him to defend the interests of the Army in France single-handed since stout old Wully had gone and his place been taken by a soldier unable to see the Army's dilemma otherwise than as a problem to be resolved in a way that would absolve and please the Prime Minister. He did not see himself as he really had been, searching every theatre for men, always more men, with which to plug the bleeding hole torn by the enemy in our line, nor did he commiserate with himself for having had to play the role of doctor in a mental hospital, whose patients were Ministers, at one time refusing to take elementary safety precautions and the next threatening suicide. He only saw the fact that a blow had been struck at the Army and that he had not parried it. He had not even known at the time that it had been struck, and he felt very guilty. It was as incomprehensible to him as it had been to the Army that Mr Lloyd George should, in his speech to the House of Commons on 9 April, have stated that the Army in France was considerably stronger on 1 January, 1918, than it had been on 1 January, 1917, and that the combatant strength of the whole German Army on the Western front was not quite equal to the total combatant strength of the Allies. In other words a lesser number of Germans had beaten a greater number of Allies. He could not but share the Army's indignation, for he knew, as they knew, that on 21 March the total of Allied Divisions had been 165 to 191 German. This was the equivalent of saying that the Army, either through faulty generalship or lack of fighting qualities in the troops, had, man for man, Division for Division, been licked by an enemy inferior in numbers, when every man in the Army knew that before the German attack the Army had been so weakened that after the break-through we had had to reduce six of our Divisions for the simple reason that this cannibalisation was the sole means available to us to make good the losses we had suffered.

And Maurice knew, as did Douglas Haig and the Army Commanders, that the Government had refused to send more men from England and to cancel the plan for an offensive campaign in Palestine so as to send reinforcements to France before the German attack. At GHQ he had to listen to the bitter complaint that the Government, with which in a way he was felt to be associated, was deliberately making out that the appalling reverse we had suffered was in no way their responsibility but that of the Army.

Such officers as he saw made it clear to him that the Prime Minister's speech had done the Army a very real mischief and inflicted a wound that would not easily be healed. He told those who raised the matter with him that he greatly regretted not having done more than read press reports of Mr Lloyd George's speech, but he undertook to read it carefully in *Hansard* on his return, and to consider what steps could be taken to correct the misleading statements he was told the Prime Minister had made.

Although he must have been glad to hear it, it did not put an end to his preoccupations to be told by Sir Douglas Haig that he hoped to reconstitute the 5th Army and that, instead of appointing General Maurice to a Division, he wanted him to be Major-General on the Staff of that Army.

We do not know the reactions of this very tired man when he first found himself back in London. He was met at Victoria Station by the Prime Minister's Private Secretary, Sutherland, who took him to the House of Commons. There he met Mr Lloyd George and heard him make what he described in his diary as a good speech on Irish conscription, after which the Prime Minister kept him talking until after midnight.

From France on the 16th, he had written to Wully Robertson that General Lawrence (Haig's Chief of Staff) told him that Haig had asked that he (Robertson) should become his second-in-command. Maurice added his own comment that this post without definite functions might not appeal to Wully, but that he was convinced that his presence would have a great effect both on the Army and at GHQ. To which Wully sent a typically Wullyish answer.*

It was now Wednesday, the 17th, and Maurice, who was to hand over on the following Saturday, had only time for matters requiring immediate action, but he noted, and this must have

* See p. 82.

pleased him, for he was entitled to think his talk with Foch may have influenced the decision, that Foch was sending another division to Plumer in the north. He also noted that Lord Derby was to go as Ambassador to Paris and Lord Milner to become Secretary of State for War.

On the 18th the enemy launched a heavy attack on General Horne's Army in the Bethune region.

On the same day, Maurice wrote, 'Government evidently determined to get rid of Haig as soon as possible. Plumer will probably succeed.'

On Friday, the 19th, Maurice was able to note that the enemy's attacks on the previous day had everywhere failed. What he did not know was that on the 18th a question had been put in the House of Commons to the Prime Minister by Sir Godfrey Baring, who asked whether the Prime Minister, when he said in his speech of 9 April that the British Army in France was considerably stronger on 1 January, 1918, than on 1 January, 1917, was including the labour battalions and other non-combatant units. Mr Macpherson, the Under-Secretary at the War Office, replied that the fighting strength of the Army was greater on 1 January, 1918, than it had been on the corresponding date in the previous year. The fact that this was not true was to play a very important role not only in the story of General Maurice but in the history of England.

On vacating his appointment as DMO, General Maurice had three weeks' leave. Having obtained a copy of Hansard containing Lloyd George's speech of 9 April, he went to his mother's house in the country to consider what his action should be. He read the speech on Sunday, the 21st, the day after he left the War Office.

It is typical of the man that having been taken aback by the realisation that the implications of the Prime Minister's speech were even more serious than he had at first thought, and feeling with growing concern that a decision which might involve not only his own future but that of his family was confronting him, he decided that, tired as he was, he must put Hansard away and read the Prime Minister's speech again after another night's sleep.

It is not difficult to follow the process through which his conscience groped at this stage. He knew that the Army had been mangled almost beyond recognition of its old self—tired divisions which, unlike those of the French, did not know what a quiet sector was, faced by far more German divisions than those facing

33

our Allies, holding positions where ground could not be given up owing to the lack of depth of the whole British front, a number of them being broken up to provide men for the remainder. He knew that many regiments had been bled white of men beyond their power of forming the new drafts in the old regimental moulds. He knew, what Ministers seemed unable to grasp, that the Army was a very sensitive organisation made up of regiments, each one a delicate plant with roots deep in its own past achievements, profoundly affected by the quality of its officers. He had had ample experience of the fact that Ministers could not tell the difference between a regiment and a crowd attending a football match, if each included an equal number of men, or, certainly in the case of Mr Lloyd George, of understanding the difference between a navvy, a Chinese coolie, and a trained soldier. Maurice also knew that the frightful pressure put on the Army by the enemy prevented our dwindling forces from being either rested or adequately trained. He knew how lamentably short we were of the suitable type of man to make adequate junior officers or NCOs.

The French suffered from the same disabilities owing to their fearful casualties but they had, fortunately for themselves, a vast framework of reserve officers, and conscription ensured their having many educated men in the ranks.

The Army was now held together by courage and faith, and General Maurice realised from his trip to France that these essential props to its existence had been severely undermined by the Prime Minister's speech, which questioned its courage by implying that it had been beaten by a lesser number of Germans, and by criticism of its leaders, in whom the Army on the whole had faith, to exonerate the Government of blame for what had happened. And Maurice knew that no Army could give of its best if it had lost faith in its Commanders.

I believe he thought Douglas Haig to be a good leader and although he certainly thought General Plumer was, he felt acutely that to replace Haig now would deal a severe, perhaps deadly, blow to the morale of the Army by proclaiming that the defeat just suffered was due to bad generalship. He felt that the Army in its very essence was in danger; that the fate of the nation, whose shield the Army was, was at stake.

Knowing these things, he felt that something should be done, and that if *he* could do something he must do it, whatever the cost.

He evidently felt he should give himself time to think. And this very scrupulous man decided that, whatever action he took, he must involve no one but himself and that he must act quite alone.

He knew that he was very tired and that, to act wisely, he must have some days' rest, so he stayed quietly at his mother's house to think out his problem and decide his action. And there was something else for which he needed time, and that was to have the opportunity, not of consulting his wife—that he never did—but of telling her of the crisis he was facing. He told her of the magnificent post Haig had offered him, and of his growing conviction that the war was being conducted in a way that would probably lead to defeat, that the fate of Haig lay in the balance, and that the fate of Haig was perhaps the fate of the Army. Robertson had been got rid of; next in line stood Haig, the last dike against the growing and threatening tide of Government interference, of Lloyd George's strategy, of Downing Street's assessment of manpower, of Cabinet estimation of the comparative fighting value of Chinese coolies, unarmed British navvies and trained German divisions arriving rested from the Russian front.

He told her that the truth was being withheld from the public, and of his belief that if only Parliament were aware of the facts, that body, representing, as he believed, the true and formidable resolution of the British people, would intervene, investigate, and sweep all this nonsense away, and see to it that the soldiers were allowed to do their jobs without political interference.

General Maurice believed that he was taking counsel of his wife, and that when he looked into her eyes he was looking at another conscience to compare with his. What he did not realise was that hers was merely a reflection of his own, incapable of coming to a different conclusion. This devoutly religious woman, simple and kindly, would no doubt have been shocked if she had been told that the God she really worshipped was called Freddy Maurice, a deity who dictated her conduct, was never wrong, and was incapable of a dishonourable action. Her heart told him what to do, for it echoed his own growing conviction as to where his duty lay.

General Maurice was still considering whether he should take any action, and if so what, when he read in *The Times* of 24 April, 1918, answers to questions put in the House of Commons by Mr George Lambert and others concerning the extension of the British front. They asked whether that extension had taken place contrary to the judgment of Sir William Robertson and Sir Douglas Haig. What they wanted to know was whether this extension was a contributory cause of the defeat of the Fifth Army.

Mr Bonar Law, who answered the questions, stated in the most positive terms that the extension that had taken place had been settled between the French and British Commanders without any Governmental pressure or intervention. This General Maurice knew was untrue, and he took this answer to be a clear proof of the Government's determination to avoid any shadow of responsibility for the present near disaster.

Bonar Law's answers raised the whole question of the extension of the British front, a matter I had dealt with for years as Liaison Officer. There was none that created more ill will between us and the French; none that had caused me greater personal unhappiness. It was one of the main reasons for my trying desperately, to the point of being threatened with a court martial, to be freed from the job of Liaison Officer.

Living with the French, I was sympathetic and understanding of their point of view, while fully appreciating that of the British, which I had constantly to defend. It was a fact that the French held a far higher proportion of the line than we did. It was also true that they had suffered heavier casualties than we had, and that the strain on them of the costly failure of the Nivelle offensive in April, 1917, had almost led to their Army's dissolving in mutinies provoked by hopelessness, despair, and mishandling.

To these arguments, repeated to me *ad nauseam*, I had to oppose the British case, but I never succeeded in convincing any Frenchmen. The French did not like being told that if the Germans advanced only six miles in Flanders we would lose coal mines providing ten million tons of coal a year. If this happened, Britain would have to make good the loss, which would involve a large diversion of labour from munitions to the mines, and of tonnage to transport coal across the Channel.

Moreover, the British line was little more than forty miles from Calais. This gave us no room to manoeuvre. Our lines of communication ran only some ten miles behind the front. We could not fall back even the shortest distance without endangering our vital communications. Without these the British Army could not remain in France, and if we went the war would be lost to the French even more certainly than to us.

36

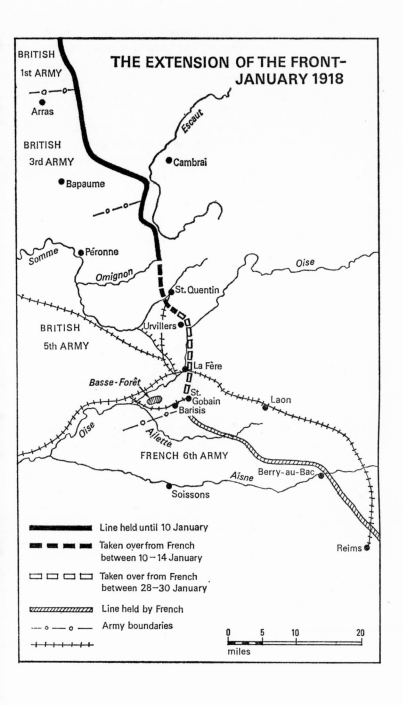

THE EXTENSION OF THE FRONT-
JANUARY 1918

BRITISH
1st ARMY

Arras

BRITISH
3rd ARMY

Bapaume

Cambrai

Escaut

Somme

Péronne

Omignon

Oise

St. Quentin

BRITISH

5th ARMY

Urvillers

La Fère

Basse-Forêt

St.
Gobain

Laon

Barisis

Oise

Aillette

FRENCH 6th ARMY

Aisne

Berry-au-Bac

Soissons

Reims

Line held until 10 January

Taken over from French
between 10 – 14 January

Taken over from French
between 28 – 30 January

Line held by French

Army boundaries

0   5   10   20

miles

On the other hand, the French, whose richest provinces were in enemy hands, could not afford to lose ground without affecting the morale of the country. Not so the Germans, who proved, as was shown when they withdrew to the Hindenburg line, how strategically effective could be a withdrawal from French lands, which involved no sentimental considerations to them.

It was, of course, impossible to make the French understand the essential importance of our having assumed the major role at sea, or the contribution we made to the Alliance by keeping our industry working at full blast. Both the French and British Governments and Commands knew that the only chance for the French Army to recover was for the British to take the greater share in the fighting; and throughout 1917 we followed an aggressive policy along the whole line. By the autumn, the French Army had recovered sufficiently, in Sir Douglas Haig's opinion, to put up a staunch defence, although it could not yet be called upon for any great or sustained offensive.

But the French insisted that it was essential to complete the cure and that the British should take over more of the line. It had to be conceded that General Pétain, the French Commander-in-Chief appointed to succeed Nivelle, was justified, as a necessary concession to re-establish discipline, to grant to every French soldier the right to ten days' leave every four months. But this reduced the total of French soldiers available in the line by some ten per cent.

From the late summer of 1917, French pressure on us to extend our line became increasingly urgent. The French Prime Minister, the gentle Monsieur Painlevé, when he pleaded with us to do this, argued that General Pétain, whom he had appointed and supported, must be given the time needed to nurse the Army back to full health.

At a meeting in a railway train at Boulogne on 25 September, 1917, attended by Mr Lloyd George and Monsieur Painlevé, the former accompanied by Sir William Robertson, and the latter by General Foch, the French strongly pressed their case. Both sides avoided expressing in words what both knew: that not only the French Army but France itself was very sick and needed not only a respite but an infusion of hope. That the British should extend their line would instil such a hope. This was evident enough to Mr Lloyd George; and I am sure he understood that when Monsieur Painlevé spoke of the people of France and their sufferings he was seeing the empty homes, the vacant chairs, the untilled fields and the multitude of aching hearts that echoed the words, 'no more, we can stand no more, there are only the children left, and who is to look after them?' No use trying to explain to villagers of Beauce or farmers in Gascony that the British on their shorter front were holding proportionately far more Germans and suffering far heavier casualties than were their own men.

The plea put forward with desperate earnestness by both Foch and Painlevé was that France would starve unless the men of 48 were released. Foch insisted that the line be extended by 1 November, so that the land could be worked in time for the harvest. The necessity for this was real, but on the moral plane. Now that America was in the war, wheat could be shipped to France, though at the cost of essential shipments of arms and munitions. What the French needed was men on the farms, better old men than no men at all, men to do the heavy work, no doubt, but far more important to give the reassurance of their presence to all those homes in so many provinces, from sunbaked Provence to misty Brittany, where even the heroic women of France, reigning over a population of children, could not carry their burdens alone any longer.

Even unsentimental Wully Robertson saw this, but he pointed out that, at the moment, the only Army carrying out aggressive action was the British, and that it was quite impossible for our Army to take over a longer line to the extent demanded by the French and at the same time carry on with the offensives in which they were engaged and to prepare for action in 1918, which was the only means by which the war could be won.

The Frenchmen understood this, but hoped, not without reason, that once the French Army was restored to health it could play a greater part in an offensive in 1918 than was possible in the winter of 1917, when it could only undertake small-scale attacks.

Both General Robertson and Mr Lloyd George were at pains to express their sympathy with the French point of view, making it clear that they conceded that some extension of our front would have to be made eventually, but stressing that no extension was possible as long as the present Ypres offensive was in progress.

Sir William Robertson, who was supported in this by the Prime Minister, said that no decision could be reached in the absence of Sir Douglas Haig, so he proposed, and it was agreed, that the Prime Minister and he should go straight from Boulogne to GHQ to inform Haig of the upshot of the Conference.

The conclusion of the Conference was reported to the War Cabinet on 27 September in the following terms:

The British Government having accepted, in principle, the extension of the line held by the British Army on the Western front, the two Governments are agreed that the question of the amount of the extension and the time at which it should take place should be left for arrangement between the two Commanders-in-Chief.*

Had the Prime Minister and Sir William Robertson been on normal terms they would no doubt have seen the Commander-in-Chief together, but they were not, and Mr Lloyd George saw Haig alone.

According to Haig the Prime Minister only informed him that Painlevé was anxious that the British should take over more line. He did, however, ask Haig for a report on the role of the British forces in 1918 in the light of a Russian collapse and the weakness of France and Italy.

This report Haig sent to London on 8 October.

It concluded: 'It is necessary, in my opinion, to refuse to take over more line, and to adhere resolutely to that refusal.'

He would not have used these terms had he been told by the Prime Minister that the discussion at Boulogne ended in a decision in principle to extend the line.

It is difficult to understand how it came about that Sir William Robertson said little or nothing to Sir Douglas concerning the discussions at Boulogne and apparently failed to emphasise to the Commander-in-Chief the desperate earnestness of the French plea for relief. Only suppositions are possible and mine may be wrong. It may be that he assumed that the Prime Minister had told Haig of what had occurred, or it may be that, as neither the Prime Minister nor the CIGS had more knowledge of the French language than is required to thoroughly misunderstand what is being said, that they did not realise, or rather perhaps General Robertson did not realise, the extent to which the French assumed that the British had committed themselves.

We do not know who interpreted. As I attempt to reconstruct what occurred I am left with the memory of how on another occasion I was the only one present, as interpreter, when the same two men, Painlevé and Lloyd George, met in great secret, also at

* Cab 24/50/181.

40

Boulogne, to discuss the Greek problem, the two Prime Ministers in the back of a taxi, I perched uncomfortably on an occasional seat to which every description could be applied save that it presented a horizontal surface. My distinct impression on that occasion was that, with but little help from me, the two Ministers understood each other quite well through the intelligent interpretation of each other's winks, frowns (whenever a Conservative was mentioned), the quick grasp of the other's meaning conveyed by a slight tap on the knee, but, above all, thanks to the extraordinarily intelligent miming these two superlatively intelligent men used to supplement the incomprehensible words with which they peppered each other as the uncomfortable and jolting taxi drove endlessly round and about up and down the hills and coastal roads in the neighbourhood of Boulogne.

Meanwhile, before Haig's paper of 8 October was sent to London, he received what he described as a great bombshell.* This 'bombshell', he wrote in his diary, was a letter from the CIGS dated 3 October stating that the British Government had 'approved in principle of the British Army in France taking over more line from the French, and details are to be arranged by General Pétain and myself. This was settled at a conference at Boulogne on 25 September at which I was not present. Nor did either Lloyd George or Robertson tell me of this decision at our interview.' And Haig proceeds to fume against Robertson whom he accuses of having quietly acquiesced at the Conference in Painlevé's demands! 'R (Robertson) comes badly out of this, in my opinion, especially *as it was definitely stated (with War Cabinet approval) that no discussions re operations on the Western front would be held with the French without my being present.*'

It is not difficult to sympathise with Haig for his sense of exasperation at receiving a letter informing him of what was described as a 'conclusion approved in principle' by the British Government concerning the extension of the British line in France, a decision he was given to understand had been taken at Boulogne by Lloyd George and Robertson on the day before they saw him on the 26th.

This was a matter of maximum importance to him, since among other things he could not pursue the offensive he was then engaged

* Sir Douglas Haig's Diary, 3 October, 1917, quoted in Robert Blake (ed.) *The Private Papers of Douglas Haig*, p. 256.

in or plan for that which it was intended he should undertake early next year if he took over more line from the French in 1917.

Although Sir Douglas's deep sense of grievance and affront is understandable I can but regret personally that he should have allowed it to develop into a feeling of bitterness and irritation against Sir William Robertson which seems to have persisted and may explain why he took no step and said no word in defence of old Wully when the Prime Minister dismissed him.

I am absolutely certain that General Robertson was incapable of letting Haig down, as he proved at the Calais Conference when he defended Haig more determinedly than Haig was prepared to defend himself. He always fought Haig's battles with a furious tenacity.

If I may hazard a guess, the fundamental reason for all the hard feeling arose from Lloyd George's failure to stress to Sir Douglas the extreme force of the French pressure for a British extension.

It would certainly have been fairer to Haig if Lloyd George had done so. As for Robertson, as I see it, he did not feel entitled to say anything to Haig before the War Cabinet had been informed, knowing he would have the opportunity of stating his views to it when it considered the matter; and it may well be that he felt that, all things considered, an extension of our line was inevitable, and that the minimum danger would be run if the length of the line to be taken over, and the timing of the operation, was left to the two Commanders-in-Chief, Pétain and Haig, to agree.

On 16 October Haig wrote to the CIGS:

In my Secret Memorandum No. O.A.D. 652, dated the 8th Instant, I have stated some of the objections to taking over more line from the French, and I regret that the British Government should have seen fit to decide a matter which may involve such serious consequences without giving me an opportunity of stating my views. In view of the considerations explained in my O.A.D. 652, I trust that the War Cabinet will reconsider the question.

This was forwarded to the War Cabinet by General Sir William Robertson with the following remarks:

At the recent Boulogne Conference between the Prime Minister, M. Painlevé, General Foch and myself, the question of extending our Front was raised by the French Representatives. The reply given was that, while in principle we were of course ready to do whatever could be done, the matter was one which could not be discussed in the absence of Sir

Douglas Haig, or during the continuance of the present operations, and that due regard must also be had to the plan of operations for next year. It was suggested that it would be best for the Field-Marshal to come to an arrangement with General Pétain when this could be done. So far as I am aware, no further formal discussion has taken place, and therefore the matter cannot be regarded as 'decided'. Further, I feel sure that the War Cabinet would not think of deciding such an important question without first obtaining Sir Douglas Haig's views. I am replying to him in the above sense.

I should add that, on the day following the Boulogne Conference, the Prime Minister verbally informed Sir Douglas Haig of what had passed, and the latter then laid stress on the necessity of settling the plan for next year and then adjusting the line accordingly. He also emphasised the great importance of our having Divisions out of the line for training purposes during the winter if we were to take the offensive next spring. He has since emphasised the necessity of giving our men who have recently done much hard fighting, adequate leave of absence.*

Sir William Robertson's explanation somewhat reassured Haig. He had started talks with General Pétain, as he had felt bound to do after the Boulogne Conference, but he asked to be informed with the least possible delay whether the War Cabinet would support him in a refusal to take over more than a 4-division front. He underlined once more that the success of the following year's campaign depended mainly on the prosecution of a vigorous offensive by the British Army.

He concluded his communication: 'You will appreciate, however, the undesirability of the Commander-in-Chief of the British Armies in France refusing a request of the French Commander-in-Chief if the British Government finds itself unable subsequently to support this refusal.' To which Sir William Robertson added ... 'if the British Armies are to undertake offensive operations early next year, it is essential that the men who have been engaged in protracted attacks throughout the present year should have adequate leave and rest and receive the training necessary to assimilate the new drafts'.

On 24 October the War Cabinet accepted Sir William Robertson's advice that while the present offensive continued it would not be possible to begin taking over more line.

At the beginning of November the Rapallo Conference was convened. Before it met, the Prime Minister informed the War

* This quotation and the preceding one are taken from Hankey's paper on *The Extension of the Front*.

Cabinet that he had learned from General Pétain that arrangements had been made by Field-Marshal Sir Douglas Haig and himself that the British should take over the front occupied by General Anthoine's army on the British left and should also take over the front occupied by 5 French divisions on the British right. But on 1 December, Haig wrote that the relief of the 3rd French Corps which was to have begun on 12 December must be postponed; and concluded: 'I do not feel justified in carrying out any extension in relief of French troops', but Robertson, keeping in the closest contact with Haig, toned this down and informed the Cabinet that Haig had arranged to study with General Pétain a possible relief down to the Barisis/St Gobain railway. But then came the order to send 2 divisions to Italy, and this offer was reduced to an extension down to the Basse Forêt/St Gobain railway, and then only if no more Divisions were sent to Italy. Robertson went on:

The present situation is that since the principle of extending the line was accepted Sir Douglas Haig has been ordered to send 5 divisions to Italy. A sixth division (4th Australian) has been converted into a draft-finding unit, whilst, as the result of the Cambrai battle, his front will have been lengthened, necessitating the employment in the line of at least one more division than before the battle. This makes a total decrease of the strength for reserve or for extension of the line of 7 divisions, while our troops have been fighting continuously from 31 July to the present time.

On the other hand, the French advance on the Ailette on 16 and 19 October shortened their front by the equivalent of 2 divisions, and they have not fought since. Further, in the north the French have relieved 4 of our divisions, while we have relieved 6 of theirs, giving them the advantage of 2 on balance. They thus have a relief of 4 divisions (2 on the Ailette and 2 in the north) to set against the 6 they have sent to Italy.

The result of these various changes is that, as compared with the situation before the Italian collapse the French are now 2 divisions to the bad and we are 4 divisions to the bad, plus the effect of the Cambrai fighting.

Clemenceau, after he became Prime Minister in November, 1917, pressed even more strongly than had Painlevé for an extension. In view of this pressure, and of the decision of the Boulogne Conference, Haig and Robertson had to accept that some extension was unavoidable.

The extent of the French pressure is shown by an entry in the War Cabinet Minutes of Saturday, 15 December, 1917:

Captain Amery* who had that morning returned from Versailles reported that on Thursday last General Pétain had discussed with the French Cabinet the question of the holding of the French line. General Pétain stated that he could not continue to accept responsibility for holding the French front unless the British were prepared to take over a considerable portion of the line now held by the French troops, and unless at the same time the French Government could find him 200,000 men from civilian sources to prepare defensive lines behind the front. This latter undertaking had been given to General Pétain by Monsieur Clemenceau, who states that he was determined to press the British Government to settle the former question at an early date and threatened to present the matter to the French Chamber in the event of our refusal to meet the French request, but Monsieur Clemenceau had been willing to submit the French case to Versailles by Thursday next.

The Prime Minister directed General Maurice to communicate the above facts to Sir William Robertson, who, it was understood, was now at Sir Douglas Haig's Headquarters. 'The Prime Minister added that he considered the matter of the utmost seriousness and importance.'

That the question was of great importance to the French there can be no doubt, but it was also of much consequence to us. Our Allies have always found a little blackmailing pressure very effective on British statesmen, though why the fear of being denounced by the French Chamber should have been so potent is not clear. A counter-threat to tell the House of Commons the facts might well have been appropriate.

On 17 December Sir William Robertson circulated to the War Cabinet the case Sir Douglas Haig intended to submit to the Supreme War Council on the subject of the extension of the line. It began by giving a detailed appreciation of the strategic problems involved in the British defensive front which had been rehearsed to them often before, and concluded:

In the above circumstances, in my judgment the utmost that can be asked of the British Armies is that they should hold their present front. To extend it now would not only involve risks which I consider very grave, but would seriously hamper and delay the development of a strong defensive system which is urgent at the moment, and which, when it has been developed, will enable me to increase my reserves considerably.

* L. S. Amery, M.P., after serving as a Staff Officer in Flanders and Salonika, was appointed Assistant Secretary to the Cabinet when Lloyd George became Prime Minister.

By that time, too, I hope that my troops will have been rested and that my drafts to fill the ranks will have been received.

Sir Douglas Haig's case included the following statement:

So far as lies in my power, with due regard to the safety of my Armies, which is as necessary to our Allies as to the British Empire, I desire to fulfil the undertaking which, subject to certain conditions, I gave to General Pétain, viz., to take over, as soon as possible, a two-Division front at least, and, if possible, a larger front extending to the St Gobain railway, a little South of La Fère.

Sir Douglas was right to emphasise the point often forgotten by the French: that the safety of the British Armies was as necessary to the Alliance as to the British Empire. Indeed it was more so, as was proved in the last war. The British Commonwealth, with the support of the United States but without the French, proved able to halt and defeat the Nazi-Fascist world. This is a thought which should not be overlooked by French historians of the First War and may well be pondered with some qualms of regret by those of our countrymen who are not so international as to regret the days when Britain was able to uphold freedom as she understood it, and to make it prevail.

In his memorandum presenting Sir Douglas Haig's statement General Robertson pointed out that he considered Monsieur Clemenceau's request that we should take over the line as far as Berry-au-Bac to be quite impossible. In this respect General Maurice's entries for 7, 15 and 17 January are enlightening.

On the 18th Mr Lloyd George informed the War Cabinet that Sir Douglas Haig and General Pétain had been unable to agree on the matter of taking over more of the French line and that the French Prime Minister proposed that the question should be submitted to Versailles. He said he would abide by that body's decision if the British Prime Minister would do the same, to which the War Cabinet answered that they had already referred the case to the Military Advisers with a view to a final decision being taken by the Supreme War Council in accordance with the Rapallo Agreement.

But Sir Douglas Haig, rightly apprehensive that the Versailles Council would opt for his taking over more line than he deemed reasonable, agreed with the French Commander-in-Chief before the Supreme Council met to take over as far as Barisis only. The relief of two French divisions was begun on 10 January and Haig said he would endeavour to take over as far as the Oise by the end of the month. The extension of the front to Barisis by the 3rd Corps was begun on 27 January and completed by the 30th. A letter from G. H. Batty a member of the DMO's staff at the War Office to General Maurice recalled on 20 May that:

There have been two extensions of the British Front this year:

   (i) From Omignon River to north-east of Urvillers—completed about *13 January, 1918.*
   (ii) Urvillers to Oise (Barisis)—completed about *3 February, 1918.*

With regard to (i), I cannot find that the War Cabinet were ever told about this extension; in fact Sir M. Hankey has put in a long scream complaining on this very point.

With regard to (ii), you reported to the War Cabinet on 8 February, 1918, that the British Front had been extended to Barisis. (War Cabinet 341, minute 1.)

The assumption is that your report to Cabinet on 8 February covered the whole of the extension of our right flank—there is only an interval of about three weeks between the two extensions.

Following extract from War Cabinet 316A, minute 1, dated *7 January, 1918;* may be of interest:

F.M. Sir D. Haig stated that he proposed to take over a two-Divisional front from the French in a few days' time, and a further two-Divisional front by the end of the month (Jan.), which would involve our right flank resting upon the River Oise.

At Versailles on 30 January the Prime Minister put the question to General Pétain point blank whether he had in fact reached agreement with General Haig on the extension to Barisis. Pétain answered that this was so but that he was now obliged to ask for a further extension. When he said this he was no doubt conscious of Monsieur Clemenceau's hard gaze riveted on him. A careful observer could have concluded that this hard gaze was the exact meaning of 'being obliged to ask for a further extension'.

It is very interesting to note how during these days Mr Lloyd George's attitude towards the Army seemed to change, or rather to be expressed in more realistic form. That he always sympathised with the ordeal of the troops is evident; his constant expression 'blood and mud' was clear evidence that it was on their behalf that he crucified the Generals. It might even be said that his strategic conceptions in favour of distant campaigns had as one of their objectives to extricate the troops from the morass of barbed wire in which they were imprisoned. But at Versailles it was as if he discerned individuals more accurately; spoke of men rather than of masses, of individuals rather than of groups; of people rather than of battalions.

He suddenly seemed to comprehend the frightful, cruel suffering of the troops, their heart-breaks, their fatigues, what it meant night after night to man the trenches an hour before dawn, practically never to have a hot meal, or to be ever clean of mud. He perceived an Army without Generals, and this beam removed from his eye he saw the truth, and his vivid imagination, his quick response to suffering led him to exert his great eloquence in an effort to save the troops from any further tortures that could be avoided. And he now really did begin to understand something of the fresh torment an extension of the line would entail. At the Supreme Council he developed better than any soldier could have done the problems inherent in the line the British already held. He spoke of our precarious communications, the closeness of the harbours to the line, the danger of losing the very important coal mines. He drew a vivid picture of the British soldiers, tens of thousands of homesick men whose only hope of survival was a wound that was not deadly—not too light a one, mind you, for that only meant you were back in the line with the smell of hospital still in your nostrils—and of how these men when out of the trenches spent their lives under the leaden drenching skies of Flanders among strangers, themselves strangers in a strange land. The French were in their own country, at home in the villages and towns, but the British troops could only hope for leave in their own land once a year; now, they heard that every French soldier was entitled to ten days' leave every four months—and it was to enable him to enjoy this enormous privilege that his ally had to take over more of his line. What, asked the Prime Minister, would the reaction of the British be? The French were not the only ones with problems of morale. Under these conditions new and very serious matters in this sphere were certain to arise.

The Military Representatives had, he gathered, recommended an extension of the line farther than the British military authorities felt they could safely agree to. Let them not forget that the British Commander-in-Chief had declared that if he had to do this he could not be responsible for the safety of his line. This responsibility would now be theirs.

Nor let the Council forget, said Mr Lloyd George, that the British had borne the brunt of the fighting during the last year. Rest and reorganisation were now imperative. Time for training and for absorbing new drafts was essential, and what training was possible for a Division in line? And he hinted at the fact that perhaps, such is human nature, the French—how do these things become known?—on a rumour that they would be relieved, had done little or no work on defensive lines, which meant additional and very unwelcome labour for our war-weary men. It would have a very dangerous effect on morale.

He suggested the transfer of a large number of Italian troops to the Western front as perhaps the best, if temporary, solution to the present problem.

But when the Prime Minister had done, General Pétain, always under the diamond-hard stare of Monsieur Clemenceau, continued to press for the acceptance of the Military Representatives' recommendation for a British extension to the Ailette river, though he conceded that the execution and method of carrying this out should be left to be settled between himself and Sir Douglas Haig.

It was the duty of Mr Lloyd George to assess these different claims and points of view. Here on the one hand was the Areopagus of Versailles, largely his own creation, demanding measures which his own Commander-in-Chief, through whom he himself was responsible to the British nation, denounced as dangerous, and there, formidable and menacing, was the French Prime Minister threatening a possible dissolution of his country, now bleeding to death. Lloyd George was, as has already been said, as frightened of Clemenceau as were most people. I have always admired how he stood up to that terrible octogenarian whose head was like a large grey rock picked up on any one of his own Vendée beaches, as shapeless, as heavy, as neolithic. On some of these occasions Lloyd George would leave the conference room and, like a lion which stimulates its courage by lashing its tail, would bound round the corridors to work himself up into a mood of the utmost determination.

This was not such an occasion. Lloyd George disappeared into the corridor, but this time, instead of working himself into furious opposition to his French colleague, he sent for Haig and obtained from him an undertaking that he would, as soon as possible, relieve the French to the Ailette river.

Haig noted that after the meeting 'Pétain came along to me and said that he had no intention to *taquiner* me over this'.*

General Maurice wrote in his diary on 2 February: 'Extension of front settled—to be left to Haig and Pétain to carry out', and on 8 February he reported to the War Cabinet that the extension to Barisis had been completed.

'This matter (the extension of the front) was not dealt with at all at the Versailles Council' were Mr Bonar Law's last words as he stood at the box in the House of Commons on 23 April, and this was a lie.

Sir Douglas Haig was as indignant as General Maurice at Bonar Law's inaccuracy. On Sunday, 28 April, 1918, he wrote in his diary that he gave Lord Milner a note:

With reference to a statement by Mr Bonar Law in the House of Commons in which he declared that the extension of the British Line had been arranged *between the Commanders in France* without interference by the British Government. My note showed clearly how on 25 September last a Conference (at which I was not present) was held at Boulogne, and the British and French Governments decided *on the principle* that the British should take over more line. To this I protested. To-day I told Lord Milner I did not wish to embarrass the Government at this time, but I must ask that a true statement of the facts be filed at the War Office. M. said he would be glad to do this, and that he recollected very well how all along I had objected to any extension. And that it was his opinion that if we had not taken over some line from the French, the blow would have fallen on them and the war would have been well-nigh lost. He (M) 'wishes to throw the blame on no one, but is quite ready to accept all blame himself'. 'Unfortunately,' said he, 'some of the members of the Cabinet are not so constituted.'†

Although Bonar Law's statements in the House of Commons were untrue, I am sure the Minister was convinced that he was speaking the truth; indeed he went out of his way to emphasise that this was his conviction. 'I am quite glad that this matter should be cleared up,' he declared. 'To the best of my knowledge—and I think I know all the facts—there is not the smallest truth in any such suggestion.' The truth was small indeed, so small as to be

* Sir Douglas Haig's Diary, 2 February, 1918, *The Private Papers of Douglas Haig*, p. 282. He noted against the word *'taquiner'* his translation: 'worry'. 'Tease' would be more accurate.
† *The Private Papers of Douglas Haig*, p. 306. See also Haig's Diary for 3 October, 1917 (p. 256).

invisible to the naked eye, imperceptible in the notes prepared for Mr Bonar Law's reply.

It was Bonar Law's answers that decided General Maurice. He reasoned that the Prime Minister's misstatements in his speech on 9 April might be accidental, but that this could not be true of a prepared answer to a parliamentary question. He concluded that the Government was determined to maintain that the blame for the defeat inflicted by the enemy on the Army was the fault of the Generals, and that Ministers, having done everything possible, had no responsibility for the disaster.

In considering what his action should be, his overriding concern was to determine where his duty lay. He had become convinced that Mr Lloyd George was steering the country to disaster. This being settled in his mind, the next thing to decide was whether there was anything he could do to avert such a calamity.

He took his decision on his own responsibility alone. He sent his letter to the press confident that once Parliament knew the facts it would demand an inquiry, which would reveal the abyss towards which the Prime Minister was steering. But it was essential that it be informed without a moment's delay, for *the flood was almost on us*. He did not underestimate either the dangers or the shortness of the time available when he decided that only the desperate cry of alarm of someone in possession of all the facts and known to be so by the country could prevent disaster. So, knowing all too well that it was useless to repeat to the Prime Minister warnings constantly disregarded, he took the only means open to him to draw the nation's attention to its plight, and sacrified himself, his career, and his family, to throw the glaring light of publicity on the facts.

It was an act of great moral courage. His sacrifice was not unlike that of the officer who threw himself over a grenade about to explode, using his body as a shield to save many men's lives.

So he immolated himself, confident that his action would force the House of Commons, in which he believed, to reassess the Prime Minister's policy and its consequences before it was too late.

This books tells the story of how he failed to get the inquiry for which he had asked; but achieved one of his principal objects—to save Haig. It tells how the Unionist War Committee, although they knew that he had told the truth in his letter, decided to support the Government in the division on the Maurice Debate because of their hatred of Asquith, the Liberal leader.

It shows how Lloyd George obtained his vote of confidence by using the reply to the Baring question to discredit General Maurice, although he knew when he spoke that the figures on which he based his argument were wrong.

It clears up the mystery of 'the burnt paper', and, for the first time, publishes all the evidence about this and the Baring question.

It shows General Maurice's vain efforts to compel Lloyd George to admit the truth; and his vindication when the Lloyd George *War Memoirs* were published.

It is a formidable indictment of Lloyd George as the political leader of the nation at a most critical period of the war. It is not less so of the Government's chief military adviser, the Chief of the Imperial General Staff, Sir Henry Wilson. To my mind he emerges as even more blameworthy than Lloyd George. I see him as he reveals himself in General Maurice's diary as a man in whom laziness first, then ambition, had destroyed all the military virtues with which he had been endowed.

There can be no excuse whatever for the support he lent to the Prime Minister's machinations in setting up the Versailles Executive Board. That Mr Lloyd George, entirely innocent of the least tincture of military knowledge, should have imagined that a war could be conducted by a Committee is understandable, just as President Kruger was convinced the world was flat, but as General Maurice says, 'Command by any Committee in War is, as history shows, condemned to failure from the beginning.' There may be some who, without approving, may condone the action of a politician in resorting to the device of setting up a board as a means of getting rid of military advisers he disliked and distrusted but was not politically strong enough at that moment to dismiss, but none can approve the conduct of the General on whom his political chief relied, and even relied to the extent of using him against other Generals in conniving at the setting-up of machinery that might well have jeopardised the outcome of the war. Ambition has never justified less adequately an historic crime.

Again, what excuse can be made for General Wilson, the most responsible soldier of all, saying on the very eve of the German offensive that smashed our front that the 'Western front is safe, and two or three Divisions from Palestine could make no difference'?

And what can be advanced in favour of a CIGS who on 4 March (the German attack was launched on the 21st) told General Maurice 'he was afraid the German attack would not come' and when it did come told the Cabinet it might be nothing more than a big raid?

What has struck me personally as unspeakably mean is the way in which Sir Henry Wilson, having based his entire career on Foch, took underhand steps with Mr Lloyd George's connivance to obstruct any further extension of the French General's powers once Foch had become Generalissimo, as these might tend to limit his own.

Nor can there be any excuse whatever for the Government's principal military adviser, on the third day of the German offensive, assuring the War Cabinet that the opposing German and allied forces could be estimated as being approximately equal, although the DMO and DMI had reported that the Germans had 191 divisions to the Allies' 165.

Henry Wilson had a very arresting personality and a fascinating ugliness of which he was quite proud, boasting that somebody having addressed a postcard to the ugliest man in London it had come straight to him.

He was immensely tall and zigzagged upwards indefinitely. From the top of the last angle a shapeless terracotta-coloured face peered down. From the large mouth which slashed it under a nondescript greying moustache came words flowing upwards musically from well below his belt. They fell with a soft thud on your alerted consciousness, for you could not but be interested in what he had to say. He had a special fascination and was certainly very intelligent, which was proved by the high posts he had held in the Army. When war was declared he sailed with the BEF as Deputy Chief of the General Staff.

This strange man loved clowning and, curiously enough, this had an unexpected attraction for many people; it certainly mesmerised Lloyd George. I have often seen Wilson reverse his cap, peak to back, so that only the red band showed like that of a German soldier, and crouch, his face level with the table, using his cane as a gun, hopping round taking pot shots at the spectators; the idea being to illustrate trench warfare. Some people found this irresistible.

My first shattering disillusionment with him was when, accompanied by General Macdonogh, he met General Franchet d'Esperey on the eve of the Marne. It was clear that Wilson, only two removed from the Commander-in-Chief himself, was quite unaware of the position of our own forces.

After the first few months of the war, I do not remember seeing him again until he commanded a Corps on the Vimy Ridge when I was liaison officer with the French Command in that most unpleasant area. It was a period when exploding mines were an almost daily occurrence. It was intensely unpleasant. Enormous craters would shake the ground like an earthquake and whole sections of the line would disappear.

General Sir William Robertson told me later that Wilson, who had been gaining more and more influence over Mr Lloyd George, had himself sent on a mission to Russia, which was certainly less unpleasant than the Vimy Ridge, and had declared that to add weight to his mission he should be appointed a temporary full General. When he returned Sir William Robertson, then CIGS, offered him the command of a Corps once more, but he declined on the grounds that he was now a full General.

And so he became Chief Liaison Officer with the French Commander-in-Chief, General Nivelle, with whom he was on very friendly terms.

What was the basis of General Wilson's character? He was certainly not stupid, nor can he have been unversed in his profession. I am inclined to think his career followed the strangely fortunate course it did, in spite of a complete failure to achieve any military success, owing to two causes: the one a fundamental laziness or mental indolence of the type that will take immense pains to avoid what looked like hard work, that will walk a mile rather than tackle the problem of climbing a short ladder or creeping through or over a fence. The other was the discovery of his innate powers of persuasion, which removed all difficulties from his path. His enormous ambition found encouragement from the ease with which his very fertile imagination devised ways of steering round, over or under obstacles, always providing means of avoiding tackling them frontally.

In later years he always made me think of an occasion when, as a young Member of Parliament, I visited the prison of Wandsworth. There I met two young men in a workshop who looked like pure angels. Their seraphic appearance made me feel there must be here some appalling miscarriage of justice; such cherubs could not possibly have been guilty of more than a childish prank, and I asked to see the Governor. He sent for the Padre who gave me the clear impression he could only feel pity for the constituency that had elected so credulous a member. 'Cannot you see', he said, 'that it is the very characteristic which has made you fall a victim to their plausible innocence which is the explanation of their being here? They realised early that they had the gift of inducing trust and belief by their very appearance. Everyone believed anything they said. Deception was too easy.' Since that day I have always avoided inviting kind fairies to be godmothers to babies I was interested in. I felt that Sir Henry Wilson must have had the doubtful benefit of having as godmother a fairy who was overkind and bestowed on him the gift of smoothing away all obstacles in the path of his ambition by disguising his purpose by his charm.

Nevertheless this strange man might have gone down in history as a considerable military figure had he not unmasked himself in his diaries. It is as if a living creature were to tear off skin and muscle from its own face, revealing the grimacing skull that lies underneath.

It is rather trying to the diminishing number of men who have survived both wars to hear self-appointed experts apportion praise or blame for the now remote battles of the First War without ever having incurred the mortal risks that were faced by those involved. I wonder if such sham historians realise how foolish they appear to those who stood beside the Commanders who had to assume the terrible responsibilities involved in operations in that war.

My own judgment is that our Generals of the First War acquitted themselves remarkably well, and extremely well compared with Allied and enemy Commanders, in view of the formidable tasks they were faced with. They did not lead their troops to victory through forests of barbed wire, nor did the French, nor the Germans. Of course they made mistakes. It was not always the Generals who were right and the politicians wrong; but the fact is that the real responsibility for the holocaust of trench warfare lay with the politicians, the newspapers and finally the public, who wanted victories but had failed to provide the Commanders with the means of winning them.

The Generals? It is amazing they were as good as they were. What opportunities did they have for training? Men on bicycles representing a Corps. A corporal wandering off the road at manoeuvres leading to furious complaints by farmers and reproofs by authorities loth to pay compensation. What means were Commanders provided with to win victories? Guns? No. Shells? No. Finally all they were left with was men, poor chaps, clerks, industrial workers, a few yokels; but the great public at the back whose point of view was so accurately represented by the Press and of course by Parliament clamoured for victories. So the Commanders used the only fighting element they had in their armoury, men, and the public that had refused to arm these men, who had denied them weapons, training and equipment, yelled in horror when they saw the blood of the men they had inadequately protected flow in torrents against the barbed wire they had been hurled at.

This book is a clear exposition of how demagogy can undermine and indeed murder modern democracy, of the terrible danger of politicians attempting to wage war, of how untutored political prejudice can so blind a people that it may stumble into disaster, of how the denial of past knowledge and experience, the casting aside of proved leadership, may be as cruel to a nation as to break a blind man's stick, or to poison his dog.

The story has a suggestion of the inevitable ending of a Greek tragedy, the self-immolation of a simple soul who, believing in truth and loyalty, found it difficult to believe that any other weapons could be used in a war waged to vindicate these principles. To soldiers steeped in Army traditions and who love what the Army stands for, it carries the consolation that General Maurice, who was one of its martyrs, was vindicated by his becoming the trusted leader of all old soldiers, the President of the British Legion.

But to many ordinary people this book will convey a deep sense of the rightness of things, a happy realisation not only that there is justice in this world but that it is sometimes manifested in a most touching way, that it is General Maurice's daughter whose filial devotion to her father and faith in what he stood for has enabled her so successfully to unravel a seemingly insoluble mystery, and finally to reveal her father in his true light as an able, brave, if perhaps almost unbelievably guileless and simple soldier.

Part 2

Foreword

In May, 1918, the Maurice family were living in a large house in Kensington Park Gardens lent them by friends for the duration of the war.

Major General Sir Frederick Maurice had been Director of Military Operations at the War Office from December, 1915, when Sir William Robertson became Chief of the Imperial General Staff, until 20 April, 1918.

There were five children in the family. Nancy, the eldest, had just had her eighteenth birthday and was studying at Queen's College, Harley Street, founded by their great-grandfather, Frederick Denison Maurice, in 1848 'for the higher education of women'. Freddy, the only son, aged $16\frac{1}{2}$, was at Dartmouth, due to pass out later in the year into the Royal Navy. The three younger girls were all at day schools in London.

General and Lady Maurice left London for his mother's house at Camberley on 6 May. He was having a few days' leave before going to France, where he was to take up an important appointment.

Late that night the telephone rang, and Nancy answered it. It was *The Times* asking to speak to General Maurice. When Nancy said he was away and she did not know where he was, the voice said 'We have a letter purporting to be from General Maurice, and we wish to be certain that it is authentic.'

Nancy, eager to be helpful, offered to go to Printing House Square 'to identify the signature', but *The Times* did not think this necessary, and, puzzled, she went to bed.

Next morning, she asked Clare, her father's devoted but not very intelligent Irish batman, who had seen off her parents at Waterloo Station, if he had any message for her from the General. He said he had not, but later, under cross-examination, produced from his pocket an envelope addressed to her which he had 'forgotten' to give her.

Meanwhile 20 Kensington Park Gardens was in a state of siege. Some thirty reporters and photographers kept watch on the front door, and the telephone never stopped ringing.

Nancy opened the envelope and this is what she read.

*H.V.,
5 May, 1918

Dear Nance and Freddy,

I have decided to take a very important step which may make a great difference to our lives, and I want you to know about it before it happens; but you must not tell a soul before you hear about it in the papers.

You know that for some time past, the Government has not been telling the truth about the War. Their object is to show that they did everything possible and that the blame rests with the Generals. This is absolutely untrue, and I am one of the few people who know the facts. I am, in fact, the only soldier who knows them and is not employed. I have therefore decided to write the letter, which I enclose, to the papers, and I hope it will appear on Tuesday. This is, of course, a breach of military discipline; but there are occasionally—not often, thank God!— times when duty as a citizen comes before duty as a soldier; and after long and careful thought, I am convinced this is one of them. They may turn me out of the Army and you may suffer in consequence, though I will do my best to see that you don't. I hope you will think that I am right. Mother has never wavered since I told her, and that has been a great support to me.

I am persuaded that I am doing what is right, and once that is so, nothing else matters to a man. That is, I believe, what Christ meant when he told us to forsake father and mother and children and wife for his sake. It has been a difficult decision for, as you know, I love the Army and I have you all and Mother to think of, but it is made now, and you must help me to make the best of it.

Your loving
Father

The enclosure, very badly typed by Lady Maurice, was a copy of General Maurice's letter to the Press, which appeared on Tuesday 7 May in *The Times*, *Morning Post*, *Daily Chronicle* and *Daily News*.†

The announcement of his retirement from the Army appeared on 13 May.

General Maurice died, at the age of 80, in May, 1951.

Many years after his death, a box of papers was found in the

---

* Highland View in Camberley, the home of Lady Maurice, the widow of Major-General Sir (John) Frederick Maurice.   † See page 97.

house in Cambridge where he died. They included a diary, written in pencil in a *Collins Scribbling Diary* beginning on 1 January, and ending on 20 May, 1918; and a long paper, dated 22 May, 1918, headed 'Secret', entitled *The Story of the Crisis of May, 1918*. These are now published, as a contribution to history, and to honour his memory.

1 The Diary of Sir Frederick Maurice

1 January, 1918–20 April, 1918

Tuesday 1 January

Cambrai report. Completed covering minute reviewing the operations for CIGS. War Cabinet decided report to go to Smuts for his opinion before communicating to France.*

Wednesday 2 January

War Cabinet. LG still harping on Jerusalem. He won't be satisfied with anything short of Aleppo and thinks we can fly there. He is convinced we didn't want to go to Jerusalem and are doing our best to belittle the results of the capture. Quite untrue.† Completed paper on Home Defence. Now that Jellicoe is gone we get the present ridiculous scale reduced, particularly as War Cabinet want some excuse for not giving us men.‡

Thursday 3 January

War Cabinet. A rather rambling discussion on War Aims. Completed paper for War Cabinet in answer to their question on present military situation, pressing for more men.

* On 5 December, 1917, the War Cabinet asked Haig for a report on the Battle of Cambrai. The politicians were concerned at the way in which the German success seemed to belie previous official reports of poor German morale. Haig, in a report dated 24 December, attributed the setback to the tiredness of the men resulting from operations early in November. Smuts thought that the trouble lay in a shortage of trained men, especially NCOs and junior officers. Robertson agreed with Haig. The several Cambrai reports are in the Public Record Office, WO32/5095B.

† For a brief discussion of Lloyd George's views on Palestine at this time see Brian Gardner, *Allenby*, London, 1965, Chapter 8.

‡ The pessimistic Jellicoe resigned on 27 December, 1917, and was succeeded by Sir Rosslyn Wemyss as First Sea Lord.

Friday 4 January

Sent on Haig's report on system of defence on British front. He reads well. Hope the Boche will give us time to complete it. Weather very favourable for work. Frost hard enough to make it easy to get material up.

Saturday 5 January

Got copy of Cabinet Committee on manpower. Most depressing. Navy—Air service—food—ship-building—timber-felling all given precedence of the Army. We shall get little or nothing.*

Monday 7 January

Haig over. Discussion on extension of front which French are pressing for. Haig asks to be left to settle with Pétain. Clemenceau wants us to go to Berry-au-Bac. Absolutely impossible. Haig told the War Cabinet that he did not think Germans would attempt a break-through—very rash. War Cabinet agreed to reduce Home Defence to meet an enemy attack of 30,000. Hurrah!

Tuesday 8 January

War Cabinet. Barnes† wanted to know whether the Germans were going to invade England.

CIGS to France to see Pershing about incorporating American troops in our army.‡

Wednesday 9 January

Haig note on future prospects received. He regards next few months as critical and thinks Germans may attempt to force a decision. That's better.§ War Cabinet nothing of importance.

* A draft report from the cabinet committee on manpower was circulated to the military members of the army council by Lord Derby. For Robertson's criticisms of the committee's report, see *Soldiers and Statesmen 1914–1918*, (2 vols), London, 1926, Vol. I, pp. 317–326.
† G. N. Barnes joined the War Cabinet in 1917.
‡ See *Soldiers and Statesmen*, Vol. I, pp. 326–331.
§ According to Robertson, Haig's paper was tossed aside by Lloyd George as being entirely inconsistent with his testimony two days before. (*Soldiers and Statesmen*, Vol. I, p. 324.)

Thursday 10 January

Breakfasted with LG. Tried to ride him off Aleppo but I fear with no success. Told him that Versailles Council would be of no use as a means of coordinating command in battle and that we must have coordinated command if the Germans attacked as heavily as they seemed likely to do. Suggested Joffre with Robertson as his chief of staff and Italian and American staff officers under them as a suitable arrangement. He seemed impressed. I wonder whether anything will come of it.

Friday 11 January

War Cabinet. Told them that signs of a German offensive on Western front were increasing but it was not likely to take place before end of February. Cabinet don't believe in this offensive and think Germans really mean to attack Italy and perhaps Salonika.

CIGS back. He didn't get much out of Pershing who thinks of nothing but getting a huge army for himself in the distant future. Meanwhile the war will be over.

Saturday 12 January

We have had to reduce our divisions to 9 battalions, as we can't get men. LG deceives himself into thinking this is really a good arrangement because both the Germans and the French have done it. It means wiping out 120 battalions, the infantry of 10 divisions, at a time the Germans are daily growing stronger.

Monday 14 January

Indian Cavalry to go to Egypt to replace Yeomanry. Completed paper for CIGS asking for decision as regards Palestine. We shall not get it as LG knows Wilson will report in favour of a campaign there and won't do anything till he gets Versailles to back him.

Tuesday 15 January

Haig's reply to Versailles proposal that he should extend his line to the Ailette has come in. He sticks to it that he can't do more than to Barisis and is quite right. This shows futility of referring this question to Versailles whose point of view is necessarily academic.

Wednesday 16 January

News as to American assistance is gloomy. They are behind-hand in everything though they bucked about their aeroplanes. They haven't got a single squadron in the field and no one knows when they are likely to have one.

Thursday 17 January

Position as regards Palestine is getting serious. We have far more men and guns than are required for defence and not enough for an effective advance which on all grounds is impossible. Cabinet won't decide and have referred question to Versailles who know nothing about it.

Versailles want us to extend our front to Ailette. Clemenceau says Berry-au-Bac, we say the Oise is the maximum. Versailles splits the difference but there is no logic in their decision. It is all paper, they forget we are New Army, short of training.

Friday 18 January

Include in weekly summary a statement showing recent increase in German strength. LG won't like it. He does nothing but count heads and reckons a Portuguese, a Belgian, or an untrained American is the equivalent of a trained German soldier.

Monday 21 January

Goeben–Breslau* come out. Breslau sunk and Goeben ashore. Good business.

Tuesday 22 January

It appears the Navy was caught napping at the Dardanelles and the damage to the Goeben and Breslau was pure good luck when they were returning from a successful raid.

CIGS to France to meet Haig, Foch and Pétain re allied general reserve. PM has put this question down for the next Versailles meeting so our talk on the 9th has had some result.

Wednesday 23 January

Attacks on Wully and Haig developing. Chief cry at present is that brains of New Army are not used. Real reason is to get rid of Wully

* The nominal sale of these two German cruisers to the Turks, after thay had eluded the British Fleet in the Mediterranean, did much to bring the Turks into the war on the side of the Germans.

because he insists on more men and won't go to Aleppo. A dirty business.

Versailles paper no 12 on this year's campaign. As I expected they plump for a decisive campaign in Palestine.

Thursday 24 January

Took Dawnay* to breakfast with LG so that he should see that Allenby's views agreed with ours as to Palestine. Impossible to reason with him on this matter, his mind is quite made up to go to Aleppo coûte que coûte. Seeley and Winston came in and backed him. Seeley, speaking of the war, said 'Burn all books, this war is different to every other war—no history or previous experience is of any value.' What an ass!

Friday 25 January

War Cabinet. A perfunctory consideration of Versailles paper on Palestine. Versailles proposes a decisive campaign against the Turks provided Western front is not weakened. Tried to explain to War Cabinet that it was impossible on those conditions, but spoke to deaf ears. LG and Milner† given carte blanche to settle the question at Versailles, that means Aleppo. We might have had three divisions on their way to France by now! Versailles maintains that Western front is safe.

Saturday 26 January

Smuts is to go to Palestine to settle the plan of campaign on the principle that when the PM can't get the advice he wants from his proper advisers he finds someone else to give it him. LG much perturbed about Repington articles in *Morning Post* and has written to Derby accusing us of giving Repington secret information.‡ Relations between LG and WR rapidly becoming impossible.

---

* Probably Brig-Gen Dawnay, architect of the attack on Jerusalem who had been moved from Palestine to the Western front.
† Lord Milner had been a member of the War Cabinet since December, 1916.
‡ Colonel Repington wrote in his diary on 24 January: 'My article, exposing the failure of the War Cabinet to maintain the Army, came out in the *Morning Post* to-day without going to the Press Bureau and caused much excitement. It is a thorough exposure of the procrastination and cowardice of the Cabinet.' (Lieut-Col C. à Court Repington, *The First World War 1914–1918* (2 vols), London, 1920, Vol. II, p. 197.)

Sunday 27 January

To Paris to meet Wully prior to Versailles council. Goeben back in Constantinople after all.

Monday 28 January

Paris. Wully has had attack of bronchitis but is getting better.

To Versailles and saw their war games. They expect big German attack by 96 divisions on Arras/La Bassée front about May. Said I thought Cambrai front more probable.

They all believe in the Palestine madness. Wully gave me an account of his meeting with Foch and Pétain; both agreed that he (WR) and Foch were the best organisation for controlling inter-allied reserve. Prepared note for LG on question of reserves.

Tuesday 29 January

Preliminary meeting with LG, Milner, Haig, Robertson and Wilson. Saw Pershing as to American troops. He agrees to 6 divisions coming over to train with us if we provide shipping. LG very distant with WR and is evidently going to take Wilson's advice, that means Aleppo and Versailles to run the reserves. Had a talk with LG; it appears he has sent Smuts on a four-day tour of the Western front. Smuts reports Western front safe, except for a little anxiety as to Portuguese front.* S's advice is of course preferred to WR's though former knows nothing of European war.

Wednesday 30 January

1st meeting of Supreme War Council.† Great gathering to look at but useless for military decision. Meeting consisted of a wrangle over manpower. Haig and Pétain both maintained that if enemy attacked and they lost as heavily as they would expect they would both have to reduce divisions in considerable numbers.

LG expressed amazement and implied that he had produced

---

* Colonel Hankey, who accompanied Smuts to the Front, recorded on 24 January that the Portuguese troops in the flat, marshy country north of the La Bassée Canal were 'a tempting and easy objective'. (Lord Hankey, *The Supreme Command 1914–1918* (2 vols), London, 1961, Vol. II, p. 758.)
† For the background and proceedings of this meeting see *The Supreme Command*, Vol. II, Chapter LXXIV.

plenty of men, he asked for fresh tables showing allied and enemy strengths by tomorrow morning. At French War Office till a late hour preparing these tables.

Thursday 31 January

2nd meeting. Foch attacked LG on question of manpower and maintained England had not done what France had done. LG waved this aside and referred to Navy, shipping, finance, etc. Discussion then turned to Palestine. Clemenceau and Foch opposed the Aleppo plan. LG repeated the amazing statement that he had previously made that we were and always had been 'over-insured' in the West.

Friday 1 February

LG had preliminary meeting with Clemenceau and Sonnino and squared them as to Palestine promising not to weaken Western front. Point is to strengthen it! At meeting of SWC Versailles note No. 12 with all its heresies as to safety in the West and the decisive campaign against Turks is passed. Wully protested. LG very angry with him and told him that having put in a protest in writing to him (LG) he had no business to disagree with the Prime Minister before the foreigners. In afternoon question of general reserves came up. Foch and Wully's proposals put in but turned down.

Saturday 2 February

Sent in to LG an alternative proposal for control of reserves. CIGS to join Versailles Council for this purpose and be represented by a deputy when he couldn't be there. Meantime LG had drafted with Wilson an alternative putting all power into an executive board at Versailles, Wilson to be British representative. This was agreed in view of LG's remarks yesterday. Wully did not protest but agrees with me that scheme absolutely unworkable. Wilson without War Office machinery cannot control British troops. Extension of front settled—to be left to Haig and Pétain to carry out.

Back to London. LG–WR very distant. Present position cannot continue.

Monday 4 February

WR referred question of command of allied reserves to Army Council with opinion that ultimate control of British troops must be in hands of AC. Military members agree. This comes back to proposal for CIGS to be member of executive board with a deputy at Versailles when he cannot be there.

LG issues orders that Press are not to refer to the Versailles decisions, nominally on grounds that it will be of use to the enemy, really to prevent discussion which would be harmful to government.

Tuesday 5 February

Derby says he will stand by WR and will resign if Government insist on Versailles proposals.

Wednesday 6 February

War Cabinet. Nothing of importance. Smuts leaves for Palestine and Kirke* accompanies him. LG has talked Derby round and proposes to get over difficulty by making the Versailles representative an Army Councillor.

Thursday 7 February

Army Council except Whigham† and Furse‡ now against Wully. Civil members don't understand the position. They think the man at Versailles can be given all the information he may require from here. They won't see that he must be in daily touch with Admiralty—shipping controller—foreign office etc.: besides the various departments of the War Office.

Friday 8 February

Wilson recalled from Versailles to be in readiness to step into WR's place as soon as LG can get rid of him. Cowans§ who has been

---

* Colonel W. M. St. G. Kirke (1877–1949) was Deputy Director of Military Operations, 1918–1922.
† Major-General Sir Robert Whigham had been appointed to the Army Council early in 1918 having been Deputy CIGS since 1916. In April he was given a division in France and was replaced as DCIGS by General Harington.
‡ Major-General Sir William Thomas Furse had been Master-General of Ordnance since late in 1916.
§ The Quartermaster-General, Lieutenant-General Sir John Cowans, was the only man who remained a member of the Army Council throughout the war.

away has returned and LG has nobbled him. The military members are beginning to weaken except Whigham. WR is to be left to fight his own battle practically alone as the civil members will go with Derby.

Saturday 9 February

Heard from Kirke. Smuts has been to Versailles and consulted Wilson. Smuts appears to have instructions to press through the Palestine plan and is not as I supposed to judge the question on the spot and there decide. Kirke writes that Wilson says Western front is safe and two or three divisions from Palestine could make no difference; how can a soldier make such a statement?

Monday 11 February

Repington has article in *Morning Post* re Versailles. War Cabinet propose to prosecute. Nothing in the article of use to the enemy, but it is embarrassing to the government.*

LG offers WR to go to Versailles at his present pay. Government to take a house for him and Lady Wully in Paris. Wilson to be CIGS. This is sheer bribery as in any case Wilson's advice is what LG means to follow. WR will simply be selling himself. He decides to refuse. For a man absolutely dependent on his pay this is a splendid decision.

Tuesday 12 February

LG offers post of CIGS to Plumer,† Wilson is to be member of executive board at Versailles.

Wednesday 13 February

At Bow Street for Repington case—case adjourned. Find that German papers have published much fuller account than the

* According to Sir Gordon Hewart, the Solicitor-General, Repington had published information about the disposition of forces, revealed a plan or supposed plan, and also revealed information likely to be of use to the enemy. Major-General Sir George Macdonogh, the Director of Military Intelligence said that he would find it difficult to testify that any information 'likely to be of any great use to the enemy' had been published. Nevertheless, it was decided to prosecute Repington. If the *Morning Post* were let off, it would be impossible to deal with revolutionary newspapers, Lloyd George concluded.

† General Plumer commanded the 2nd Army, BEF, from May, 1915 to 1917, and was GOC Italian Expeditionary Force, November, 1917–March, 1918. He took command of the 3rd Army, BEF, in 1918.

1 *Major-General Sir Frederick Maurice.*

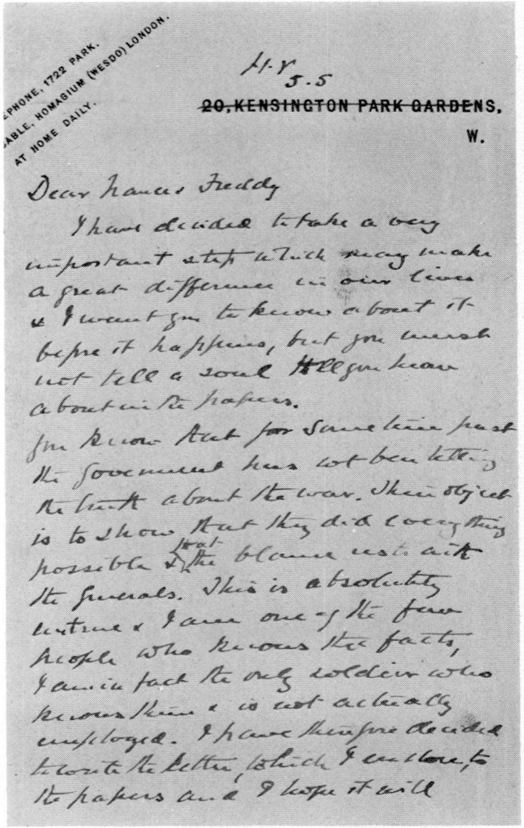
EPHONE, 1722 PARK.
CABLE, HOMAGIUM (WESDO) LONDON.
AT HOME DAILY.
11.V
5.5
~~20, KENSINGTON PARK GARDENS,~~
W.
Dear Nancie Freddy
I have decided to take a very important step which may make a great difference in our lives & I want you to know about it before it happens, but you must not tell a soul till you hear about it in the papers.
You know that for some time past the Government has not been telling the truth about the war. Their object is to show that they did everything possible & that the blame rests with the generals. This is absolutely untrue & I am one of the few people who knows the facts, & am in fact the only soldier who knows them & is not actually employed. I have therefore decided to write the letter, which I enclose, to the papers and I hope it will
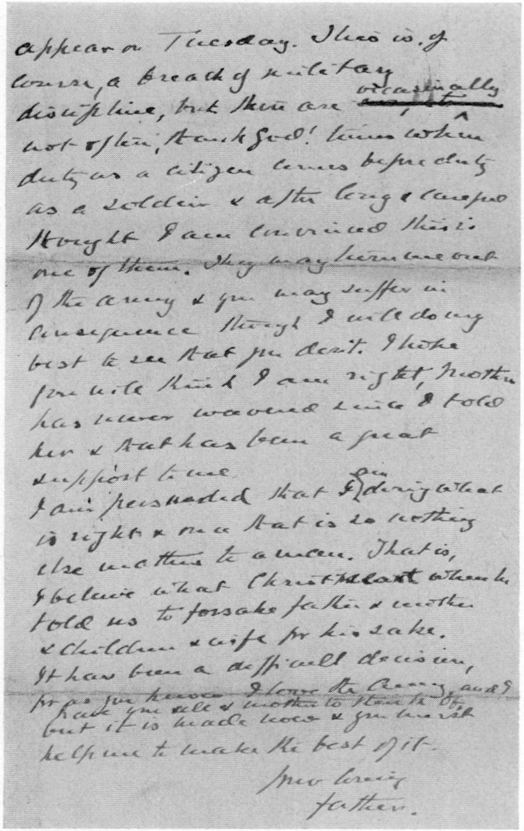
appear on Tuesday. This is, of course, a breach of military discipline, but there are occasionally, not often, thank God! times when duty as a citizen comes before duty as a soldier & after long & careful thought I am convinced this is one of them. They may turn me out of the army & you may suffer in consequence though I will do my best to see that you don't. I hope you will think I am right, Mother has never wavered since I told her & that has been a great support to me.
I am persuaded that I am doing what is right & once that is so nothing else matters to a man. That is, I believe what Christ meant when he told us to forsake father & mother & children & wife for his sake.
It has been a difficult decision, for as you know I love the Army, and I hate you all & mother to think of, but it is made now & you must help me to make the best of it.
Your loving
father.

Morning Post of Versailles, so that prosecution will now be limited to disregarding the Government's order issued through the Press Bureau not to refer to the matter.

Thursday 14 February

Plumer refuses CIGS.

Evidence is accumulating that the enemy are preparing a big attack on the Cambrai front; it is not likely to be ready before the middle of March, but meanwhile all this squabbling is a good preparation for it.

Friday 15 February

War Cabinet on Foch's recommendation decides to send 2 of the British divisions in Italy to the Western front. LG now offers Wully to go to Versailles as member of executive board with Wilson as CIGS or Wully to remain CIGS with Wilson independently of him at Versailles. In either case LG means to use Wilson and throw Wully aside. So he, rightly, has decided to refuse. Hear from *Morning Post* that they will not call me as witness. Very glad.

Saturday 16 February

Morning Post fined £100. WR sings his swan song to the War Cabinet pointing out that he believes their arrangement unworkable and that he cannot accept it. His principle is that only a man with all the information and machinery of the War Office at his back can control movements of troops, therefore he would equally stultify himself if he remained as CIGS with Wilson moving troops at Versailles or went to Versailles to move troops with Wilson as CIGS at home.

Smuts proposals arrive. Government publishes an announcement that WR has resigned—he denies this. Is offered and accepts Eastern Command.

Monday 18 February

Wilson takes over. WR says goodbye. Rawlinson is to be British member of Versailles Board.* Wilson's power of issuing orders to

* General Rawlinson commanded the 5th Army, BEF, before being released by Haig for the Versailles appointment.

troops is to be abolished. This is mere camouflage as exactly the same procedure as before will be followed, telegrams going out in the name of Secretary of State instead of CIGS. All it means is that Secretary of State becomes responsible for matters he knows nothing about.

Tuesday 19 February

Put in note on Smuts proposals to CIGS. Smuts is asking for a great campaign which will eat shipping, men and railway material all of which we want on the Western Front. It is contrary to LG's express promise at Versailles that Western Front shall not be weakened.

Meanwhile position on Persian front is not at all happy.* Smuts, who knows nothing of this, proposes to gut Mesopotamia for the benefit of Palestine.

Wednesday 20 February

Wilson told me that he wishes to bring in 'a man from the trenches' in my place and that Haig has promised to give me a division. I shall be delighted to get out of the War Office where I have been for too long. LG in his speech in the House definitely implied that both Haig and Robertson had agreed to Versailles executive board at the meeting because they had not expressed their dissent. As LG expressly told Robertson he could not do this if he had previously expressed his dissent in writing this is pretty cool. Idea given is that Robertson was opposed to unified control which is quite untrue. He was only opposed to unworkable machinery for exercising control.

Thursday 21 February

The Italians have objected to the withdrawal of the two British divisions from Italy on the grounds that the matter had not been referred to Versailles executive which was charged with question of reserves. It appears Foch took action because he thought the matter

* Sir Charles Marling, British Minister in Teheran, had urged a military occupation of NW Persia 'against the Tartars, Bolsheviks and Persian Extremists'. The Persian Committee of the Cabinet deprecated this proposal. The War Office supported military action even though it was tantamount to a declaration of war on Persia. Difficulties in Persia were a result of General Dunsterville's forced withdrawal from Transcaucasia.

urgent quite rightly. Wilson was away from Versailles and we were squabbling. Meanwhile more delay. Luckily our divisions under way and cannot well be stopped.

Friday 22 February

Allenby has captured Jericho. LG delighted since he had heard of Jericho before Passchendaele. Jericho consists of a few mud hovels and 1 third rate hotel.
    CIGS to GHQ and Versailles.
    He sends letter to Rawlinson directing that all executive orders for moves proposed by Executive board should come from War Office. This is practically Wully's proposal.

Saturday 23 February

German divisions already moving up on Western front. This can only mean attack though most of War Cabinet think Germans won't attack because they said they would. This is sometimes not bad camouflage particularly as they are now spreading reports of attacks on Italy, Salonika etc.

Wednesday 27 February

War Cabinet. Mainly concerned with supply of anti-aircraft guns for London.

Thursday 28 February

War Cabinet. Ministers still disinclined to believe in attack on Western front. Told them Germans would be ready by March 15th and that it was probably coming on Cambrai front. They still believe in an attack on Italy because nothing much is heard about it. LG wants another review of the war. Suggested that he had first better settle his policy as to Palestine which has been in abeyance for three months.

Friday 1 March

CIGS back. So are Smuts and Kirke. Latter tells me Smuts practically told Allenby it had been decided to carry out a big offensive in Palestine and asked him what he would want. Smuts then proceeded to see how the troops would be collected without weakening the Western front. It is impossible to skin Mespot as he proposes. The question of the allied general reserve has now dwindled down to 20 divisions of which eleven are in Italy. What a farce. The question of bringing the second British division from Italy has been referred to Versailles. The Boche will attack before this settled.

Monday 4 March

We may expect big German attack on Cambrai front before very long now. Probably as soon as the Easter moon begins. Weather extraordinarily dry for the spring; it may break before they begin.

Told CIGS I thought attack certain. He says he is afraid it won't come and doesn't think Cambrai/St Quentin front likely because of the devastated area and the Somme. I go by evidence of preparation—point of junction of French and ourselves always a favourite with the Germans and the road to Paris.

Tuesday 5 March

Plumer to be recalled from Italy to take Rawlinson's place, that is good. War Cabinet are at last beginning to think attack on us likely.

Wednesday 6 March

Haig says he can't contribute to general reserve. Foch therefore proposes to dissolve Executive War Board. War Cabinet in position of either having to sack Haig or disregard executive board they have set up. They don't feel strong enough to sack Haig so the SWC is to meet in London and regard Haig's refusal as an appeal to them.

Thursday 7 March

Orders to Allenby as to his offensive in Palestine. 1 Division from Mesopotamia to Palestine instead of Smuts' 2 and a cavalry brigade. Allenby will get to Haifa and will be in no better position than where he is now. So we make war.

Friday 8 March

Executive War Board refuses to decide as to move of 2nd British division from Italy on grounds that Haig having refused to contribute to general reserve it has no locus standi. This puts our government in an awkward position. Wully was sacked because he did not agree with Executive War Board and now it commits suicide.

Tuesday 12 March

Wilson tells War Cabinet that he puts no certainty that attack on us is coming. I have no doubts about it. The Germans are not piling up divisions in the West for fun.

Wednesday 13 March

War Cabinet. Questioned as to attack on Salonika front. Ministers still looking for attack anywhere but in the West.

Haig arrives for meeting of Supreme War Council. He has his toes in about giving up any divisions for allied general reserve and as he is likely to be attacked very shortly in great strength he is probably right but that doesn't alter the necessity for an effective allied command. CIGS inclined to put responsibility on Haig. Am not at all happy about situation.

Thursday 14 March

Supreme War Council in London. Foch lashed out into attack on Haig for not complying with orders of executive board. Clemenceau shut him up. He and LG evidently arrived at a compromise.

Friday 15 March

SWC decides that Haig and Pétain are to be left alone to make their own arrangements for reserves. Executive Board is to confine itself to making recommendation as to reserves for Italy and are to visit that country with Maistre* taking Foch's place.

So we finally end with no general control at all on the eve of the Boche attack.

Saturday 16 March

Saw Foch end Weygand† before they left, both very sad at the situation. I agree. It comes of LG having forced through an unworkable scheme in order to get rid of Wully or at least have

* General Maistre had previously commanded the French 6th Army.
† General Weygand was Foch's Chief of Staff.

another adviser. The proper machinery for running the war was with him a secondary matter. He looks on himself as the proper machinery.

Monday 18 March

Rawlinson and Co have gone off to Italy, so Versailles remains empty for the present. It is now as certain as it can be in war that the Germans will attack before the end of the month.

Meanwhile the situation on the Persian front is going from bad to worse. Owing to state of passes we cannot get troops in and the government has no policy.

Tuesday 19 March

Italians are panicking about an attack on their front. There is no immediate sign of it and the Germans are all coming away. This is probably a manoeuvre to prevent us from drawing divisions to France.

Wednesday 20 March

Rawlinson reports that a reserve of 10 divisions all in Italy will be formed. This won't be much use to meet a heavy attack on us.

Thursday 21 March

GHQ reports heavy bombardment on whole front between the Scarpe and the Oise. Rang up and asked if infantry had attacked, was told yes. Told Wilson the battle had started. He still doubtful; cannot get rid of his conviction that attack would be further north. He told Cabinet that this might be nothing more than a big raid. He hasn't got our manpower position into his head and in spite of his Versailles war game wants the Boche to put in a heavy attack on us. So would I if we had the men but we haven't.

Friday 22 March

News of yesterday's fighting appears satisfactory. North of St Quentin he appears to have done nothing more than driven us back from our outpost line. South of St Quentin he has penetrated our battle zone and we have retired behind the St Crozat canal.

Later news comes in that he has broken through our battle Zone north of St Quentin. This is serious.

Saturday 23 March

The whole fifth army is retiring to the Somme and the Germans are reported to be across the Somme at Ham. 5th Army have lost many prisoners and guns. All our drafts in France are already exhausted and by stripping England of men we can just about replace our casualties. War Cabinet in a panic and talking of arrangements for falling back on Channel ports and evacuating our troops to England.

Sunday 24 March

Enemy has broken our front north of Peronne. LG is steadier and doing everything possible. The rest panicky. CIGS and Milner to France.

Monday 25 March

At War Cabinet. Enemy is evidently trying all he can to separate us from the French. He is skinning our front to the north and the French front to the south and staking everything on knocking us out. The situation is decidedly critical but not desperate.

Tuesday 26 March

War Cabinet. 3rd Army and left of 5th Army have to go back to the Ancre, real danger of a breach on this part of the front. I am not afraid of the South of the Somme as French reserves will be in time to prevent anything really dangerous happening there. We must maintain our touch with the French—any idea of falling back on the Channel ports and separating from the French is madness.

Wednesday 27 March

Orders to Allenby to adopt defensive in Palestine and send one division to France as soon as possible. The Boche is a good teacher of strategy and forces us to do the right thing too late. CIGS back. Foch has been appointed 'to coordinate the action of the allied armies of the Western front'. Foch takes Weygand with him and Rawlinson goes to 5th Army. So Versailles disappears.

Thursday 28 March

Enemy are still pressing south of Somme. I have not at present much anxiety as to this as French reserves should be in time to stop this. Government busy with manpower proposals.* Great hesitation as to conscription in Ireland.† Cannot get anything definite out of the Americans as to what they mean to do. Pershing's one idea is to have a great army of his own which will be ready when the war is over. Marshall has had a real success beyond Het.‡

Friday 29 March

Germans yesterday made a very heavy attack on the Arras front which has been completely repulsed. This materially improves the situation as this attack was hanging over Haig's head. The situation south of the Somme appears unsatisfactory. No one knows who is really in charge. GHQ are leaving it to the French who are leaving it to us because Rawlinson is there. If we are not careful the Germans will walk into Amiens merely for want of proper organisation.

Saturday 30 March

The French are happier about the situation south of the Somme. They checked the enemy yesterday and their reserves are arriving well.

Sunday 31 March

To France to GHQ and Foch. After lunch at GHQ to Beauvais to see Foch. He in good form but his staff as yet very rudimentary and he hasn't got hold of things. He wants help from us and should have a good English staff.

Monday 1 April

Saw Haig in the morning. Told him I did not think situation south of Somme satisfactory and pressed him to go and see Foch about it.

* See Hankey, *The Supreme Command*, Vol. II, Chapter LXXII.
† The question of Irish conscription was revived in Cabinet on 25 March and discussed over the next few days. The Chief Secretary, H. E. Duke, argued that it would be unwise to force the issue: 'we might as well recruit Germans' he told his colleagues. It was decided to take power in the new National Service Act to extend conscription to Ireland by order-in-council; but conscription was not to be attempted without simultaneous Home Rule legislation.
‡ General Sir W. R. Marshall was Commander-in-Chief, Mesopotamia.

He agreed. He is very calm and looks well, says he won't ungum Gough* who was given too long a line to hold and his troops were overwhelmed in the fog. Saw Wilson and PM on my return and urged importance of a senior British officer being appointed to Foch. Wilson inclined to demur. He really wants to reconstitute Versailles and is shy of giving Foch too much power.

Tuesday 2 April

Wilson is decidedly against giving Foch more power but it appears to me that having appointed him we must support him and see that he is properly informed as to the British army. He must therefore have a suitable British staff.

PM and Wilson to France to discuss Foch's position again with Clemenceau.

Wednesday 3 April

War Cabinet. Tried to make Bonar Law understand that Germans' object was not to take Amiens or any other town but to destroy our army. He thinks a town is a necessary military objective. Things are quieter on the battle front, Germans are trying to bring their guns up before beginning again.

Thursday 4 April

Germans have renewed their attack south of the Somme and taken Mont Didier. This is beginning to make railway communications through Amiens very difficult. PM and Wilson back. Foch is now charged with 'general strategic control on the Western front'. Why not say he is commander-in-chief at once. Grant† is to go to Foch as liaison officer but no proper English staff. Foch can't direct the British army unless he knows all about it.

Friday 5 April

Enemy made heavy attacks both North and South of the Somme. On the Albert front he was completely repulsed but made some ground South of the Somme. He is gradually eating his way to Amiens.

* General Sir Hubert Gough commanded the 5th Army which was smashed by the German offensive.
† Colonel Charles Grant was married to the elder daughter of the Earl of Rosebery. He won the DSO in 1915; and served on Allenby's staff in France.

Saturday 6 April

Another lull on the front. Curzon* very tiresome at the War Cabinet. Wants to know why he can't be told at once the number of prisoners we lose and why he should have to go to the German communiqués for this. This has been explained to him a dozen times but he either can't or won't understand. Made out a statement for PM's speech on Tuesday.

Sunday 7 April

Pershing still very obstinate about American assistance.

Monday 8 April

Enemy has started bombardment on Armentières front. GHQ don't expect a heavy attack here but Portuguese are a tempting bait and most of our divisions have already fought on the Somme and made up hastily. CIGS at last agrees to send a senior officer to Foch. Du Cane is to go.†

Tuesday 9 April

War Cabinet. News of attack on La Bassée–Neuve Chapelle–Bois Grenier front. Portuguese not likely to stand a big attack. Therefore more strain on us to replace them. Owing to fog not much known of situation. CIGS to France.

LG's speech on manpower. Age limit raised to 50. Conscription for Ireland. Very moderate about soldiers but as usual he is working sub rosa against Haig. Curzon made a number of absolutely untrue statements in H of L.

Wednesday 10 April

War Cabinet. Every one very agitated about situation at Armentières. We have only tired troops there. I told them that if France did not at once take a larger share in the battle we ran a grave risk of defeat. PM for sending Milner over at once, I suggested better wait and hear what Wilson said. Got on the telephone to Wilson who had seen Clemenceau and apparently was satisfied. Does not want

* Lord Curzon had been a member of the Asquith coalition government and joined Lloyd George's war cabinet in December, 1916.
† Major-General Sir J. Du Cane joined Foch's staff in April. He had previously commanded XV Corps. 'His one disability', General Spears wrote (*Prelude to Victory*, London, 1939, p. 60), "was that his body lacked the agility of his brain.'

Milner over. I don't like situation on 2nd Army front, we have skinned it for the Somme and have nothing left of much use. Told Wilson so on telephone.

Thursday 11 April

War Cabinet. Germans have got into Steenwerck and are well across the Lawe and the Lys. We are sending a division to counter attack at Steenwerck. We evacuate Armentières. CIGS arrives with Radcliffe.* Foch is sending troops north to help but he is late. His counter-attack should have got off three days ago, now it is useless and will have no effect on the situation in the north.

Friday 12 April

News from France serious. The Germans in Neuville and on the outskirts of Bailleul. If he presses his advance on Hazebrouck we shall have to withdraw from Ypres. Unless Foch hurries up there is serious danger of a break on our front. All our reserves have been drawn south and the Boche is now attacking in the North. Trenchard's resignation is accepted.† This is a real blow.

Saturday 13 April

News from France slightly better. Enemy has made no material progress. He is probably bringing up troops for another effort. Leave at short notice with Milner for Folkestone.

Sunday 14 April

Cross at 6 am in bad storm. Breakfast with Haig, he looks tired and worried as do Lawrence‡ and Davidson.§ Saw Plumer. He looks

* Major-General Percy de B. Radcliffe, an artillery expert, had served on the General Staff in France and at the War Office.
† General Sir Hugh Trenchard, after a protracted struggle with his Minister, Lord Rothermere, submitted his resignation as Chief of the Air Staff on 19 March. He agreed to Rothermere's request to defer the effective date of his resignation for a short time but refused to serve under Rothermere any longer. The fusion of the Royal Naval Air Service and the Royal Flying Corps into the Royal Air Force was announced on 1 April. Rothermere himself resigned on 25 April. (See Andrew Boyle, *Trenchard*, London, 1962, Chapters 10 and 11.)
‡ Major-General the Hon Sir Herbert Lawrence was appointed Haig's CGS in January, 1918.
§ Brigadier-General J. H. Davidson was Haig's head of Operations. He was elected MP for Fareham in December, 1918.

splendid and is more satisfied as to position. He has decided to withdraw from Ypres. Talk with him about troops from Italy.

Monday 15 April

Spoke Milner at Paris on telephone. He wants Wilson to come over as Haig wants more French troops in the north and Foch is not disposed to give them. Saw Horne* at 1st Army HQ, he looks worried. He expects attack on Bethune shortly but says he has not sufficient reserves. To Beauvais where I met Milner and gave him Horne's and Plumer's views. At his request went to see Foch who is in excellent form and confident of holding the enemy. He is naturally anxious to hold his reserves but doesn't quite appreciate condition of our troops. People here very dissatisfied with LG's speech of 9 April.

Tuesday 16 April

Heavy enemy attack on Bailleul–Wytschaete front. Enemy take Bailleul and Neuve Eglise and enter Wytschaete. Plumer's withdrawal from Passchendaele successfully carried out. Met Wilson at Boulogne and gave him situation. He goes with Haig to meet Foch and Milner. Crossed 5 pm. Met at Victoria by Sutherland† who took me to H of C to meet LG. Heard his speech on Irish conscription. Good. He kept me talking till after mid-night.
 Wrote Robertson re situation:

The situation is grave but not desperate. The real gravity lies in the steady exhaustion of our army, which is of course what the Germans are aiming at . . . I had a long talk with Lawrence (CGS) last night and he told me that Sir Douglas has asked that you should come out as 2nd in command. It may appear to you that this is only a nominal position without any definite functions and you may not feel inclined to take it. I am convinced however that your presence would have great effect both in the Army and at GHQ . . .

Wully replied:

I am ready to help, but it's no use *pretending* to help. I must have a definite status. I don't like the term '2nd in command', though perhaps something on the lines of Lord K (Kitchener) and Bobs (Roberts) in S.

* General Sir Henry Horne had commanded the 1st Army since August, 1916.
† William Sutherland, Lloyd George's press secretary since 1915, was elected as coalition Liberal MP for Argyllshire in December, 1918.

Africa might help. But I don't think anyone can help unless Ministerial control and hourly interference is rigorously suppressed . . . I practically left WO on this point, and I'd like to get it put right when next I get into harness . . .

Wednesday 17 April

Heard from Wilson that Foch is sending another division to Plumer and that Foch went to see Plumer himself this morning, that is good. Germans take Meterun. They are getting near the Mont des Cats ridge. Later news is better. Germans checked at Meteren and near Wytschaete—French should arrive in time. Wilson returns evening. Derby to go to Paris. Milner to War Office.

Thursday 18 April

Enemy is putting in heavy attack on Horne's front E & N of Bethune but does not appear to be making progress. Government evidently determined to get rid of Haig as soon as possible. Plumer will probably succeed.

Friday 19 April

News of yesterday's fighting is good. The Germans failed everywhere with heavy loss. The French have made a useful gain on the Somme. Today as a result of his failure yesterday the enemy has been quiet. Completed plans for reinforcing France from the outside theatres of war. This is my swan song.* I have done in one month with the help of the Boche what I failed to get through in two years.

Saturday 20 April

Went through LG's speech again. Pity I didn't read it before. It is clearly an attempt to shovel off responsibility on the soldiers while appearing to treat them generously. Must always get Hansard for important speeches. Newspapers no good.

Note

The diary runs to 20 May, but as only passing references are made to the central theme of this book, it is not printed in full.

* See *Reinforcements for France from Outside Theatres* on the next page.

2. Reinforcements for France from Outside Theatres

C.I.G.S.

1. You have decided that two divisions complete are to be transferred from Palestine to France and that as a general principle other reinforcements for France shall take the form of infantry with the object of reconstituting the divisions in France reduced to cadre in the most rapid and economical way.

2. The following movements from Palestine have been ordered:

    I The 52nd division has arrived in France complete.
    II The 74th division begins embarkation on 1 May. This movement cannot be expedited owing to lack of shipping. The 74th division will be followed by:
    III $5\frac{1}{2}$ batteries Heavy Artillery.
    IV 5 Machine Gun Companies.
    V Australian and New Zealand reinforcements.
    VI $4\frac{1}{2}$ Yeomanry M.G. Battalions.
    VII 2/Battn Royal North Lancs.
    VIII 9 British battalions released on 15 May, and replaced by 9 Indian battalions now in Egypt.

3. In addition to the above it is proposed to ask General Allenby to release a further 14 British battalions to follow the above as shipping becomes available. This will leave General Allenby with:

    1 British Division.
    6 Indian Divisions (complete by the end of June)
    2 British Cavalry Divisions
    1 Indian Cavalry Division.

or a rifle strength of over 76,000 and a sabre strength of over 15,000. The transfer of the proposed 14 battalions will involve some further temporary weakening of General Allenby's force, as while re-organisation is in progress, it may be necessary in order not to delay the flow of reinforcements to France to anticipate slightly the arrival of the Indian battalions, which are to replace the British battalions in Palestine; but the risk involved is slight and should in my opinion be accepted.

4. The total force which the Turks can bring against General Allenby at the present moment is:

	Germans	Turks Rifles & Sabres
West of Jordan	950	26,000
East of Jordan	650	8,700
In the first reserve at a few days call	2,000	2,600
Total	4,500	37,300

It is in the highest degree improbable that the Turks can maintain a rifle and sabre strength of more than 50,000 on General Allenby's present front, while it is quite clear that no Turkish offensive can hope for success without considerable further German assistance and so long as Germany seeks a decision in France, such assistance will not be forthcoming.

5. I have ascertained from the Director of Movements that Infantry can be transferred from Salonika without interference with the above movements from Palestine.

The second of the newly mobilised Greek divisions is now at Salonika and a third is arriving. In one month's time, say about 15 May, it should therefore be safe to reduce the divisions at Salonika to a 10 battalion basis. This will release 12 British battalions. This matter should be taken up with General Guillaumaut at once.

6. If the above proposals are accepted our forces in France should by the end of June be reinforced by 2 complete divisions, 36 Infantry battalions, a number of machine gun units and some heavy artillery. This will enable us to restore completely 4 of the 6 divisions now reduced to cadre, and will give 2 new divisions to replace 2 cadre divisions. We may expect that by the end of June some American infantry will be sufficiently trained either to reconstitute the remaining 2 cadre divisions or to increase the strength of the other divisions to 12 battalions, and that from then on American infantry will be available to reconstitute any further divisions we may have to reduce, until such time as the new manpower legislation takes effect.

7. The only remaining further infantry reinforcements which we can obtain from overseas apart from a few garrison battalions consist in the 2 British divisions it is proposed to leave in Palestine and Mesopotamia and in the force at Salonika. I submit that the 2 divisions in Palestine and Mesopotamia should not be touched for the present but that we should retain the power of expanding them with further Indian battalions as a potential reserve for the East.

As regards Salonika I suggest that our policy should be to convert the 4 divisions there into Anglo-Indian divisions with one British and 3 Indian battalions per brigade. This will eventually release 24 more British to be replaced by 36 Indian battalions and with the gradual development of the Greek Army this policy should, by restoring our brigades to a four battalion basis, make our position in Macedonia secure, if, as is possible, the enemy turns against that theatre when he has been checked in the West.

There remains our force in Italy to consider. I consulted Sir H. Plumer as to this when I was recently in France. He said that he was unable to speak on the political aspect of this question, but he was strongly of opinion that there would be no difficulty with the Italian soldiers if we said to them, 'The enemy is clearly trying to finish the war on the Western Front and we are hard pressed there. We helped you when you were in trouble, we now ask you to release our troops and send us any of your own you can spare. You are more than able to hold your own against the Austrians and if Germany is held in the West, and turns against you we will come and help you again.'

We are now only in the month of April and we must expect the

3 *General Sir William Robertson.*

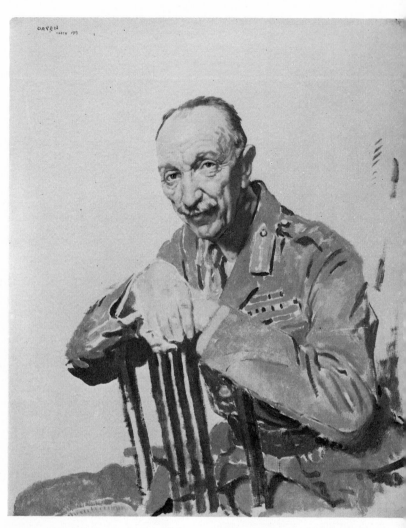

4 *General Sir Henry Wilson. Painting by Sir William Orpen.*

Germans to keep up these attacks for many months to come. The loss of the Channel Ports or the loss of Amiens would almost certainly have greater effect in Italy than the withdrawal of our troops. We must take risks elsewhere if we are to save the situation in the West and I submit that the risk of withdrawing British troops from Italy is one which we can and must accept.

9. In addition to the reinforcements from France we can probably obtain a certain number of good garrison battalions from the Garrison of Egypt and one or two from the Mediterranean and Bermuda. This completes the extent of the possible reinforcements for France, which amount to the following:

2 Divisions complete from Palestine (already ordered)
3 Divisions complete from Italy (not yet ordered)
10 Battalions from Palestine (ordered)
$5\frac{1}{2}$ Batteries Heavy Artillery from Palestine (ordered)
$4\frac{1}{2}$ Yeomanry Machine Gun Battalions (ordered)
4 Machine Gun Companies from Palestine (ordered)
14 Battalions from Palestine (not yet ordered)
12 Battalions from Salonika (by reduction to 10 bns per division; not yet ordered)
24 Battalions from Salonika for replacement by Indian Battalions (not yet ordered)
6 Garrison Battalions (number not yet certain)

20.4.18

Part 3

1. The Story of the Crisis of May, 1918

by Major-General Sir Frederick Maurice

At the end of December, 1915, I came home from France and was appointed Director of Military Operations at the War Office. I held this appointment until 20 April, 1918. During that period I was intimately associated with the Chief of the Imperial General Staff in his capacity as Military Adviser to the Government, I was in constant touch with the Prime Minister and the War Cabinet, and it was my duty to be conversant with all matters affecting the conduct of the War.

On 18 February, 1918, Sir William Robertson was dismissed from his post of Chief of the Imperial General Staff, by the Government, in consequence of his disagreement with the War Cabinet on the question of the formation of an Executive Board of the Versailles Supreme War Council to control the forces of the Allies in France and Italy. He was succeeded by Sir Henry Wilson, who informed me at once that he considered that the Director of Military Operations should be a man of more recent experience of the Front, that he intended to find such an officer to succeed me, and would endeavour to get me suitable employment in France. I cordially agreed with this view, as I considered that I had been quite long enough at the War Office, and I was delighted at the prospect of more active employment.

Accordingly I made all necessary preparations to proceed to France, but owing first to the threat and then to the development of the great German attack which began on 21 March, my successor could not at once give up his duties in France, and he did not actually arrive in the War Office until 11 April.

Meantime, on 9 April, the Prime Minister made a speech in the House of Commons dealing with the situation which arose out of the reverse to the Fifth Army, and recounting the measures which the War Cabinet had taken, and were taking, to meet the German menace on the Western Front.

As is explained in a statement which I sent to the Press, and which appears later, it happened that the day on which the Prime Minister spoke, was also the day on which the enemy opened the second phase of his offensive of 1918 by an attack in Flanders on the La Bassée/Armentières front, and I had no leisure to read through the full report of the Prime Minister's speech until after I left the War Office on 20 April.

The circumstances which caused me to examine the speech carefully were these:

On 13 April I went to France, returning late on the 16th, and while there I heard from a number of officers in important positions, grave criticisms of some statements which the Prime Minister had made on 9 April, and I was informed that these statements were having a bad effect on the Army. The two statements particularly mentioned were, one in which the Prime Minister indicated that the British Army in France in 1918 was stronger than it had been in 1917, and the other in which he said that all except three divisions in Palestine contained a very very small proportion of white troops.

I undertook to go into the Prime Minister's speech carefully on my return, and to see what steps were necessary to correct these statements.

Now, while I was in the War Office I had been asked to prepare, for the Prime Minister's speech of 9 April, a statement of the military events on 21 March and the following days. I was not asked for and did not give any figures as to strengths. On Sunday, 7 April, Sir Henry Wilson told me that the Prime Minister had rehearsed his speech to him; and that he (the Prime Minister) was going to maintain that the Government had sent plenty of men to France, and that the Army was very considerably stronger in 1918 than in 1917. Sir Henry Wilson mentioned that the Prime Minister had produced some figures showing that some 413,000 more men had been provided for the Army in 1917 than in the previous year, and that he had warned the Prime Minister that these figures probably included a large amount of coloured labour. I replied that the statement in question was a very dangerous one to make, as it was notorious in France that owing to the failure of the Government to provide men, it had been necessary to make very large reductions in the establishment of the Army between 1 January, 1918, and the German offensive of 21 March.

I at once got the correct figures and found, as I had expected, that there had been an increase in total numbers in France of about 325,000 men, and that this was almost entirely accounted for by an increase in British and coloured labour. I gave the figures to Sir H. Wilson for the Prime Minister.

While I was considering the Prime Minister's speech of 9 April and thinking over the best course of action to take, I saw in the paper a notice of answers given by Mr Bonar Law in the House of Commons on 23 April to questions regarding the extension of the British front in France. I realised that, particularly in these days of shortage of paper and reduced size of newspapers, the Press summaries of speeches and answers in Parliament did not always convey a correct impression of what had been said, I was away in the country at the time, and I determined to suspend judgment until I could get the official report.* I returned to London on 29 April and got a copy of Hansard's report of speeches in the House of Commons on 23 April. I then saw that the effect of Mr Bonar Law's answers was to produce the impression that there had been no protests either from Sir Douglas Haig or from Sir William Robertson as to the extension of the British front, and that the extension had been made by Sir Douglas Haig and General Pétain without any pressure from the French or British Governments. Mr Bonar Law further conveyed the impression that there had been no intervention by the Versailles Council in the matter.

These impressions I knew to be completely incorrect, and I was very greatly influenced by Mr Bonar Law's answers in deciding upon the course which I undertook. It appeared to me that incorrect statements made in the course of a long speech by the Prime Minister might be accidental and not by themselves be a fair indication of Government policy, but that the same consideration could not possibly apply to a deliberately prepared answer to questions in the House.

This view was confirmed by an examination of Lord Curzon's speech on 9 April in the House of Lords, which I did not read until after I had seen Mr Bonar Law's answers.

I will deal with Lord Curzon's speech later, but I may say here

* But see the exchange of letters between F. M. and Sir William Robertson on pp. 117–19.

that it crosses the t's and dots the i's of certain portions of Mr Lloyd George's speech of the same date.

Now ever since January, 1918, I had formed the conviction that the Government's policy was fundamentally wrong and was leading us to disaster. In spite of repeated representations by the General Staff, the Government view was that the Western front was safe. (The Prime Minister told me on 10 January that he had always been convinced that we were over-insured on the Western front. He repeated this statement later at Versailles.) They had met the persistent demands of the Army Council for men during the latter half of 1917 with a wholly inadequate contribution which was announced in the House of Commons by Sir Auckland Geddes in his speech of 14 January. This contribution amounted to an addition of 100,000 men in 1918 for the Army, a number which barely equalled the casualties of the first fighting which began on 21 March. The Government had, despite military advice to the contrary, hugged the belief that casualties could be reduced by acting on the defensive, ignoring altogether the obvious fact that this must depend upon the enemy's action, which could not be definitely foreseen, and was contrary to recent experience on the Russian and Italian fronts. Further, again despite the repeated and persistent representations by the General Staff, the Government insisted upon an offensive policy in Palestine, and refused to permit the withdrawal from that theatre of troops who might, if a defensive policy had been adopted there, have been in France in time for the battle of 21 March. Simultaneously with this refusal to meet the demands of the military authorities for men and for the reduction of our overseas commitments, the Government was compelled to accede to pressure from the French Government upon us to extend our front in France. The one practical step which the Government took to meet the German menace was to set up the Versailles Executive Board. This was a Committee composed of representatives of four Nations of whom the French representative alone had at his disposal the machinery required for effective command. The remaining representatives were not and could not be in that intimate and close touch with the Central Military Executive and with the great Government Departments concerned in the conduct of the War, which alone makes control in War possible. Command by any Committee in War is, as history shows, condemned to failure from the beginning. The bare thought of command by an International Committee which could not in any circumstances be vested with the powers necessary to enable it to execute its decisions, makes anyone acquainted with the realities of war shudder. On this matter the Government rejected the advice and the counter-proposal of their military adviser, and, as I have already said, it was because of disagreement with the Government on this vital question that Sir William Robertson was dismissed from the War Office.*

Having all this in mind I was convinced that the Government were primarily responsible for the events which followed the German attack on 21 March, and I was also convinced by the Government pronouncements of 9 and 23 April that they had persisted in their erroneous views, were determined to continue in the future the same policy as in the past, had made up their minds that they were in no way to blame, and were putting responsibility which should be theirs upon the soldiers. I made up my mind that this policy and these views were likely to lead us to disaster, but that as official representations on these vital questions had been repeatedly made and disregarded nothing could be gained by repeating them. I knew, however, that I had information in my possession which would enable me to challenge certain statements of fact recently made by the Government. I knew that these statements were creating a very bad effect on the Army in France and while I could not disclose in a public announcement my whole case against the policy of the Government, since it depended upon secret information, I believed that I could produce a case which would convince Parliament of the necessity for such an enquiry as would bring to light the fundamental errors in the policy of the Government. I had to consider very carefully my own position in the matter. I was an officer on full pay and therefore I could only indite the Government publicly by committing a grave breach of military discipline which would involve the sacrifice of my military career. Such a step could only be justified by an earnest and sincere conviction that the present policy of the Government was disastrous to the interests of the Nation. Possessing that conviction I felt that no private interest and no peace-time regulations should be allowed to stand in the way of an honest attempt to put right what I believed

* It has been generally assumed that Sir W. Robertson objected to unity of command. This is quite untrue; he objected to command by committee; but at the same time put forward a definite proposal for unity of command which he had previously submitted to Haig, Foch and Pétain. All were agreed that it was a sound and practical scheme and were prepared to carry it out.

to be wrong. I had further to consider whether my action would produce the result which I hoped to obtain.

I was known to have held an important and confidential position which made it my duty to be cognisant of the facts of the case and I could not be accused of being actuated by any motives of self-interest. I was, when promoted not quite two years ago, the youngest Major-General in the Army and had received more than ample recognition of such work as I had been able to do during the period of the War. I was known to all my acquaintances to be a poor man, dependent almost entirely upon my pay. Though unemployed at the moment I had been promised and was about to take up important employment in France, and I had the prospect before me of a brilliant military career.

As an officer on full pay in war-time I could not resign my commission before taking the step which I contemplated nor could I go to my superiors and say that I proposed to commit a breach of military regulations. That, of course, would only have resulted in my incurring severe penalties and could have prevented the disclosure of the facts which I wished to make known. I also felt that the penalties which I was incurring by my action were so serious to myself that I could not ask anyone to share my responsibility, and I therefore determined that I must act alone. I decided, however, that as the effect of the Government statements on the Army in France was a new fact that it was my duty to bring it to the notice of my late chief and to point out to him those Ministerial statements which I knew to be incorrect. Accordingly, on 30 April, I sent the following letter to Sir Henry Wilson, then Chief of the Imperial General Staff:

My dear CIGS,

When I was last over in France I was told by many officers both at GHQ and elsewhere that certain of the Prime Minister's statements in his speech of 9 April had had a very bad effect on the Army, because a very large number of all ranks knew them to be incorrect.

The two statements chiefly quoted were those in which it was stated that the Army in France in 1918 was stronger than in 1917 and that all except three divisions in Egypt and Palestine were either Indian or contained a very very small proportion of white troops.

As you know the first of these statements is literally true because the Prime Minister referred to the date of 1 January, but he was speaking of the situation at the beginning of the battle of 21 March, and very shortly after 1 January, 1918, as you also know, the Army in France was reduced in establishment by about 140 infantry battalions and 2 cavalry divisions. This is perfectly well known to the Army, which regards the statement as very misleading.

The second statement as to the troops in Palestine is incorrect and is known to the Army to be incorrect.

I have now just heard that a similar impression has been produced by Mr Bonar Law's answers on 23 April to questions as to taking over the line.

The statement that this question was not referred to Versailles, as you know is incorrect, and other statements in Mr Bonar Law's reply are misleading and give the impression that responsibility rests with Sir Douglas Haig alone.

The general effect has been, I am told, to produce a feeling of distrust and lack of confidence in France. You probably know this already but although I have ceased to be your DMO I think it right to make certain that you are aware of it.

(sd.) F. Maurice

I decided that if I received an answer to the effect that the matter had been brought to the notice of the War Cabinet and that the Cabinet were determined to consider favourably the idea of correcting the false impression produced by these Ministerial statements, I would rest content, but, being, as I have said, convinced that these statements were the indication of a settled policy, I did not expect such a reply, nor did I receive it. Accordingly, after waiting until 6 May I sent the following letter to *The Times*, *Morning Post*, *Daily News*, *Daily Chronicle* and *Daily Telegraph*:*

Sir,

My attention has been called to answers given in the House of Commons on 23 April by Mr Bonar Law to questions put by Mr G. Lambert, Colonel Burn, and Mr Pringle, as to the extension of the British front in France. (Hansard, Vol. 105, no. 34, p. 851.) These answers contain certain misstatements which in sum give a totally misleading impression of what occurred. This is not the place to enter into a discussion as to all the facts, but Hansard's report concludes:

'Mr Pringle—Was this matter entered into at the Versailles War Council at any time?'

'Mr Bonar Law—This particular matter was not dealt with at all by the Versailles War Council.'

I was at Versailles when the question was decided by the Supreme War Council to whom it had been referred.

---

* It was published in all these papers except the *Daily Telegraph*.

This is the latest of a series of misstatements which have been made recently in the House of Commons by the present Government.

On 9 April the Prime Minister said:

'What was the position at the beginning of the battle?'

Notwithstanding the heavy casualties in 1917 the Army in France was considerably stronger on 1 January, 1918, than on 1 January, 1917. (Hansard, Vol. 104, no. 24, p. 1328.)

That statement implies that Sir Douglas Haig's fighting strength had not been diminished on the eve of the great battle which began on 21 March.

That is not correct.

Again in the same speech the Prime Minister said:

'In Mesopotamia there is only one white division at all, and in Egypt and Palestine there are only three white divisions, the rest are either Indians or mixed with a very very small proportion of British troops in these divisions—I am referring to the infantry divisions.' (ibid., p. 1327)

This is not correct.

Now, Sir, this letter is not the result of a military conspiracy. It has been seen by no soldier. I am by descent and conviction as sincere a democrat as the Prime Minister and the last thing I desire is to see the government of our country in the hands of soldiers.

My reasons for taking the very grave step of writing this letter are that the statements quoted above are known to a large number of soldiers to be incorrect, and this knowledge is breeding such distrust of the Government as can only end in impairing the splendid morale of our troops at a time when everything possible should be done to raise it.

I have therefore decided, fully realising the consequences to myself, that my duty as a citizen must override my duty as a soldier, and I ask you to publish this letter in the hope that Parliament may see fit to order an investigation into the statements I have made.

I am,
Yours faithfully,
F. Maurice,

20 Kensington Park Gardens,   Major-General.
    6 May, 1918.

Now it was suggested in many of the comments which this letter provoked that I charged Ministers with deliberately lying. There is nothing in my letter to warrant that assumption. What I did charge Ministers with, and what I hoped to prove had I been given an opportunity, was that they had drawn incorrect deductions from facts, that these incorrect deductions were the outcome of a wrong method of conducting the war to which, as was shown in their recent statements the Government despite the experience of 21 March, still adhered, that the method of conducting this war was wrong because it was not based upon military advice tendered in the only way in which such advice should be tendered to a Government in time of war, and that the deductions were incorrect because they were drawn from a variety of military opinions sifted and pieced together by the Government themselves.

I will take Mr Bonar Law's answers of 23 April first, as they are the first matter I deal with in my letter of 6 May. They are as follows:

Mr G. Lambert asked the Prime Minister if he can offer the House any explanation of the failure of the Fifth Army to hold the line of the Somme; and whether this portion of the line was taken over by the British troops contrary to the judgment of Sir William Robertson and Sir Douglas Haig?

MR BONAR LAW: I cannot at present make any statement in regard to the first part of the question. There is not the smallest justification for the suggestion that this portion of the line was taken over contrary to the judgment of Sir W. Robertson and Sir D. Haig. The arrangements in the matter were made entirely by the British and French military authorities.

MR LAMBERT: Is it the fact that this portion of the line was taken over after the War Cabinet had ordered it to be taken over, and that, therefore, the objections of Sir W. Robertson and Sir Douglas Haig were thereby overruled?

MR BONAR LAW: The answer which I have given is an answer to the supplementary question. The suggestion is absolutely without foundation. The arrangement was a military arrangement, made between the two military authorities.

COLONEL BURN: Will the right hon Gentleman say whether the Commander-in-Chief of the British Force at the time did not make a protest, owing to the short number of divisions at his disposal, against taking the extra line from the French?

MR BONAR LAW: I am glad that this matter should be cleared up. To the best of my knowledge—and I think that I know all the facts—there is not the smallest truth in any such suggestion. Naturally, there have been differences of opinion as to the extent of line which should be taken over, but such representations as occurred between the two Governments on that subject always were left to the military authorities to decide. Of course, if they had not agreed, a decision would have had to be made by the Governments, but that did not arise.

MR LAMBERT: Did Sir William Robertson and Sir Douglas Haig make no objection at any time to taking over any part of the line?

MR BONAR LAW: The answer which I have given is clear—that, though obviously there may have been different views as to the proper course, such differences were always left to be decided by the military authorities. If they did not agree, then the Government would have had to take a final decision, but the need for such a decision did not arise.

MR PRINGLE: Was this matter entered into at the Versailles War Council at any time?

MR BONAR LAW: This particular matter was not dealt with at all by the Versailles War Council.

Mr G. Lambert's first question is that of which notice was given, and Mr Bonar Law's first answer is the considered official reply. The remainder are supplementary questions and answers given on the spur of the moment.

Now I suggest that the inference which anyone, not cognisant with the facts, would draw from Mr Bonar Law's replies to these questions is that the question of the extension of the British front was settled between Sir Douglas Haig and General Pétain without any pressure from their respective Governments, and that no protests had been received either from Sir Douglas Haig or Sir William Robertson. I do not suggest that the extension could have been avoided but I do suggest that the action of the Government exercised great influence over Sir Douglas Haig and that the Government should have accepted their share of the responsibility. The Government were in fact announcing to the Army in France that Sir Douglas Haig, of his own volition, had agreed to an extension of his front at a time when a great attack by the enemy was expected, and when the forces at his disposal only enabled him to hold the new front thinly. Such a statement could only affect detrimentally the confidence of the Army in France in their Commander-in-Chief.

Now the facts are these:

Between the middle of October and the end of December three protests were received from Sir Douglas Haig against carrying out the extensions asked for by the French.

Sir Douglas Haig was first informed that the matter would be referred to an Allied Conference, but before such a Conference could be assembled, the Italian collapse occurred, followed by the Rapallo agreement and the institution of the Versailles Council which was designed to take the place of the Allied Conferences hitherto held.

The next step was that in the first half of December the French Government began to exercise the greatest pressure upon us to carry out a very large extension of our front. It was then decided by both the French and British Governments that their cases should be submitted to the Versailles Supreme War Council. This decision was arrived at before the extension of the Fifth Army front, which is in question, was carried out. After this decision was reached Sir Douglas Haig's third protest was received, giving military reasons for not carrying out more than half the extension which was actually completed and stating that he could only carry out the extension which he promised if his forces were kept up to strength, which was not done. This protest was endorsed by Sir William Robertson and sent to the War Cabinet, who a second time decided that the matter must be referred to the Supreme War Council, again before the extension was carried out. At the same time the military advisers of the Supreme War Council were instructed to go into the question and to report upon it. Under pressure of these events Sir Douglas Haig met General Pétain and agreed with him to carry out half the extension actually completed by 10 January and said that he hoped to be able to take on the remainder by the end of January.

On 10 January the report of the Military Representatives of the Versailles Supreme War Council was received and it was found that they recommended a considerably longer extension than that agreed upon by Sir Douglas Haig and General Pétain, but a shorter one than that for which the French Government were pressing. This report was considered amongst others at the Session of the Supreme War Council, which assembled on 1 February and was approved by the Council with the stipulation that any further extension beyond that agreed upon by Sir Douglas Haig and General Pétain should be left to the two Commanders-in-Chief to arrange. This was the final decision on a question which had been under consideration for some months and it was ratified by the British War Cabinet. Until then the question had not reached the stage of final agreement. I suggest that a suitable answer to Mr George Lambert's question would have been that the question of the extension of the British front had been considered by the French and British Governments with the assistance of the Versailles Supreme War Council and that after hearing the views of the French and British Governments Sir Douglas Haig and General Pétain had agreed upon the extension subsequently carried out. Such an answer would have put upon the French and British Governments their fair share of responsibility in the matter, and would have removed the false impression which the answer actually given created on the British Army in France.

I now come to the two statements of Mr Lloyd George's speech of 9 April, which I challenged.

The first of these is: 'What was the situation at the beginning of the battle? Notwithstanding the heavy casualties in 1917 the Army in France was considerably stronger on 1 January, 1918, than on 1 January, 1917.'

Now it is true that by counting heads it will be found that the British Army was stronger on 1 January, 1918, than on 1 January, 1917. I therefore stated expressly in my letter to Sir Henry Wilson that I did not challenge those figures, but by beginning this statement with the words 'What was the situation at the beginning of the battle?' I maintain that the impression conveyed is that our Army in France entered upon the battle which began on 21 March stronger for fighting purposes than it was in 1917. That this was the view entertained by the Government is shown by statements made on the same day 9 April in the House of Lords by Lord Curzon who said 'There seems to have been a tendency in some quarters to suppose either from a reluctance to tamper with available sources of manpower in this country, or from a failure to appreciate military advice, the British Army in France had been allowed to decline numerically to a point that was fraught with peril. There is no foundation for such a suspicion; nor were any apprehensions of such a character either entertained or received.' And again later: 'The Western front was well equipped to look after itself. If it has in any respect failed to do so, the explanation must be sought elsewhere.'

Now, as I have already said, the Army Council had during the latter half of 1917 pressed insistently upon the Government the need for more men. Sir Douglas Haig stated in the middle of December, that if he did not get more men, he would be compelled to reduce his establishments, and that in that event it would not be a question of his extending his front, but of whether his existing front could be secured. Sir Douglas Haig did not receive the men he required, he was compelled to reduce his establishments, and he had to extend his front. He also at a later date submitted a statement showing the probable extent to which it would be necessary to reduce the establishments of the Army during 1918 if more men were not received. Sir William Robertson, who as a member of the Army Council had supported the demands for more men referred to above, sent in separate memoranda, as Chief of the Imperial General Staff, in November and towards the end of December, in which the urgent need for a greater call upon the manpower of the Nation than had yet been made, was strongly impressed upon the War Cabinet. In answer to these various representations, the Government allocated to the Army a number of men wholly inadequate to keep it up to strength.

I am not aware why Mr Lloyd George selected 1 January, 1918 and 1 January, 1917 for comparison. Probably they were selected arbitrarily as being convenient dates. But they were in fact unfortunate dates to choose in order to give a fair impression of the comparative strengths for purposes of battle of the Army in those two years.

The situation on 1 January, 1917, was that the Army in France was low in strength as the result of the fighting on the Somme and on the Ancre. It steadily increased in strength during the spring of 1917 and entered upon the Battle of Arras on 9 April of that year much stronger than it had been at the beginning of the year.

The situation on 1 January, 1918, was that the strength of the Army was again low as the result of the fighting in Flanders and at Cambrai, and it was not made up to strength sufficiently to allow existing establishments to be maintained. The infantry, on the eve of the battle of 21 March, 1918, were more than 100,000 weaker than they were on 1 January, 1917. The result of this was that the infantry brigades in the British divisions had to be reduced from four battalions to three, entailing a reduction of some 140 battalions, while at the same time two cavalry divisions were broken up. There were increases in artillery, aircraft, machine guns, and tanks, but none of these increases were sufficient to compensate for the weakness in infantry and in cavalry, when it was a question of meeting a great attack on an extended front.

Now I did not and do not suggest that it is not absolutely and solely the business of the Government to decide upon the number of men and the amount of money and material which should be provided for the prosecution of the war, and how these should be allocated to the various national services. But I do suggest that when the Government decide that they cannot meet the full demands of the military authorities they should accept responsibility for the consequences, and should shape their policy in accordance with their means. I further suggest that Ministers should not put their own interpretation upon comparative statements of strengths of the Allied and enemy forces and be satisfied with an appearance of numerical equality, but should be guided solely by military advice upon what is a very intricate and difficult question, namely, the comparative fighting power of the opponents. This has been pointed out to the Government on more than one occasion.

The second of the Prime Minister's statements which I challenged had reference to the number of British in the secondary theatres of war. The whole passage runs as follows:

THE PRIME MINISTER: There is another matter to which I should like to refer, and it is the suggestion that our forces have been dissipated on subsidiary enterprises. Not a single division was sent from France to the East. With regard to Italy, had it not been for the fact that there were Italian, French, and British divisions there, the Austrian Army would have been free to throw the whole of its strength on the Western front. If there were not some there now, the Austrian Army would be more powerfully represented than it is on the Western front. With regard to Salonika, the only thing the present Government did was to reduce the forces there by two divisions.

MR PRINGLE: You increased them at first.

THE PRIME MINISTER: The present Government reduced them by two divisions. In Mesopotamia there is only one white division at all, and in Egypt and Palestine together there are only three white divisions; the rest are either Indians or mixed with a very, very small proportion of British troops in those divisions—I am referring to infantry divisions.

To appreciate the policy and views of the Government on this question it is necessary that this passage should be read in conjunction with the corresponding passage in the speech made by Lord Curzon on the same day in the House of Lords.

Lord Curzon said:

There is another criticism, equally fallacious, which I must note in passing—namely, that the Western front has been stinted or drained for the more distant campaigns in other parts of Europe or Asia—campaigns which the Imperial responsibilities of Great Britain or her obligations to her Allies have compelled her to undertake. Such is not the case. Our military commitments in Salonika were made long before the present offensive was so much as dreamed of. They dated from the year 1915;

and it will be within your Lordships recollection that instead of being blamed for undertaking them, the late Government were reproached both here and elsewhere for not having undertaken them earlier and in greater strength. I have never met anybody who recommended their complete or even their partial abandonment. So far from our forces at Salonika having been increased, it is a matter of common knowledge that they have been considerably reduced for the sake of the Western front.*

Now I suggest that the inferences to be drawn from these statements are that the forces at Salonika were reduced for the benefit of the Western front and that forces were not kept in secondary theatres which might without detriment to vital national interests have been employed in France.

The facts are these:

During the summer and autumn of 1917 two divisions were withdrawn from Salonika, but they were sent to Palestine to reinforce General Allenby, and to enable him to carry out his offensive, which resulted in the capture of Jerusalem. I am speaking from memory, but during the two years I was in office I cannot recall a single instance of the reduction of these forces at Salonika for the benefit of the Western front.

As regards the forces in Egypt and Palestine, the General Staff had recommended consistently at the end of 1917 and in the beginning of this year that after the capture of Jerusalem we should adopt a defensive policy in Palestine, that it was urgently necessary that our commitments in secondary theatres should be reduced to the bare minimum, and that three British divisions could be withdrawn from Palestine for the benefit of France, without detriment to our defensive position in the East. This advice the Government rejected, and decided on an offensive campaign in Palestine. Had the advice of the General Staff been followed, these three British divisions might have been in France before 21 March. But the Government were of opinion that three divisions more or less would make no difference to France, and in coming to this conclusion they relied upon the approximate numerical equality of the forces on the Western front, and upon the establishment of the Versailles Executive Board.

Again I could not state these views in public, but I hoped by challenging the Prime Minister's statement that all except three divisions in Egypt and Palestine were either Indian or contained

* For the full text of Lord Curzon's speech see p. 120.

a very very small proportion of white troops to be enabled to bring before an enquiry the larger question of War policy.

On the eve of the battle of 21 March, there was in Egypt one Indian division, which contained some 7,000 white and some 13,000 native troops. There were in Palestine 7 infantry divisions which contained about 100,000 white troops as against 6,000 native troops. There was in addition a large force of white mounted troops. It is true that arrangements had been made to replace in all but three of the white divisions in Palestine a certain number of British battalions by native battalions from India, and therefore I did not challenge the Prime Minister's statement as to the three white divisions. I did challenge the whole passage and especially that part relative to the proportion of British and native troops. I expected to be able to show that while the Prime Minister's statement conveyed the impression that there was a bare minimum of white troops in Egypt and Palestine, there were in fact ample white troops to make our defensive position in Palestine secure, and at the same time allow of the despatch of a considerable force of white troops from Palestine to France in time to meet the menace to the Western **front**.

In fact after the German attack of 21 March a defensive policy was adopted in Palestine and two white divisions and more than the equivalent in infantry of a third division were ordered from Palestine to France.*

Such then were my reasons for sending my letter to the Press and my justification for doing so.

The immediate effect of my letter was that the Government

---

* At the War Cabinet meeting on 23 March (WC 361), the CIGS stated that 'there were 3 British divisions in Egypt'. In his speech on 9 April, Lloyd George had said 'in Egypt *and* Palestine there are only three white divisions; the rest are either Indian or mixed with a very, very small proportion of British troops in these divisions'.

Although Lloyd George informed the War Cabinet on 7 May that the CIGS was his authority for saying that 'all but three white divisions in Egypt and Palestine were either Indian or mixed with a very, very small proportion of British troops in these divisions', in the Minutes of W.C. 361 the CIGS is not reported as having made any such statement, and Lloyd George did not refer to this in his speech in the Maurice debate, having no evidence to support it.

Lloyd George seems to have been carried away by the same 'Celtic temperament' which had caused him to stretch the figures of the strength of the forces in France in January, 1918 'to their extreme limits'. (*The Supreme Command*, Vol II, pp. 198–9.) He was particularly vulnerable to exposure in regard to the British forces in Palestine, since he had refused repeated requests from his military advisers to bring 3 divisions from there to reinforce the Army in France before the German attack in March.

announced in the House of Commons that they proposed to appoint a commission of two judges to investigate my charges. I was prepared to go before any impartial commission appointed by Parliament, and I believed that my main object had been achieved. Unfortunately, a commission of two judges did not appeal to Mr Asquith, nor apparently to the House of Commons generally. Mr Asquith refused it and proposed instead a Select Committee of the House. This the Government rejected, and made the matter a question of confidence. I saw at once that this would mean that I should fail to obtain an enquiry, and without an enquiry I was helpless.

The remainder of my story is, with the exception of some con-structive proposals at the end of this paper, more personal. I was prepared for the abuse which was heaped upon me in a certain section of the Press, and I decided to take no notice of it. I had appealed to Parliament, and had determined to stand or fall by that appeal.

I was not however prepared for the methods pursued by the Government to defeat my request for an enquiry. My case depended upon the production of secret information and documents, and it was not possible for me to make a full reply to attacks made upon me except before an authoritative tribunal. I was attacking the Government, and, very naturally the Government defended itself, but being in such a position that I could not state my case while the Government was free to put theirs, I think I had a right to expect more judicial treatment than I received. My case was prejudiced in the House by three statements which the Prime Minister made: Firstly, that I had not made any representations on the matters either to him or to anyone else before I left office; secondly, that I was not in a position to know what happened at Versailles when I stated that I had been there, and, thirdly, that the statements which he made on 9 April were based on information supplied by me or my Department.

The first two of these statements I replied to in a letter to the papers, dated 15 May, which appears later.

With regard to the first of them, my alleged neglect to inform those in authority before I sent my letter of 6 May to the Press, my case was further prejudiced in the House of Commons in a manner which has only recently come to my knowledge. A statement made on 9 May, the day on which the Prime Minister spoke, by his private secretary, Mr Sutherland, was understood to mean that the Prime Minister had sent Mr Sutherland for me on 9 April, and that I had heard the Prime Minister's speech from the secretaries' gallery behind the Speaker's Chair. This report was given wide circulation in the House and appeared in the Press. The incident in question happened on 16 April on my return from France, and the speech which I heard was that of the Prime Minister on Irish Conscription.

With regard to the question of my attendance at Versailles, I may add that I stated in my letter of 15 May to the Press that I received the Agenda of the Session of the Versailles Supreme War Council and that later the complete verbatim reports of the meetings passed through my hands. This was struck out of my letter by the Censor as being a reference to secret documents. My only point is to make it clear that I was fully aware of all that led up to and happened at this particular Session of the Supreme War Council.

As regards the third point, that the Prime Minister's statements as to the strengths of the Armies in France were supplied to him by me or by my Directorate, the Prime Minister devoted a considerable part of his speech to showing that his comparison of the strength of the Army in France on 1 January, 1917, and 1 January, 1918, was correct. It will be remembered that in my letter to Sir Henry Wilson I specifically stated that I did not challenge that comparison for reasons which I have already given. I may mention that figures as to the British forces in the various theatres of war are not compiled in the Operations Directorate, but in the Adjutant General's Department, and that the Operations Directorate in these matters merely acts as a medium for collecting information for the War Cabinet. I cannot recollect that, during the period that I was in office, I was ever asked to supply any information to the War Cabinet as to the comparative combatant strength of the Army on the eve of the battle of 21 March and in 1917. My attention was first called to the matter by my conversation with the Chief of the Imperial General Staff on 7 April, but I was not then aware, nor was I aware until 20 April when I read the Prime Minister's speech, that he intended to refer to the strength on the eve of the battle. In the course of his speech the Prime Minister mentioned a return prepared in answer to a question in the House of Commons on 18 April. I did not know of the existence of this return until I read the Prime Minister's speech of 9 May and it appears to be incorrect.

I fail to see how an incorrect return made on 18 April could influence what the Prime Minister said on 9 April. It is hard to understand why the Prime Minister did not have the correct figures before him when he was preparing his speech on 9 May, or why he did not know that the return of 18 April was incorrect.

The Prime Minister also referred to two statements which in the course of my duties I made to representatives of the American Press, one on 27 March and the other on 3 April, in which I referred to the approximate equality of the forces on the Western Front. These meetings of the Press representatives were held by me at the request of the Foreign Office, and with the approval of the Chief of the Imperial General Staff, for propaganda purposes, and naturally statements made at such meetings were very different in character to statements of considered military opinion made to the War Cabinet. At the time when the statements in question were made there was very general alarm at the extent of the enemy's successes, and I desired to point out that the blow had fallen on the British Army alone, that in course of time the French reserves would come up and intervene, and that there was good hope that the enemy's progress would be thereby checked. The statement did not mean that I considered that a numerical equality which included Belgians, Portuguese, and partly trained American troops meant an equality in fighting strength. Further it had been repeatedly pointed out to the War Cabinet that we might expect the number of German divisions on the Western Front to be increased to 220 and that the German heavy artillery would be very largely reinforced from the East. This meant an enemy reinforcement in divisions alone of about 30 over the number estimated to be in the West on the eve of the battle, while the Entente had no comparable reinforcements in sight.

As regards the strength of the enemy forces in Egypt and Palestine the Prime Minister stated that I had been present at a meeting of the War Cabinet at which they were informed that there were only three white divisions in Palestine, that the proceedings of the Cabinet had been forwarded to me for correction and that I had not corrected this statement. To the best of my recollection the meeting in question was held at the War Office shortly after the events of 21 March. I was called in to the Meeting while it was in progress and asked to furnish figures as to the Allied strength on the Western front; having furnished these figures I left the Meeting and I have no recollection of having been present at any discussion of the strengths of the forces in Palestine and Egypt. When the proceedings were circulated to me I followed the procedure which I had always previously adopted of checking the statement I had myself made and no others. I believe the statement in question was made by the Chief of the Imperial General Staff and I assumed that he had made any necessary corrections. I remember reading the paragraph in question and noticing that it was not literally accurate, but as the discussion turned upon the number of troops that could be withdrawn from other theatres to France, and for reasons which I have already given, not more than three white divisions could be withdrawn from Palestine, and further as very shortly afterwards orders were issued for the withdrawal of two white divisions, and a considerable number of white battalions, the inaccuracy did not seem to me to be of any moment. I have no recollection whatever of any statement to the effect that the remaining divisions in Palestine contained a very very small proportion of white troops.

One other point in connection with the Prime Minister's speech before I leave it. The Prime Minister maintained his right to include non-combatants in estimating the fighting strength of the Army. That is, I maintain, a matter upon which military opinion and military opinion alone should be taken. He instanced, in support of his contention, the achievements of General Carey's force and stated that the men of this force 'would not be treated as combatants'. General Carey's force was composed very largely of Royal Engineers, Signallers, and men from a number of the Fifth Army Schools of Instruction; they were all men hastily collected to meet an emergency, but the great majority of them were combatants, and to the best of my knowledge the number of non-combatants in the force was small. The labour units who made up the increase in total strength of the Army in January, 1918 as compared with the strength in January, 1917 were as a whole neither armed nor trained to fight.

The Prime Minister in his speech of 9 May did not reply as to the diminution of the fighting strength of the Army on the eve of the battle of 21 March, nor as to the number of white troops in Palestine and Egypt. His answer as to the extension of the front brought out the main point I desired to make, namely that the extension was carried out in consequence of great pressure from the French Government.

As regards the question of the breach of discipline, the Army Council wrote to me on 7 May asking for my reasons for writing as I had done. I replied the next day to the effect that I recognised with deep regret that the publication of the letter was a breach of the regulations and added that the writing of the letter was with me a matter of conscience. On 11 May I was informed that the Army Council had decided to place me on retired pay forthwith. To this I replied that I recognised the justice of the Council's decision. The announcement of my retirement appeared in the Gazette of 13 May and on the 14th I sent the following statement to the Press which was published the next day:

The editor of the *Daily Chronicle* has asked me to become his military correspondent, and I have accepted his offer. The *Daily Chronicle* has generously recognised that I acted as I did with a deep sense of the gravity of the step I took because I conceived it to be my duty. I was not, as has been stated, a disgruntled soldier turned out of a job. I had been promised and was about to take up important employment in France, which of all things I most desired, and I think I may say without vanity that I had a promising career before me. That is all behind me, and I have left a service I love. I have therefore made a very real sacrifice, I hope not in vain.

I do not intend to indulge in any recriminations. My sole object will be to help my readers to get on with the war. If in the future I have occasion to be critical, my criticism will be constructive.

I appealed to Parliament to order an inquiry into the statements I had made. I failed in my appeal, and my case has not been heard. The 'explanations' referred to in the official notice of my retirement had reference only to the breach of discipline, to which I, of course, pleaded guilty. I have paid the penalty for that breach of discipline which, with very deep regret, I felt myself bound to commit, and there is nothing more to be said.

After the short personal explanation which follows, I do not intend to reopen the question unless and until I am asked authoritatively to do so. Obviously a newspaper controversy as to the correctness of the facts stated in my letter of 6 May, which I was and am prepared to substantiate before a Tribunal appointed by Parliament is impossible, as proof depends upon the production of confidential information.

I feel, however, that I owe my readers a word of explanation on two comments which the Prime Minister made on my conduct, and these I can answer without disclosing secrets. The first is as to my presence at Versailles at the session in which the question of taking over the line was discussed. I accompanied the British representatives to Versailles, and I was present* at the first meeting of this session of the Supreme War Council. During the meetings held after the first I was in a corridor outside the Council Chamber, and in the intervals between the meetings was engaged on work in connection with the questions under examination. I hold, therefore, that my statement that I was at Versailles at the time is justified. As to the second point, the Prime Minister asked why I did not make any criticisms of Ministerial statements either to him or to my chief, the Chief of the Imperial Staff, while I was in office.

The Prime Minister made his speech on 9 April. I was not, as has been stated in some reports of the speech, in the House on that occasion. The day on which the Prime Minister spoke was also the day on which the enemy's attack in Flanders began. Between then and 20 April, when I handed over my work to my successor, I was very much occupied with my duties, and was part of the time in France. I had no leisure to do more than glance at the Prime Minister's speech. I did notice the statement about the forces in Egypt and Palestine, but that did not seem to me by itself to warrant my calling attention to it at a time when everyone was very much occupied with other matters. I left the War Office on 20 April on leave, and then for the first time read the full report of the speech.

While I was on leave I heard of Mr Bonar Law's answers to questions in the House on 23 April. I returned to London on 29 April by arrangement to make my official farewells at the War Office, and afterwards saw the Hansard report, for 23 April. It was then, 29 April, and not till then, that I formed the definite opinion that Mr Bonar Law's replies and those statements of the Prime Minister's which I have questioned, taken together, put upon the soldiers responsibility that, in my judgment, should be borne by Ministers, and it appeared to me a matter of urgency to correct that impression.

As the Prime Minister indicated in his speech of 9 May (Hansard, Vol. 105, p. 2348, line 13, *et seq.*), I wrote the next day, 30 April, after I had left office, to my late Chief, the Chief of the Imperial Staff, pointing out that the statements which I quoted in my letter of 6 May were incorrect. I had not made up my mind before then that action on my part was necessary. I waited for a reply until 6 May before sending my letter to the Press, and that I conceived to be as long as I could wait, because I had been warned to expect orders to go to France on or after 10 May, and I did not wish to make such charges on the eve of leaving this country.

As suggestions have been made that I was working in concert or collusion with other soldiers or with opponents of the Government in Parliament or in the Press, I wish to add that I acted entirely alone, and

---

* In the original letter I added here 'I received the agenda of all the meetings, and later the complete verbatim reports of the meetings passed through my hands.' This passage was deleted by the Censor.

that the responsibility for what I did is mine alone. Nothing was further from my mind than to serve any partisan political purpose.

This closes the story of what happened. But I did not take the step I did without having definite constructive proposals in mind.

The first of these is one of secondary but still of considerable importance. It is the practice of the Prime Minister, and of the Leaders of the House of Commons and the House of Lords, to make from time to time statements on military operations which often go into great detail. It is the custom of members of the War Cabinet who intend to make statements, to apply to the War Office for such information, and I have during my term of office prepared many notes for speeches by Ministers. I have found, however, that additions have sometimes been made to the notes sent in from the War Office and the additions presumably have been based upon information obtained from other sources. I have also found that I have not always been aware of the purpose for which the notes were required, or of the arguments which Ministers propose to use. The military situation at times varies so quickly that information supplied at one time and for one particular purpose, may be incorrect for another time or for another purpose. I would therefore suggest that all statements concerning military details which members of the War Cabinet propose to make should be first checked at the War Office. It would be preferable, if the normal practice in regard to naval affairs were followed in the case of military affairs and statements involving military detail were made only by the Minister in charge of the War Office just as detailed statements on naval affairs are made as a rule by the Minister in charge of the Admiralty. The present system arises from the heresy that the conduct of war on land is less technical than the conduct of war on sea. Ministers are, of course, best able to judge as to what the effect of their words will be in Parliament or on the public at home, but they are less well able to judge of the effect upon the Armies in the field, and any statement made by them which appear to the men at the front to be inaccurate are almost certain to create a bad impression there. The plain fact is that members of the War Cabinet, not being in charge of the departments concerned with the fighting forces, have not the time or the opportunity to make themselves thoroughly conversant with details before they speak and they select for themselves statements to support their policy which are not always in accordance with facts.

This brings me to my second proposal. After more than a year's association with the War Cabinet as at present constituted I am convinced that it is over-loaded with work and that the machinery of Government is over-centralised. The War Cabinet is charged not only with the conduct of the war, but with the general administration of the Empire. It has to supervise not only the general conduct of operations in a number of theatres of war and the arrangements for co-operation with our Allies, but also a large number of social and political problems concerning the entire government of the United Kingdom and the Empire generally. The result is that they are unable to give the time necessary to purely naval and military policy, and to the maintenance of our armies and fleets. They are competing with an enemy organisation which, with fewer and less intricate military and naval problems to deal with, is able to devote its whole time to their solution. I suggest that what is required is a small Cabinet composed of the Prime Minister, the Secretaries of State for Foreign Affairs and War, and the First Lord of the Admiralty charged solely with the conduct of the war, and that this Cabinet should have as its sole military and naval advisers the Chief of the Imperial General Staff and the First Sea Lord. A second Cabinet composed of other Ministers to deal with all the multifarious questions not directly concerned with the conduct of naval and military operations. Co-ordination of the work of the two Cabinets might be arranged by the Prime Minister being Chairman of both or by the Leader of the House of Commons being Chairman of what I may call the Political Cabinet, and also an additional member of the War Cabinet. All members of both Cabinets should receive reports of the proceedings of both Cabinets.

My third proposal is that the War Cabinet should receive naval and military advice only through one naval and one military adviser. This is the only means by which a definite continuity of naval and military policy can be obtained. If the Cabinet are not satisfied with the advice tendered to them, the advisers should be changed, but other advice should not be sought while they remain in office. This does not mean that the War Cabinet should be debarred from obtaining the advice of any Commander in Chief, or other naval or military officer, but that such advice should be tendered to them through their responsible adviser, if necessary with his comments or remarks. Further, plans or proposals for naval or military operations should reach the Cabinet only through their responsible advisers, to whom any such proposals put forward by individual Ministers or other persons should be addressed. British Ministers have never been able to grasp the difference between the opinion of individual soldiers, however distinguished and experienced, speaking for themselves alone and the opinion of a responsible military adviser speaking as the head of an organisation established and designed for the preparation of considered and co-ordinated views on military questions. It is to this that most of our troubles in the present and in other wars are due. Until Ministers do grasp this vital difference our troubles will continue. If Ministers seek advice on the conduct of the war from a number of soldiers, taking this man's advice on one point and that man's on another, they are impressed chiefly by each individual soldier's power of expressing himself and of urging his views and not by the one consideration which gives the advice value, namely whether it is the resultant of careful and detailed examination of all the factors involved in the problem in question. Only the soldier with the machinery at his disposal to enable him to conduct such an examination can prepare advice as it should be prepared. The others may occasionally be right, they will be more often wrong. Again, under the present system Ministers have themselves to piece together a mosaic of military policy, and this they have not the necessary technical knowledge to do, while they are tempted, almost irresistibly, to select from each adviser that advice which suits best their own preconceived ideas and policy.

The principle of single military advice, based upon organised machinery for its preparation, is that which upon which our chief enemy has long waged war and waged it successfully. There are many who are now disposed to believe that a democratic government cannot compete with an autocratic in the conduct of war. We certainly cannot if we adhere to the methods we have followed in the past, but there is nothing in our constitution or system of Government which forces us to adhere to those methods. Nearly sixty years ago, another great democracy was engaged in a life and death struggle, under the leadership of a great statesman.* He groped his way slowly and painfully along the same road which we have been

* Abraham Lincoln.

following in this struggle equally slowly and equally painfully towards a sound method of conducting war. The system he eventually evolved was in principle identical with that which our enemy has followed and is following. There is no other which can guide us to victory.

F. MAURICE

22 May 1918

2 The Letters from Sir William Robertson

On Wednesday, 24 April General Maurice noted in his diary 'Wrote WR re Bonar Law's Answer in the House about extension of front.'

Robertson replied next day:

50 Pall Mall
S.W.
25 April, 1918

My dear Maurice,

Your letter of yesterday. I have seen the answer to the question, and I agree with your opinion of it. I have just returned from Cambridge and was thinking of writing to you on the subject.

I agree that something really should be done, but it is difficult to know what to do. As I remember the case, Haig first, and for a long time, considered he could not and ought not to extend. I believe I asked for Cabinet support to that. Eventually it was referred to the Military Advisers at Versailles, and they split the difference. Eventually it was settled at the last Versailles meeting I attended in Council, but whether actually *by* the Council or whether it was in a way left to the Soldiers, I cannot remember.

As you say you have the papers, I would very much like to see them. For my own part I believe I was always against extension, at any rate to the amount made. The impression given by the answer is, of course, totally misleading. I think we had better talk the matter over, but I would much like to see the papers if this can be managed. Probably it cannot. I will expect to see you on Monday—not too late. Lunch if possible.

W. W. Robertson

General Maurice wrote in his diary 'WR replies that he thinks action necessary.'

Robertson wrote again next day:

27.4.18

Dear Maurice,

In continuation of my letter of 25th: what I would like to know is what we said in receipt of the Versailles M. Adviser's proposals, whether

117

the latter were finally accepted by the War Cabinet, and ditto later by the Versailles Council when it came up at my last meeting.

Yours

W. W. Robertson

I am expecting you to lunch on Monday unless I am away. Will tell you later.*

It is clear from Sir William Robertson's next letter that at their meeting on the 29th General Maurice had told him of his intention to write his letter to the press.

General Maurice noted in his diary for 29 April:

Saw WR and put proposals to him. He wants to sleep over it.

And on 30 April:

Saw WR again and he agrees to my suggestion to write Wilson. Did so. He suggests I should see Asquith before writing to the papers.

On the 30th, Robertson wrote:

My dear Maurice,

I have been thinking further and am not sure that I like the Asquith idea after all. The case is rather one for your own judgment. The thing to do is to decide irrespective of what the results may be, unless you feel sure that the results will certainly be nil. I shall be interested to know what reply, if any, you get to your letter to the CIGS. Let me have your address whilst away in case I want to write to you. I shall be away on Saturday till Monday morning and expect that I shall be going away on Monday evening for 24 hours.

Yours very truly,

W. W. Robertson

On the same day as he received this letter Maurice wrote in his diary: 'On second thoughts decided not to see Asquith. Must take sole responsibility for action myself.'

On Thursday, 2 May, he wrote: 'Made up my mind to write letter and composed it. Will not send it if I hear from Wilson, but do not expect to.'

Robertson wrote again on 4 May:

My dear Maurice,

Everyone I see swears that the days of LG are numbered, but I don't attach much confidence to these statements. The point of this is to

* In a letter dated 28 April Robertson wrote that he had to be away until 6.30 on Monday 28th.

repeat what I have said already, namely, be quite sure of your facts and do not say a word that cannot be conclusively substantiated or that can be twisted to your disadvantage.

You are contemplating a great thing—to your undying credit.

Yours very truly,

W. W. Robertson

3 Lord Curzon's Speech

In Lord Curzon's speech on 9 April, he 'crossed the t's and dotted the i's' of certain portions of Lloyd George's speech of the same date, which General Maurice had challenged.

Regarding the strength of the opposing forces on 21 March Curzon said:

Along the entire Western Front there was an approximate equality between the combatant strength of the Allies and the Germans in respect of infantry; the enemy were slightly inferior in artillery, and considerably inferior in aircraft. The Germans, however, had so organised their forces as to produce a considerably larger number of divisions out of an equal or a smaller number of men. That, as your Lordships will understand, is a question of organisation, apart from numbers, though it had the consequence of enabling them to constitute a powerful reserve of more than 80 divisions, the greater part of which were concentrated in the rear of the right and centre of their line. Moreover, owing to the position of the Germans on interior lines, they were able to move their reserves from the centre of a great arc to the circumference either of the British or of the French front more rapidly than the Allies could do because of the greater distances which the latter had to cover. This is an advantage which the enemy forces have almost consistently enjoyed by reason of the geographical factor alike in the larger and in the local aspects of the entire European campaign. The possibility to which I alluded just now of an attack on the French front in Champagne necessitated the retention of a great part of the French reserves in rear of that front, thus rendering it impossible for the Allies, acting on exterior lines, to prevent the enemy from achieving temporary superiority at any one point in the line where he might choose to attack.

My Lords, I have made the above remarks about the approximate numerical equality of the opposing forces along the entire Front *because there seems to have been a tendency in some quarters to suppose that, either from a reluctance to tap the available resources of manpower in this country or from a failure to appreciate military advice, the British Army in France had been allowed to decline numerically to a point that was fraught with peril. There is no foundation for such a suspicion; nor were any apprehensions of such a character either entertained or received. Our Commanders were equally satisfied with the numbers, the equipment, and the morale of their forces.** Nor is it in any of those respects that fault has been found. Up to the very eve of the battle the Government continued to receive the most confident and gratifying assurances from the Allied military authorities on the spot.

In regard to the forces in theatres other than the Western Front, he went even further than Lloyd George.

There is another criticism, equally fallacious, which I must note in passing—namely, that the Western Front has been stinted or drained for the more distant campaigns in other parts of Europe or of Asia—campaigns which the Imperial responsibilities of Great Britain or her obligations to her Allies have compelled her to undertake. Such is not the case. Our military commitments in Salonika were made long before the present offensive was so much as dreamed of. They dated from the year 1915; and it will be within your Lordships' recollection that, instead of being blamed for undertaking them, the late Government were reproached both here and elsewhere for not having undertaken them earlier and in greater strength. I have never met anybody who recommended their complete or even their partial abandonment. *So far from our forces at Salonika having been increased, it is a matter of common knowledge that they have been considerably reduced for the sake of the Western Front.** Equally does everybody know that the Allied Armies there, though operating in a secondary theatre of war, are performing a military service of primary importance, desistance from which would have involved the abandonment of Greece to the Germans, the disappearance of our staunch ally and friend M. Venizelos, the restoration of King Constantine, and, still more, the handing over to the enemy of the most formidable group of naval and submarine bases to be found in the Eastern Mediterranean.

Similarly as regards Palestine and Mesopotamia, I do not think that I need enter on this occasion into a defence of either of these campaigns.

Our advance upon Palestine, pursued with a success that still continues, was the alternative—and a very preferable alternative—to the passive defence of Egypt and the locking up of a large number of troops there. In these campaigns we have not only taken two of the capital cities of the Turkish Empire, but we have practically destroyed an entire Turkish

* Editor's italics.

Army. We have forced the Turk to withdraw the whole of his fighting forces from Europe, and we have even compelled the Germans to spare not only a German Field-Marshal and German units to assuage by their presence the discomfiture of their Turkish Allies, but even German regiments—an entire German battalion having been discovered only during the past few days in occupation of an important position to the east of the Jordan. *I mentioned these two Eastern campaigns only in order to point out to your Lordships that neither of them has been allowed to affect the fighting strength of the forces in France or in Flanders.* No British troops have been taken from France for any Eastern theatre of war.

There is no question here of Western as against Eastern strategy. *The Western Front was well equipped to look after itself; and if it has in any respect failed to do so, the explanation must be sought elsewhere.*

It will not be found in denouncing the secondary campaigns of our Armies, the full value of which will, perhaps, be even more visible at the Peace Conference of the future than it is now.

The Unionist War Committee met on the evening of 8 May to consider their attitude in the Debate on the Maurice letter. Some 230 members attended. Much sympathy was expressed for General Maurice, as it seemed that this was to be a battle between the politicians and the soldiers, the former trying to make a scapegoat of the latter in order to cover up the shortcomings of the Government in not attempting to provide the necessary men, and for forcing the Commander-in-Chief to take over 45 miles of front from the French when he had not the men to do so. From the point of view of discipline General Maurice came in for some condemnation but on balance he had much support. However the committee decided that they could not support Asquith in the division; Carson told Col. Repington that 'he had been for three hours with the Unionists today; their hate of Asquith overrides all other considerations and they will not back him tomorrow in the Maurice Debate'.

Part 4

1 The Maurice Debate and the Baring Question

> Therefore, waiving a strict enquiry into the cause of these
> things, let us apply ourselves to the remedy, which is most
> necessary. And I hope we have such true English hearts, and
> zealous affections towards the general weal of our Mother Country,
> as no Members of either House will scruple to deny themselves,
> and their own private interests, for the public good.
>
> From *Cromwell's first speech* in the House of Commons, 1654

Lloyd George's speech in the Maurice Debate was a parliamentary triumph—one of the greatest of his career.

Asquith had played into his hands by rejecting the offer of an enquiry by two judges and demanding a debate on the motion to set up a Select Committee of the House. By so doing he made it inevitable that there would be no inquiry, and that the Government would not fall, since Lloyd George had only to treat the Motion as a vote of censure on the Government to make certain that it would be defeated.

General Maurice's own actions did nothing to forward his cause. Lloyd George is reputed to have said 'Maurice went away for the week-end. Any man who goes away for the week-end I can deal with.' General Maurice did, deliberately, go away. He made no attempt to brief the Opposition as to the facts, and left London before the Debate so as to be unavailable to provide answers to Lloyd George's statements for the speakers who followed him. His motive was his desire to avoid any implication of being involved in a political intrigue. He had sacrificed his military career in the hope that Parliament would order an inquiry to which he would be able to disclose secret information which would justify his charges. He hoped, by so doing, to bring to an end the pursuit by the Government of a policy which he believed was fatal to the successful prosecution of the war. If Parliament did not choose to order an inquiry, he would accept their decision. But he would do nothing more to influence it than he had done by writing his letter. This was a fatal error of judgment, but completely in character; simple, honourable, no match for the politicians, and quite unversed in Parliamentary procedure.

So he stayed away from the debate, but he got a ticket for his daughter Nancy, who sat next to Mrs Asquith in the Speaker's Gallery.

Margot noted in her diary:

A pretty girl sitting next to me said 'I suppose, Mrs Asquith, my poor father's case will never be heard!' M. Is your father General Maurice? The girl 'Yes.' M. 'No, my dear, the Government will take good care of that.'

The Debate was opened by Asquith, in a long, dull, inept and irrelevant speech, devoted almost entirely to his reasons for preferring a Select Committee of the House to an inquiry by two judges.

Mrs Asquith noted in her diary:

H (Mr Asquith) made an admirable speech unanswerable but of course he could not give the facts as it would have betrayed Haig and other soldiers.

This was wifely loyalty. No one else who heard Asquith's speech seems to have agreed with her.

Lloyd George was at his brilliant best. His speech was a mixture of prevarication, distortion and special pleading, in which even when he could not deny the truth of General Maurice's accusations, he convinced the House that it was not he, but General Maurice himself who was to blame.

In his letter to the press, General Maurice had made the mistake of not stating that he had only seen the Ministerial statements he challenged after he left the War Office. Lloyd George took full advantage of this. In a most telling passage in his speech, he said:

A general, a distinguished general, who, for good or for bad reasons, has ceased to hold an office which he has occupied for two years challenges, after he has left office, statements made by two Ministers during the time he was in that office. During the time he was in such office he never challenged those statements, when he had not merely access to official information, but when he had access to the Ministers themselves.

General Maurice was in office for weeks after I delivered that speech in the House of Commons. He attended a meeting of the Cabinet, in the absence of the Chief of the Staff, the very day I delivered the speech. He never called attention to it; he never asked me to correct it. It may be said, perhaps, that at that time he had had no time to read it. He was there the following day, but he never called my attention to the fact that these statements were inaccurate. Supposing he did not care to do it in the presence of the whole Cabinet, I was in daily contact with General Maurice on the business of the War. I was under the impression, in fact, that he was a great friend of mine. We were constantly discussing these questions of figures, because as the Director of Military Operations, he was the authority. Was it not his business to come to me—especially if he thought that this was so important that it justified a great general in breaking the King's Regulations and setting an example of indiscipline— was it not his business, first of all, to come to the Cabinet, or, at any rate, to come to the Minister whom he impugned, and say to him, 'You made a mistake in the House of Commons on a most important question of fact'? He might have put it quite nicely. He could have said, 'I dare say you were misled, but you can put it right.' Never a word was said to me! Never a syllable until I saw it in the newspapers!

I say that I have been treated unfairly. I will say more than that. I thought that probably General Maurice had not talked to me about it, because he thought that it was his business to talk to his immediate Chief first of all—either to the Secretary of State for War or perhaps to the Chief of the Imperial General Staff. Perhaps he thought that it was not his business to talk to me. I therefore inquired; but until he left office, during the whole of the time that these questions were being discussed, he never made any representations to his Chief on the subject.

This last sentence was Lloyd George's formula for informing the House of Commons that General Maurice had written to the CIGS on 30 April and had received neither acknowledgment nor reply.

In dealing with General Maurice's criticism of his statement on 9 April, Lloyd George played his trump card.

He said:

Let me read the statement made by General Maurice:

On 9 April, the Prime Minister said: 'What was the position at the beginning of the battle? Notwithstanding the heavy casualties of 1917, the Army in France was considerably stronger on 1 January, 1918, than on 1 January, 1917.'

This is his [General Maurice's] comment:

'That statement implies that Sir Douglas Haig's fighting strength on the eve of the great battle which began on 21 March had not been diminished. This is not correct.'

126

Lloyd George went on:

The issue is a very clear one. I said that the fighting strength of the Army had increased. General Maurice says that it had diminished, as compared with the previous year. The figures that I gave were taken from the official records of the War Office, for which I sent before I made the statement. If they were incorrect, General Maurice was as responsible as anyone else.* But they were not inaccurate. I have made inquiries since. I am not sure what he quite means. There is absolutely no doubt that there was a very considerable addition to the manpower of the Army in France at the beginning of 1918 as compared with the manpower at the beginning of 1917. There was a great increase in the manpower of the British Army throughout the world in 1918, as compared with 1917, but the increase of the manpower in France in 1918, as compared with 1917, was greater than the average throughout the whole area. I do not know whether General Maurice had in his mind that, when he talks about fighting strength, you must draw a distinction between what are known as 'combatants and non-combatants'. I am going to take that later on as well, but before I do so, let me say at once I do not accept that distinction. When you talk about 'fighting strength', who are the combatants and who are the non-combatants? AN HON MEMBER: 'Oh!' I am going to take the non-combatants as well. My hon Friend need not be afraid that I am going to shirk it.

Let me first of all deal with the question, Who are the combatants? Are those men who stopped the advance of the German Army to Amiens the other day combatants? (HON MEMBERS: 'Yes!') They are not, if you begin to make a distinction between combatants and non-combatants—I am speaking of General Carey's force†—they would not be treated as combatants. Are the men who are under fire every day, making and repairing roads and tramroads and railways, and who suffer severe casualties, combatants or non-combatants? In most lists that have been drafted they would be non-combatants. Does anyone mean to tell me that they are not part of the 'fighting strength' of the Army? Take the men who, when the British Army retreated, and had to abandon trenches which took months to repair, and who had to improvise defences under shell-fire to relieve the Infantry—are those men no part of the fighting

* General Maurice's Department had no responsibility for the figures which Lloyd George gave in his speech on 9 April. The Prime Minister had made his own analysis of a return from the Adjutant-General's department, and had included in the fighting forces available to Haig to meet the German attack 410,897 non-combatants, of whom some 300,000 were Chinese coolies and unarmed British labourers. He admitted to Sir Maurice Hankey that 'speeches dealing with facts and figures were not his strong point, and that his Celtic temperament made him unable to resist stretching them to their extreme limits'. (*The Supreme Command*, Vol II, pp. 798–9.)
† See *The Story of the Crisis*, p. 91.

strength of the Army? When you have not got them, you have to take Infantry out, and set them to that work. As a matter of fact, one of the things I came back with from France was a demand for more of them, and they are not part of the 'fighting strength' of the Army! I decline absolutely to accept that interpretation.

But I will leave that. Take the ordinary technical distinction between combatants and non-combatants. A question was put in the House of Commons by the hon Member for Barnstaple on 18 April, eight or nine days after I delivered my speech—I delivered my speech on 9 April, and this question was put:

Sir Godfrey Baring: To ask the Prime Minister whether when he said that the British Army in France was considerably stronger on 1 January, 1918, than on the 1 January, 1917, he was including the Labour battalions and other non-combatant units, and whether the combatant strength of the British Army was greater or less at the beginning of this year than at the beginning of last year?

My hon Friend [Mr Macpherson], whose duty it was to answer this question on behalf of the War Office, sent that question to General Maurice to be answered. I am not going to read the answer which he gave, because that is on the records of the House,* but I will give the note that came from General Maurice's Department. This is the actual document from General Maurice's Department.

MR GEORGE LAMBERT: Is it initialled?

THE PRIME MINISTER: It is initialled by his deputy! (Laughter) My right hon Friend is going to draw that distinction, is he? That shows what sort of impartiality you get! This is the note. First of all we have the figures inside. I cannot give those to the House, but this note is a summary of them:

From the statement included, it will be seen that the combatant strength—

LORD HUGH CECIL: The right hon Gentleman is reading from an official paper. I quite understand his motive for not disclosing the whole of it, but is it not contrary to the Rules of Order to read part of a document and not to disclose the whole of it to the House?

THE PRIME MINISTER: The Noble Lord is not very helpful. On the question of order, if the House wants this from which I am reading I am perfectly prepared to put it on the Table. (HON MEMBERS: 'No!') I am not going to put the note which I am not going to read on the Table—for that is the document which is inside, and gives the actual details.

* MR MACPHERSON: The combatant strength of the British Army was greater on 1 January, 1918, than on 1 January, 1917. My right hon. Friend the Prime Minister did not necessarily include the labour and other non-combatant units, but their inclusion would, of course, make the increase more marked. *Hansard*, 18 April, 1918

That, of course, I cannot give—but the document I am reading from I am perfectly prepared to put on the Table of the House—

From the statement included, it will be seen that the combatant strength of the British Army was greater on 1 January, 1918, than on 1 January, 1917.

This comes from General Maurice's Department, nine days after I made that statement! I am not depending on the fact that all these men who were ruled out as 'non-combatants' are an essential part of the strength of the British Army in France. I have this statement, that, as regards those who were technically treated as combatants, we were better off on 1 January, 1918, than on 1 January, 1917. As a matter of fact, there was an increase as between 1 January, and March, 1918, but it just happened that I thought I would take the first month of the year.

This was deadly. The Prime Minister appeared to be citing the DMO's own department to confirm the accuracy of his statement which General Maurice had challenged. In the heat of the debate no one realised that it was not the January figures which were relevant, but the situation in March.

Sir Sam Hoare (later Lord Templewood) has described the effect.

I scarcely ever went to the House of Commons. Once, however, I did attend an important debate to vote in a decisive division. While on leave from Italy I received an urgent Whip asking me to be in the House for the Maurice debate on 9 May, 1918. I had known General Maurice when he was Director of Military Operations and I was serving under his colleague, General Macdonogh, the Director of Military Intelligence. I was, therefore, all the more impressed by his letter of 7 May to *The Times* and the *Morning Post* in which he accused the Prime Minister of giving a false account of the strength of the Army in France. I knew the Director of Military Operations to be an excellent staff officer, I went to the House strongly prejudiced in his favour. I shall never forget what happened. Lloyd George made the speech of his life. Maurice stood convicted out of his own mouth, and the Opposition was so completely demoralised that although it was expected that Runciman or McKenna would make some kind of defence, not a word was said from the Opposition front bench in reply to the Prime Minister's charges.

After that, Lloyd George had no difficulty in justifying to the House the other statements General Maurice had said were 'not correct'.

It will be remembered that at the War Cabinet meeting on 8 May Lloyd George admitted that he had been wrong, and General Maurice right, in regard to the number of white infantry divisions in Palestine and Egypt.* He had said there were only three white divisions whereas there were, in fact, five.†

In his speech, he justified his statement by saying that General Maurice had been present at the meeting of the War Cabinet at which 'a member of the Staff (actually Sir Henry Wilson) had stated that there were only three white divisions in Egypt' (in his speech on 9 April he had said 'Egypt *and* Palestine') and that when the Minutes were sent to General Maurice, he telephoned to Sir Maurice Hankey that he had 'no remarks'. So Lloyd George made General Maurice responsible for endorsing the statement which he challenged in his letter.

This was typical of Lloyd George's tactics.

The facts are that General Maurice was not present at the meeting of the War Cabinet at the actual time when the CIGS made the statement regarding the forces in Palestine and Egypt. He had been called in earlier to give the figures of the Allied strength on the Western front, and having done so left the meeting. When he received the Minutes, he followed the procedure he had always adopted of checking the statement he himself had made, and no others. It was neither his duty nor his business to correct statements made by the CIGS.

Lloyd George used the same methods in dealing with General Maurice's allegations in regard to Bonar Law's statement on 23 April about the extension of the front.

He dealt at length with this question, and any informed listener would have realised he was admitting that Bonar Law's statement that 'this particular matter (the extension of the front) was not dealt with at all by the Versailles War Council' was untrue; but he convinced the House that it was General Maurice, not Bonar Law, who did not know the facts.

He said:

General Maurice says:

'I was at Versailles when the question was decided by the Supreme War Council, to whom it had been referred.'

In the first place, I think, anyone reading that would say that General Maurice was present at the meeting. He was at Versailles, it is true, but

* See Cabinet Memo, p. 232.

† When Lloyd George spoke on 9 April, there were five complete British infantry divisions in Palestine. A sixth division, the 75th, contained 9 British and 4 Indian Regiments. A seventh, the 52nd, had embarked for France on 4 April. Lloyd George was given this information by the War Office on 8 May, the day before the Maurice debate.

the implication is that he was in the Council Chamber. He was not there. I have looked at the Official Record since. He was at Versailles—he was in a building with several others, who were then assisting the various generals, but he was not in the Council Chamber when the question to which he refers was discussed.

In point of fact, General Maurice *was* present at the first meeting of the Council, and received the Agenda and verbatim reports of all the meetings. He had far more knowledge of the facts than Bonar Law.

Successful, however, as Lloyd George was in convincing the House, he did not succeed in meeting the wish of the War Cabinet that he should so word his speech 'as to give satisfaction to Field-Marshal Sir Douglas Haig'. In a letter to his wife, Haig wrote: 'How terrible to see the House of Commons taken in by a claptrap speech by Lloyd George. The House is really losing its reputation as an assembly of commonsense Britishers.'

Lloyd George ended his speech with an impassioned appeal to the House:

I wonder whether it is worth my while to make another appeal to all sections of the House and to all sections of the country. These controversies are distracting, they are paralysing, they are rending and I beg that they should come to an end. It is difficult enough for Ministers to do their work in this War. We had a controversy which lasted practically for months over the unity of command. This is really a sort of remnant of it. The national unity is threatened—the Army unity is threatened—by this controversy. Days have been occupied in hunting up records and minutes and letters and *procès verbaux*, in interviews, and in raking up what happened during a whole twelve months in the War Cabinet. And this at such a moment! I have just come back from France. I met some generals and they were telling me how now the Germans are silently, silently, preparing perhaps the biggest blow of the War, under a shroud of mist, and they asked me for certain help. I brought home a list of the things they wanted done, and I wished to attend to them. I really beg and implore, for our common country, the fate of which is in the balance now and in the next few weeks, that there should be an end of this sniping.

The result was a foregone conclusion.

In the division the Government had a majority of 187—for the Government 293, against 106.

In the 1918 General Election, every leading Liberal who had

voted against the Government in the Maurice Debate lost his seat. It was a blow from which the Party never recovered.*

Colonel Burn MP, one of Lloyd George's strongest critics, wrote to General Maurice after the debate:

When Asquith made his indictment he did it in such a faltering way and with no confidence—indeed I have never heard him so feeble. He was answered by Lloyd George in his best form and with no one in a position to counter him with the evidence you must have had in your possession; it was inevitable that he should carry the House with him.

Those present could only form an opinion on what LG said ...

I can't tell you how disappointed your many friends were, but as it all turned out what could be done in face of the statement made by LG?

But if the Debate was a victory for Lloyd George and a death blow to the Liberals, it had one important consequence which alone would have justified General Maurice's action.

One of his motives for writing his letter was that he had learnt before he left the War Office that the Government had decided to dismiss Haig. He believed that this would be a blow to the morale of the Army which must by all means be prevented.

To create a vacancy, Field-Marshal French was appointed Viceroy in Ireland on 6 May. Haig was to have been brought home to succeed him as Commander-in-Chief, Home Forces. As a consequence of the Maurice debate, Haig was not moved, and Sir William Robertson was appointed to the Home Command.

On 7 May Brigadier-General John Charteris wrote:

There are strange rumours here that LG had intended to remove DH to succeed Lord French as Commander-in-Chief at home, and that Maurice's

* For the 1918 General Election (the Coupon election) Lloyd George issued lists of 'authorised Coalition Candidates', who were provided with a letter signed jointly by himself and Bonar Law 'stating they were the recognised Government Candidates in their constituencies'. 159 Liberals received the coupon, of whom 156 were elected. Only 29 Liberals who did not receive the coupon were elected. The defeated included Asquith, McKenna and Runciman, all ex-Ministers in the last Liberal Government, and Gulland, Howard, Walter Rea and Marshall among the Whips. Several forfeited their deposits. All had voted against the Government in the Maurice debate, and Lloyd George claimed that 'the Mauricites were annihilated at the polls'.

In an analysis of the result of the election on the 108 Liberals, including tellers, who voted against the Government in the division on the Maurice debate Dr Trevor Wilson in *The Downfall of the Liberal Party* has shown that 25 did not stand for re-election, 12 did not stand as Liberals, 6 stood in constituencies where no coupon was given, only 54 were refused the coupon and 11 received it. He argues that the voting in the division on 9 May had little to do with the Liberal defeat. But it marked the cleavage between pro- and anti-Coalition Liberals, which resulted, as has been stated above, in 136 Coalition Liberals and only 29 Opposition Liberals being returned.

letter has at least stopped that scheme, and DH remains here for the time being; his letter has done much good. His facts were strictly correct, and he was fully justified in everything he wrote, and also, I think, in writing it. He has plenty of moral courage. Whatever happens to him, I do not think the Cabinet will wish a repetition.*

On 9 May, Margot Asquith wrote in her diary:

We hear Haig has been given the sack, but I bet this won't be announced yet.

And on the opposite page, in red ink, she wrote:

Haig *was* dismissed, but they wired him to stay on as the Government was terrified after the Maurice Debate.

On 11 May Haig wrote to his wife:

Many thanks for telling me what the gossips say about my being selected to succeed F. M. French as C.-in-C. Home Forces . . . I think they will find it difficult to find a successor *at this moment*.†

On 10 May, General Maurice noted in his diary:

Prime Minister's speech in House full of prevarication. He makes a casual reference to my letter to Wilson which deceived the House. Conceals the fact that I knew all about Versailles and refers to a report sent in by my directorate which I never saw.‡

If Lloyd George's use of the reply given by Macpherson to the Baring question was a shock to General Maurice, it must have been still more so to the member of his staff who had supplied the Prime Minister with the weapon he had used so effectively against his Chief in the debate. This was Colonel Walter Kirke, the senior GSO I in the DMO's Department, who when General Radcliffe took over from General Maurice had been promoted to Deputy DMO.

On 18 April, Macpherson had asked the DMO's Department for the information, which was required in a great hurry. Kirke obtained the figures from the Adjutant-General's department, and the clerk who prepared them included in the combatant strength of the Army

* Brigadier-General John Charteris, *At G.H.Q.*, London, 1931, p. 508.
† *The Private Papers of Douglas Haig*, p. 309.
‡ Macpherson's reply to Baring's question.

in France 86,000 men in the British Army in Italy. Kirke, without checking the figures, added 'From the statement included, it will be seen that the combatant strength of the British Army was greater on 1 January, 1918, than on 1 January, 1917.'

By producing this statement in the House, and stating that it came from General Maurice's department, Lloyd George was able to discredit General Maurice, and to evade the point of his charge that the Army was greatly weakened between January and March, since Haig had to break up 141 infantry battalions and two cavalry divisions for lack of drafts. It was due to it that he achieved his triumph in the debate. But did he know that the answer was wrong?

Evidence which is now available proves that he received from the War Office on 8 May the correct figures of the combatant strength of the Armies in France in 1918 compared to 1917, and that he was informed before he spoke in the Maurice debate on 9 May that the figures given in the answer to the Baring question were wrong.

It will be remembered that at the meeting of the War Cabinet on 8 May he had produced the reply to the Baring question as providing him with a complete answer to General Maurice's charge in his letter to the press that the Prime Minister's statement on 9 April about the strength of the armies in 1918 compared to 1917 'was not correct'.

On the same day, 8 May, the Director of Military Operations, Major-General P. de B. Radcliffe, sent to Lloyd George's secretary, Philip Kerr, a return from the Adjutant-General's department dated 7 May, headed 'British Forces in France' which showed that the combatant forces were 88,332 less on 1 January, 1918, than on 1 January, 1917.*

Owing to Kirke's mistake in including 86,000 men in Italy, the answer to the Baring question had stated that they were 43,000 more in 1918 than in 1917.

On the morning of 9 May, Philip Kerr telephoned to Kirke pointing out the discrepancy in the two statements, the AG return of 7 May, sent by the DMO on 8 May, and the figures supplied to Macpherson on 18 April for the reply to the Baring question, which Lloyd George intended to use in his speech in the debate that afternoon.

It was only then that Kirke realised that the answer given by Macpherson was wrong. He went through the returns, checked the

* See p. 139.

figures and found the mistake. He telephoned Kerr before lunch on the 9th, and informed him of it.

Nevertheless, Lloyd George used the wrong figures in his speech, and ignored the correct ones which he had received on 8 May.

When Kirke read the reports of the speech on 10 May, he was horrified. He addressed a Minute to the DMO, General Radcliffe, asking that the Secretary of State should consider how best to give Sir Godfrey Baring a correct answer to his question, 'more particularly in view of the publicity which has been given to the incorrect statement signed by myself' and offered his resignation as DDMO.*

Radcliffe passed this Minute to Macpherson, with attached to it the AG return of 7 May, on which was minuted 'statement produced for PM by AG from which the error made in reply to question put by Sir Godfrey Baring was discovered'.

On 14 May, Kirke saw Macpherson and wrote to General Maurice:

War Office,
Whitehall,
S.W.1.

My dear General,

I took the course you suggested† and which was concurred in by P de B, and Macpherson is I believe seeing the PM. Former [Macpherson] seems a straight man and a friend of yours.

My appreciation of the situation is that:

a) Most people know you were right in point of fact.

b) The personal attacks made on you have disgusted all decent folk.

c) We don't want a military split at the present time.

d) You would get enormous credit, and absolutely silence criticism if you would write publicly, saying that you left the rights of the case for discussion in less critical times, and hoped that no-one would take up the cudgels on your behalf, as no useful purpose could be served—of course you can put it much better than that. I believe this would be best for Sir William (Robertson) and for yourself, and certainly for the Army.

I personally would be quite ready to go the whole hog with you, but don't believe it would do you or Sir W any good and probably the reverse—D.M.I. agrees that what I suggest would be best and greatly

---

* See p. 140.

† 'The course suggested' was to ask Macpherson to inform the Prime Minister of the mistake in the reply to the Baring question.

redound to your credit, and is in the interests of the Army—the 'big' course in fact.

Yours sincerely,
Walter Kirke

Macpherson was greatly distressed to have been the innocent cause of the injustice done to General Maurice by Lloyd George's speech, and asked the Prime Minister's permission to inform the House of Commons of the incorrect answer he had given to the Baring question. But Lloyd George forbade him to do so.

Macpherson, however, who, as Kirke had said in his letter to General Maurice, was a straight man, did not feel he could be absolved of his responsibility by Lloyd George's prohibition, and reported the facts to Lord Milner, the Secretary of State for War, as Kirke in his Minute of 10 May, had requested.

On 15 May, Milner informed Lloyd George officially.

At a meeting at the War Office attended by Lloyd George, Milner, the CIGS and Sir Maurice Hankey:

Lord Milner said that a mistake had been discovered in the figure given by Mr Macpherson as the basis of his statement in the House of Commons that the fighting strength of the British Army on the Western Front was greater on 1 January, 1918, than on 1 January, 1917. As a matter of fact the fighting strength had been less on 1 January, 1918.

It had transpired that the figures given by Mr Macpherson included British troops on the Italian Front. As the Prime Minister had used Mr Macpherson's statement in his speech on 9 May, he felt bound to let him know.

The Prime Minister [who had already been informed by Macpherson] pointed out that he could not be held responsible for an error which had been made in General Maurice's Department.*

Kirke had expected that as a result of his conversation with Macpherson on the 14th, steps would have been taken to inform the House of Commons of his mistake, and on 16 May wrote a further Minute to the DMO pointing out that

nothing has been done so far to correct the misstatement quoted in the Prime Minister's speech of 9 May as having been made by me.

I consider that such a correction should be made without delay, but appreciate that there may be political difficulties involved, in view of the manner in which the statement was made.

I request therefore that the question be referred to the War Cabinet

* Cab 25/17/5.

for consideration. If they decide that it is against the public interest to make the correction, I would ask that my request for correction and the decision be definitely recorded, in which case I should consider that my responsibility in the matter was ended.

On this General Radcliffe minuted that he had spoken to the Deputy Chief of the Imperial General Staff, to the Director of Military Intelligence and to the Director of Staff Duties.

I think that it is not in the interests of the Service that any further action should be taken on this question unless there are further developments. I consider that you have done all that is necessary or desirable in the matter, and I will take the responsibility for it.

P. de B. Radcliffe
D.M.O.

17 May/18

So Lloyd George had his victory, discredited General Maurice, silenced the Opposition, and destroyed the Liberal Party, It may be that Lord Milner also was a casualty; for he knew, having been informed by Macpherson, that Lloyd George was aware of the mistake before he spoke on 9 May, and although he kept silence till his death, Lloyd George may well have felt that he could never trust him again. Milner had been one of his most loyal supporters. Now he was excluded from meetings of the War Cabinet on the grounds that his health was failing and became completely estranged from the Prime Minister. There seems no more obvious reason for this hitherto unexplained estrangement than that Milner was another victim of the consequences of the Maurice debate.

War Office,
Whitehall, S.W.1.
8 May, 1918

Dear Kerr,
    I forward herewith:*

1. Comparative statement furnished by the Adjutant-General showing combatant and non-combatant strengths on 1 January, 1917, and 1 January, 1918.

2. Comparative statements showing length of front held by the British and French. The French figures for January, 1917, are not yet available, but they were presumably in the neighbourhood of 400 miles.

3. Telegrams dealing with the move of two British Divisions from Egypt to France. From these it will be seen that the orders for the move on the 52nd and 74th Divisions were issued on 27 March.

4. The exact dates when dilution of British Divisions actually commenced is not known and the information has been wired for to Egypt. Such information as we have shows that there were five white divisions complete at the time, excluding the 52nd Division, which was about to embark for France, but including the 74th Division which is now on the sea. I attach a statement showing the situation on 9 April.

Yours sincerely,
P. DE B. RADCLIFFE

Philip Kerr Esq.

* Only (1) is here reprinted.

SECRET

BRITISH FORCES IN FRANCE

	Fighting Troops		Non-fighting Troops		Labour*		Total Effectives
	British	Coloured (Indian Cavalry)	British	Coloured	British	Coloured	
January 1917	1,069,831	8,876	217,533	2,704	—	—	1,298,944
January 1918	969,283	11,544	295,334	2,256	190,197	108,203	1,576,817

*Labour Corps did not exist till the middle of 1917

OVERSEAS DOMINION CONTINGENTS

	Fighting Troops		Non-fighting Troops		Labour*		Total Effectives
	British	Coloured (Indian Cavalry)	British	Coloured	British	Coloured	
January 1917	204,989	—	22,249	—	—	—	227,238
January 1918	217,205	—	56,945	—	—	—	274,150

TOTAL BRITISH AND DOMINION CONTINGENTS

	Fighting Troops		Non-fighting Troops		Labour*		Total Effectives
	British	Coloured (Indian Cavalry)	British	Coloured	British	Coloured	
January 1917	1,274,820	8,876	239,782	2,704	—	—	1,526,182
January 1918	1,186,488	11,544	352,279	2,256	190,197	108,203	1,850,967

A.G.I.c.
7.5.18.

KIRKE'S MINUTE 10 May, 1918
(WO 32/10085 Code O(V).)

Copy
D.M.O.

With reference to a question by Sir Godfrey Baring, which was answered on 18 April, as to whether the Combatant Strength of the British Army was greater or less at the beginning of this year than at the beginning of last year, this question was passed by C.2 to me to answer at very short notice. Figures were produced showing the following Combatant Strengths:

January, 1917	1,253,000 Other Ranks
January, 1918	1,298,000 Other Ranks

This latter figure included 86,000 in Italy, a fact which unfortunately was not noticed, consequently Mr Macpherson made an incorrect reply.

On the morning of 9 May, Mr Philip Kerr mentioned over the telephone that the Prime Minister had a statement from us showing that the Combatant Strength was greater in January, 1918, than in January, 1917, and that it did not agree with the AG's figures. I went through the returns and found the mistake, and I rang him up and told him what the mistake was before lunch.

I much regret that Mr Macpherson should have been wrongly informed, and should have in consequence mis-informed Sir Godfrey Baring. Without in any way wishing to continue the recent unfortunate controversy, I trust that the Secretary of State will consider how best to give Sir Godfrey Baring a correct answer to his question, more particularly in view of the publicity which has been given to the incorrect statement signed by myself.

You will no doubt advise the CIGS as to the desirability, or otherwise, of my continuing in my present appointment.

W. KIRKE

10.5.18   Colonel G.S.

The original was passed to the CM, with the figures referred to, on 10/5/18.

2 Suppressing the Truth

At the meeting of the War Cabinet on 7 May, the Adjutant-General reported that he had written to General Maurice, 'asking him in the usual service manner for his reasons for having written the letter contrary to regulations'. General Maurice replied the next day that he recognised with deep regret that the publication of his letter was a breach of the regulations, but that the writing of it was with him a matter of conscience.

On 11 May, he was informed that the Army Council had decided to place him on retired pay forthwith, to which he replied that he recognised the justice of the Council's decision.

The announcement of his retirement appeared in the Gazette on 13 May.

'Am retired from the Army', he wrote in his diary.

Although he was a Major-General, he was retired on the half pay of a Major—£225 a year.

This piece of spitefulness was too much for the military authorities and in October General Maurice's retired pay was increased to that of a Major-General, £750 a year, which he continued to receive until his death.

On 11 May, the Editor of the *Daily Chronicle*, Robert Donald, offered him the post of military correspondent, which he accepted, and on 15 May, the *Daily Chronicle* and a number of other papers published the statement which General Maurice quotes in *The Story of the Crisis* (p. 91).

On 16 May, General Maurice received the following letter from Lord Milner:

Private   17 Great College Street,
                                                                                S.W.

Dear General Maurice,
    This letter is not prompted by, nor will it in any way refer, to past

events. I am dealing solely with the new situation wh. has arisen through your acceptance of the post of Military Correspondent to the *Daily Chronicle*.

I am sure that in that very responsible and important position you will be constantly guided by considerations of the public interest. Therefore I venture to impress upon you, that every word you write will be most closely scrutinised by the enemy.

They know, of course, that you are the depository of the most intimate details of the Allied military position. And they will be constantly trying to glean information from what you say, wh. it will be difficult for you to avoid giving them—of course quite unintentionally—unless you are always on your guard against a set of people, who are as minutely pains-taking, as they are clever in 'putting two and two together'.

Of course, we have always got the censorship, and it may be said that it is the business of the censor, and not of the writer who submits his article to inspection, to see that nothing, wh. might be informative to the enemy, is allowed to pass. But I am sure you will not take that narrow view of your own duty in the matter. You are necessarily in a better position than any censor to, so to speak, censor yourself. And I can honestly say it would be most repugnant to me personally, to have to sanction a frequent use of the powers of censorship in the case of your articles. The last thing I desire is to blunt the point of criticism directed against myself or any other person in authority, or to embarrass you in the discharge of your new duties. Indeed it is solely in order to avoid the necessity of any interference that I have written.

Believe me

Yours sincerely

Milner

Lord Milner submitted this letter to Lloyd George for his approval before sending it, and also showed Lloyd George General Maurice's reply.* This was as follows:

My dear Lord Milner

I fully appreciate the point of your letter and thank you for it. I may say that the same point was very much in my mind before I accepted the offer of the *Chronicle*. That offer was made to me the day after my letter appeared and I did not accept it until last Tuesday, having in the meantime taken the advice of soldiers whose opinion I value. Having had some experience of censorship in the course of my duties, I came to the conclusion that I would, as you put it, censor myself and I further thought that such knowledge and experience as I possessed could be put to good use in enlightening the public as to the conduct of the war. You may

* Cab 23/17.

possibly have seen my first article in today's *Chronicle* and that will give you an indication of the general lines on which I propose to work.

I can say that I intend to adhere strictly to the statement I made in my letter to the papers of the 15th that I would not indulge in any recriminations nor attempt to reopen my case until I am asked authoritatively to do so. I hope you will allow me to add that in taking the course I did I was actuated by no personal considerations whatever and my letter was in no way directed against either yourself or Sir Henry Wilson, who has always treated me with the greatest consideration.

P.S. I may add that I shall regard the Censor as a help and not as an enemy, as it is always possible that I may quite inadvertently hint at something which it is not in the public interests to have published.

F. Maurice

On 16 May, General Maurice wrote in his diary: 'Donald tells me it was Sutherland who spread report of my presence in the House on 9 April.'

Sutherland, later the Rt Hon Sir William Sutherland, MP, KCB, Chancellor of the Duchy of Lancaster, was one of Lloyd George's Secretaries. It was, perhaps, natural that these should be eager to help their Chief in discrediting General Maurice, and in this Sutherland was zealous.

On 16 May, Robert Donald wrote:

My dear Maurice,

I have traced the origin of the statement which appeared in some newspapers that you were present in the House of Commons on 9 April, when the Prime Minister made his speech. This statement was given publicity by our Parliamentary Correspondent (Mr Harry Jones) and other correspondents. I have asked Mr Jones who his authority was for making the statement and I enclose a copy of his reply. You have already answered this misstatement, but there may be another opportunity for making a further exposure. . . .

Believe me,
Yours very truly,
Robert Donald

Enclosure

15 May, 1918

Mem. Mr Donald

My assertion in House and Lobby that General Maurice heard the Prime Minister's speech on 9 April was based on a conversation I had with Mr Sutherland (Mr Lloyd George's private secretary) in the Lobby on the evening of 9 May. Mr 'S' told me he could not understand General

Maurice's action in writing the letter; the relations between M and Ll G had always been cordial; he (Sutherland) liked General M very much; it was he (S) who met the General at Victoria Station on the night of 9 April and escorted him to the PM's room in the House of Commons. He added that General Maurice heard the PM's speech from the Gallery behind the Speaker's chair.

H.J.

General Maurice wrote to Sutherland on 17 May:

My dear Sutherland,

Mr Donald of the *Chronicle* has written to tell me that he has been informed by his Parliamentary correspondent, Mr Henry Jones, that a statement which the latter circulated in House and Lobby and published, to the effect that I was in the House on 9 April emanated from a conversation with you. Mr Jones says that you informed him that you met me at Victoria Station on the evening of 9 April and escorted me to the Prime Minister's room, and that I heard the speech from the gallery behind the Speaker's Chair. You will recollect that the incident in question occurred on 16 April and that it was the Prime Minister's speech on Irish conscription which I heard and not the speech of 9 April.

I have no doubt but that the mistake was made bona fide but as it was given wide publicity and has done me considerable injury, I should be obliged if you would make the necessary correction publicly in a letter to the papers at the earliest possible date.

F. Maurice

P.S. I enclose a copy of Mr Henry Jones' explanation to his Editor.

As he received no reply, he wrote again on the 21st:

My dear Sutherland

I wrote to you on the 17th but as I have received no reply, I think it possible that my letter may have miscarried.

I therefore enclose a copy of my letter of the 17th and must ask for an early reply.

Yrs sincerely
F. Maurice

to which Sutherland at last replied:

North British Station Hotel,
Edinburgh
26 May, 1918

My dear General,

Many thanks for your letter. I have to apologise for being so long in writing but owing to the urgent pressure of work, my private correspondence has fallen into arrears.

I recollect the conversation with Mr Harry Jones. He approached me in the Lobby and asked what I thought of the Maurice letter. I replied that I could give no explanation of it; that the relations between the Prime Minister and General Maurice had always been of the best, and mentioned in this connection that General Maurice was the very General to whom the Prime Minister made reference a few days before in the House, at the end of his speech when he said that he had now to leave the House in order to meet a General just back from France who was waiting for him. I added that, on that occasion, I had myself gone to Victoria Station in order to meet General Maurice and bring him straight to the Prime Minister. I said that I had always had a great respect for General Maurice.

No mention was made of dates.

Yours sincerely
Wm Sutherland

General Maurice sent Sutherland's letter to Robert Donald, who wrote on 28 May:

My dear General,
   I fear our friend Sutherland is prevaricating. I am sending a copy of his letter to Harry Jones and will send you his comments on it. . . .

Believe me,
Yours very truly,
Robert Donald

Among General Maurice's papers was found a letter to Lord Milner dated 18 May. Although there is no indication whether it was sent, it is reproduced here, as it shows his feelings at the time.

My dear Lord Milner,
   In my letter to you of the 16th I said that I intended to adhere to my decision to avoid recriminations. I am still as anxious as ever to avoid any discussion of my letter of 6 May in the Public press, but certain facts regarding the Prime Minister's speech on 9 May which have come to my knowledge, together with others which I know already, have forced me to reconsider my position and therefore though I am loth to trouble you with personal matters in these times, I feel compelled to put certain facts before you.

   I make no complaint as to the action of the Army Council—I have officially recognised its justice and I expected nothing else when I took the step I did. I have endeavoured throughout the whole affair to behave according to my lights in an upright and patriotic manner. Pending the decision of the Army Council on my case I refused to make any statement of any kind, though I was besieged with requests accompanied in some cases by considerable financial inducement. I did not attempt to reply to the vilifications of me which appeared in a portion of the Press. I recognised before I sent my letter to the Press that I would be subjected to such attacks, and had previously decided on my course of action.*

I find:

1. That the Prime Minister's Private Secretary Mr Sutherland, stated incorrectly in the precincts of the House that he had brought me at the Prime Minister's request to the House of Commons on 9 April and that I had heard the Prime Minister's speech of 9 April from the Secretaries' Gallery behind the Speaker's chair. This is not the case and I have written to Mr Sutherland asking him to contradict it publicly as the statement was given wide circulation in the House and Lobby, and appeared in the Press. The incident which Mr Sutherland apparently had in mind happened on 16 April.

2. That the Prime Minister made great play in his speech of 9 April with a return dated 18 April which appears to have been prepared during my absence in France, which return I never saw, or was aware of, before the Prime Minister spoke. I feel that it is due to me that this fact should be made known, preferably in the House of Commons. The information on which this statement is based did not come to me from the War Office.

3. That though I had expressly stated in my letter of 30 April to Sir Henry Wilson that I did not criticise the Prime Minister's comparison of the strengths of 1 January, 1917 and 1 January, 1918, and though I did not challenge that comparison in my letter of 6 May to the Press the Prime Minister devoted a great part of his speech to that comparison and laid great emphasis on the fact that the figures had been supplied by my directorate.

4. That a very important portion of my statement of 15 May was censored for no apparent reason except to support the Prime Minister's statement that I was not in a position to know the facts that occurred at Versailles which statement the Prime Minister would by enquiry beforehand have found to be incorrect.

5. That the Prime Minister referred to the fact that I had written to Sir H. Wilson on 30 April in such a way as to be incomprehensible to any one who did not know the facts.

As the above are all matters which affect my credibility and honour, I state them to you and leave myself in your hands.

Signed
F. Maurice

Whether or not this letter was sent, no acknowledgment of it has been found.

* I did not expect however that the Government would adopt the methods which it pursued against one who was debarred by his position from reply.

General Maurice was being hounded by the Establishment. Their vindictiveness and lack of scruple was a measure of the fear which the publication of his letter had inspired in them.

But he had his defenders. There were many who were not deceived by Lloyd George's prevarications, and who were outraged by the way General Maurice had been treated.

On 2 July, George Lambert put a question to Mr Forster, Financial Secretary at the War Office:

what were the emoluments of General Sir F. Maurice as Director of Military Operations; and what is his present allowance from Army funds?

who replied:

As Director of Military Operations General Sir Frederick Maurice received £1,500 per annum. He is now in receipt of £225 per annum retired pay.

which drew from Pringle, one of Lloyd George's most persistent critics:

Are we to understand that this is the price of General Maurice for telling the truth?*

When he had finished *The Story of the Crisis of May, 1918*, General Maurice showed it to a few of those upon whose discretion he could rely.

Before sending his letter to the press, he had consulted no one except Sir William Robertson, and had held no communication with any politician or member of the press.

After the Maurice debate and his dismissal from the Army, he felt it his duty to do all in his power to enlighten those who were in a position to influence opinion as to the dangers which had led him to the action he did.

One of those to whom he sent the paper was the Duke of Northumberland, who was one of his staunchest champions. He had been GSO I on his Staff, but left the War Office in July.

On 21st July, the Duke of Northumberland wrote:

> 17 Princes Gate
> S.W.7.

My dear General
    I have asked Salisbury to return your paper if he has finished with it. I

* Hansard, 2 July, 1918.

have explained that if he can still make further good use of it, he can keep it a little longer, but otherwise you wish to have it back.

With regard to my comments, I have only one to make. I think that perhaps the degree to which the Government were acting contrary to the advice of the General Staff is not quite sufficiently brought out. You lay stress on the fact that all our reverses and misfortunes are due to the Government pursuing their own policy in direct opposition to the views of their military advisers. They have really been doing this ever since the beginning of 1917 and the present situation is due not so much to their neglecting to get the men (for which excuses can be found) as in their pursuing a policy of side-shows. If they had taken the advice of the Gen. Staff we might have had sufficient divisions in France to have prevented the disaster to the 5th Army—L-G knows this and is intensely anxious that it should not leak out. His defence is that the Gen. Staff persisted with the Ypres offensive contrary to his advice and it was this drain on our man-power resources which has brought about the present situation. This view he has expressed in a memorandum written in answer to a paper by the A.G. in which the latter enumerated the various demands for men which he had made and expatiated on the Government's neglect of these warnings. L-G was very angry and threw all the blame on the Gen. Staff. We have written an answer to this which I should like to show you confidentially.

My point is, however, that in order to convince people of the truth we must point out the fatal consequences of civilian control of the War and the substitution of political for military objects, because that is really what it amounts to.

If we can convince a large section of the Unionist party of this, they may, under the threat of exposure, be able to induce the Government to modify their Cabinet system.

I hope this is clear.

Yours ever
Northumberland

Less than five months after General Maurice had accepted Robert Donald's offer of the position of Military Correspondent of the *Daily Chronicle*, both he and Donald had to find other employment.

Lloyd George bought the newspaper, largely from the monies he had acquired from the sale of honours.* He had for at least two years wanted a paper of his own, and had been trying since June, 1916, to acquire the *Westminster Gazette*. Its Liberal Editor, J. A. Spender, had incurred his ire because of Spender's loyalty to Asquith and

---

* Trevor Wilson, *The Downfall of the Liberal Party*, p. 108.

criticism of himself. But these efforts failed because, at the moment when they were on the point of succeeding, Lloyd George gave mortal offence to its proprietor, Lord Cowdray, who was a member of the Government and President of the Air Board. Lloyd George tried to buy the support of Lord Northcliffe by offering *him* the post of President of the Air Board: Lord Cowdray knew nothing of this offer until he read in *The Times* an open letter to the Prime Minister from Northcliffe rejecting it in most offensive terms. Cowdray never forgave Lloyd George, resigned from the Government, refused to sell the *Westminster Gazette*, and retained Spender as its Editor.

Foiled in his efforts to buy off Northcliffe and remove Spender, Lloyd George turned his batteries on Robert Donald at the *Daily Chronicle*. Donald had at one time been one of his intimates, his near neighbour and frequent golfing companion at Walton Heath. But Donald, who was an Editor of principle and integrity, had become one of Lloyd George's most forthright critics. Moreover he had committed in Lloyd George's eyes the unforgivable offence of employing General Maurice, and had added to his crimes by attacking Lloyd George in September, 1918, in a leader for his 'small mind' in 'petulantly' refusing to congratulate Haig on his recent victories.

So by buying the *Daily Chronicle* Lloyd George was able not only to fulfil his ambition of having 'his own' newspaper, but to take his revenge on Donald and Maurice.

General Maurice, however, was immediately offered by A. G. Gardiner, the Editor of the *Daily News*, the same position as he had enjoyed on the *Daily Chronicle*, and in his new Editor he found as congenial and appreciative a chief as he had in Robert Donald. He took up his new post on 8 October, 1918.

By this time the end of the war was only a few weeks away, Haig's position as Commander-in-Chief of our victorious Armies was impregnable, and while continuing his claims to be 'the man who won the war', Lloyd George was powerless to impose his will on the Army, or even to carry out one of his minor objectives, to damage General Maurice.

This latter objective, however, he pursued when the opportunity offered, as it did in 1925. Spencer Wilkinson, the Chichele Professor of Military History at Oxford, resigned in 1923. This was the senior Chair in this subject in England, and General Maurice applied for the post, for which, as a distinguished military historian, he was

admirably qualified. To the surprise of all who knew of the require-
ments of the position, the Professorship was conferred, not on
General Maurice, but on Major General Sir Ernest Swinton, a
charming individual whose only publications, apart from *Eye-
Witness*, his despatches as official war correspondent, were a book
entitled *The Defence of Duffer's Drift*, published in 1904 under the
pseudonym of 'Backsight-Forethought', and some delightful short
stories under the pseudonym 'Ole Luk Oie'.

The reason that he, and not General Maurice, obtained this
academic plum was that Sir Maurice Hankey, the Secretary of the
Cabinet, who was a member of the Board of Electors representing
the Committee of Imperial Defence, informed the Board, which
met in 1925 to fill the vacancy, that 'General Maurice was persona
non grata with the Admiralty and the War Office'.*

General Maurice was convinced that Hankey's intervention was
instigated by Lloyd George, who, although out of office, had been
Prime Minister when General Maurice was DMO and had been
dismissed from the Army because of his letter to the Press.

When the war ended, General Maurice was appointed by the
Daily News as head of their team to report on the Peace Conference,
and was in Paris in that capacity from the middle of January, 1919,
until the end of June. When President Wilson returned to the
United States, the *Daily News* did not consider it necessary to keep
so high-powered and expensive a team in Paris and he returned to
London to continue his work as Military Correspondent.

The Peace Conference dragged on for another six months, and

---

* General Maurice gave me this account in 1925. His brother-in-law, C. T. Atkinson,
Fellow of Exeter, gave the same account to other members of the family. Sir Charles
Oman, who was a member of the Board of Electors, was a close friend of Atkinson.
There can be no doubt that he was their informant.

Sir Maurice Bowra in *The End of an Era*, writes: 'In 1925 the chair of Military History
was vacant, and an obvious candidate for it was Sir Frederick Maurice, who was a
learned and acute historian with a special appeal for classical scholars because he had
worked out the probable size of Xerxes' Army by calculating how much water it needed
on its advance into Greece. Denniston had served under him in the War Office and
spoke warmly of his charm and integrity. But Maurice had been involved in a famous
episode in 1918 when he provided Asquith with evidence that Lloyd George had lied
about the number of troops in France. It lost him his job, and it began the break-up of
the Liberal Party. But he acted on the highest motives, and everyone knew it. However,
it was enough to keep him out of the chair, which was given to Sir Ernest Swinton, an
amusing and friendly man, who had taken a leading part in the invention of the tank,
but was intellectually much inferior to Maurice.

5 *Field Marshal Sir Douglas Haig.*

operations,
ed back to
The enemy
oraniyeh on
pulsed. On
was begun,
ntered the
rmans and
d been sent
the Jordan
north of the
Juoraniyeh.
to prevent
ents from
ause a force
he Shechem
river and
Nine light
iver valley,
column was
afterwards
lt without
l from the
forcements,
down the
lly caused
ordan. We
ast night's
dvance our
thousand
ns that we
Jordan, and
y to with-
front have
of the two
which were
he winter.
extremely
ided check

tter.

Government
Bill. That
one concrete
the almost
PLUNKETT
We entirely
t should be
in carrying
transitional
l be the last
public of a
because the
were unable
lves. Their

MINISTERIAL STATEMENTS.

TO THE EDITOR OF THE TIMES.

Sir,—My attention has been called to answers given in the House of Commons on April 23 by Mr. Bonar Law to questions put by Mr. G. Lambert, Colonel Burn, and Mr. Pringle as to the extension of the British front in France (Hansard, Vol. 105, No. 34, page 815). These answers contain certain misstatements which in sum give a totally misleading impression of what occurred. This is not the place to enter into a discussion as to all the facts, but Hansard's report of the incident concludes :—

Mr. Pringle.—Was this matter entered into at the Versailles War Council at any time ?

Mr. Bonar Law.—This particular matter was not dealt with at all by the Versailles War Council.

I was at Versailles when the question was decided by the Supreme War Council, to whom it had been referred.

This is the latest of a series of misstatements which have been made recently in the House of Commons by the present Government. On April 9 the Prime Minister said :—

What was the position at the beginning of the battle ? Notwithstanding the heavy casualties in 1917 the Army in France was considerably stronger on the 1st January, 1918, than on the 1st January, 1917. (Hansard, Vol. 104, No. 24, page 1,328.)

That statement implies that Sir Douglas Haig's fighting strength on the eve of the great battle which began on March 21 had not been diminished.

That is not correct.

Again, in the same speech the Prime Minister said :—

In Mesopotamia there is only one white division at all, in Egypt and in Palestine there are only three white divisions, the rest are Indians or mixed with a very, very small proportion of British troops in those divisions—I am referring to the infantry divisions.

This is not correct.

Now, Sir, this letter is not the result of a military conspiracy. It has been seen by no soldier. I am by descent and conviction as sincere a democrat as the Prime Minister and the last thing I want is to see the Government of our country in the hands of soldiers. My reason for taking the very grave step of writing this letter are that the statements quoted above are known to a large number of soldiers to be incorrect, and this knowledge is breeding such distrust of the Government as can only end in impairing the splendid *moral* of our troops at a time when everything possible should be done to raise it.

I have therefore decided, fully realizing the consequences to myself, that my duty as a citizen must override my duty as a soldier, and I ask you to publish this letter in the hope that Parliament may see fit to order an investigation into the statements I have made.

I am yours faithfully,
F. MAURICE, Major-General.
20, Kensington Park-gardens, May 6.

before the li
could have
Mr. Montagu
to exploit
preted India
who desired
that any had
spirit. Whe
was being st
that India
Empire. Th
ference. He
like men. Th
declaring tha
mote the spir
activity. and
secure victor
Lord Chel
large comm
other on re
journed mee
The first inc
Meyer, Sir
Kashmir, B
officials, am
Jinnah, Dr.
Hassab Imn
second incl
Barnes, Sir
Scindia, the
Sahib of Na
men, Europ
Great int
of the Confe
certain Hom

FINAN

STATE
(FRO)

The State
assembling
Wednesday.
An exten
the problem
to obtain th
Some of the
lian market
ment have
States are u
fearing th
incurred.
A large de
increased ta
fairly certai
the new ta
new appoi
Federal Tre
warns the
bound to co
Owing to
of meat, att
the New Sc
the opening
The Fede
napers to

6 *The letter to* The Times, *7 May, 1918.*

until it was over General Maurice felt bound by the resolution he had taken that he would not reopen the controversy in regard to his letter to the Press until peace had been ratified.

When he was free to do so, he decided to challenge the false version of events which Lloyd George had given to the House of Commons in the Maurice debate.

On 1 January, 1920, he wrote to Mr Balfour, the Secretary of State for Foreign Affairs:

Personal
Dear Mr Balfour,

I want you to be good enough to give me your advice on a matter of some public importance. You will remember that the Prime Minister replied on 9 May, 1918, in the House to the letter which I wrote to the papers on 6 May challenging, amongst other statements made by Ministers statements which he had made on 9 April. In his speech on 9 May (you will find the passage in Hansard, Vol. 105, No. 44, pp. 2352–2353), the Prime Minister produced an answer which had been prepared in my department in reply to a question put by Sir Godfrey Baring on 18 April. That answer stated that the combatant strength of the British Army was greater on 1 January, 1918, than on the 1 January, 1917. Mr Lloyd George specifically stated that this was proof that a similar statement made by him on 9 April was correct. Now in fact I knew nothing of either question or answer until I read Mr Lloyd George's speech on 9 May. I had been in France from 13 to 16 April; my successor had arrived in the War Office and I was occupied from the 17th to the 19th in winding up and handing over to him. I left the War Office on the morning of the 20th. My deputy did not therefore think it necessary to trouble me with Sir G. Baring's question and I only found out what happened some time afterwards.

Private notice had been given of the question and the answer was required in a hurry. The figures asked for were not those with which my deputy usually dealt and he asked another department for them. The figures submitted to my deputy shewed an increase in the combatant strength in January, 1918, as compared with January, 1917, and he endorsed the answer accordingly. Some days later* it was discovered that in the hurry of typing out the figures a clerk had included in the strength on the Western Front in France the strength of our forces in Italy, which then amounted to 5 divisions and a considerable force of artillery. On finding out the mistake my deputy informed Mr Macpherson, then Under Secretary of State for War who had given the

* Whatever Kirke may have told Maurice in May, 1918, it is now known that the mistake was not discovered until the morning of 9 May.

answer and Mr Philip Kerr. Both were informed of the facts before the Prime Minister spoke on 9 May.* I have no evidence that either of these Gentlemen said anything to Mr Lloyd George on the subject and I assume that they did not do so, but I have evidence that on the appearance of my letter in the papers the War Cabinet asked the War Office for the correct figures which were furnished in a statement dated 7 May.† That statement shewed that the combatant strength in January, 1917 was 88,332 greater than in January, 1918. Mr Lloyd George therefore knew that in producing to the House the reply to Sir G. Baring's question he was producing an incorrect statement as proof that what he had said on 9 April was correct.

I made up my mind after the division of 9 May that I would not reopen this question except in the way of ordinary comment until peace had been ratified. As that will shortly happen I am now writing to ask you two questions:

   (i) Is there some explanation of Mr Lloyd George's use of the Baring answer of which I am not aware?
   (ii) Is it at the present time a matter of vital public interest that Mr Lloyd George's position should not be shaken?

I find it hard to believe that a man who can act as Mr Lloyd George appears to have acted is a fit person to be Prime Minister, but I am not actuated by any desire for revenge and I have tried according to my lights to act in this matter throughout in what I believed to be the public interest. I should therefore be most grateful if you would answer my two questions for I have the very highest respect for your judgement and probity and your opinion would have great influence with me.

Believe me
Yours sincerely
F. Maurice

Mr Balfour replied to General Maurice's appeal in a friendly and sympathetic letter, but the only advice he gave was that General Maurice should write to Philip Kerr.

Whittingehame,
Prestonkirk, N.B.

Private   7 Jan, 1920
My dear General,
   I have given much thought to your letter of the 1st, but without finding anything to say on the subject which is likely to be of value. I have many disqualifications for giving you the advice you ask for.

---

* Kirke only informed Macpherson *after* the Maurice debate. There is no evidence that he informed Kerr or anyone else before 9 May.
† General Maurice has not disclosed the source from which he received this information.

In the first place, the controversy of the Spring of 1918 is one on which I am not specially competent to speak, for I know nothing more than the broad outlines, with which the public is now familiar; and the statements contained in your letter are quite new to me.

In the second place, you desire my advice in order to make up your mind whether, in the public interest, you are justified in making an attack on the Prime Minister. It is evident that I cannot approach this problem in an attitude of abstract impartiality. The Prime Minister is my colleague and my friend. Together we have gone through most difficult times; and few would be bold enough to say that those difficulties are nearing their end. I could not but deplore, both on public and on private grounds, anything which should damage his position in the country.

If then you ask if you are to sit down silently under what you believe to be a great injustice, I reply that I make no such statement. I merely point out that I am disqualified from offering an opinion on the point by the peculiarities of my position.

May I, however, make one observation, not based upon any special information of this case, but upon my general experience of political misunderstandings and controversies.

You believe, rightly or wrongly, that the Prime Minister's statement gave a wholly false impression of your case, and you assume that this was done deliberately by the Prime Minister, who was prepared to sacrifice your character in the interest of political expediency. Now I am quite confident that this view is most unjust. The Prime Minister no doubt felt very strongly upon the subject, and it is possible, as sometimes happens in the heat of controversy, that he may not have measured his language. On this point I make no pronouncement, as I do not recollect what he said; but of one thing I am quite confident, which is, that he thought *you* were the doer of a wrong, and that *he* was the victim of it. Whether he was correct in holding this view is, of course, the precise point which you want re-opened; but that he did hold this view when he spoke, I do not for an instant question.

One other thing let me say. It is clear from what you tell me that there are some questions of fact known to Mr Philip Kerr in regard to which you are in doubt. Why not communicate with him directly?

I am afraid you will think that your appeal to an old friend receives a very poor response in this letter; but, after anxious reflection, I am quite unable to see what more, or better, I can do. In any case pray believe that if I fail to help you, it is from no lack of personal goodwill—nor is there any forgetfulness on my part of the anxious hours we have passed together, or of your services to the country.

Yours ever
Arthur James Balfour

Although disappointed, General Maurice accepted Mr Balfour's advice and wrote to Philip Kerr on 18 January, reminding him that it was he who had been informed by Colonel Kirke before the Maurice debate that the reply to the Baring question was wrong. It is now known that it was to Kerr that the DMO had sent the correct figures on 8 May, and he was fully aware of the injustice done to General Maurice by Lloyd George's use of the wrong figures in the debate.

Kerr's reply, dated 3 February, was as follows:

10 Downing Street
Whitehall, S.W.1.

Dear General Maurice,

I have looked into the matter raised in your letter of 18 January since my return from Paris. There does not appear to be any foundation for the imputation which you make. In his speech of 9 May the Prime Minister was dealing with your accusation that the statement he had made to the House of Commons in regard to the strength of the army in France on 9 April was not correct. He pointed out that his statement of 9 April was based upon information officially derived from the War Office and was confirmed from your own department nine days later, and he concluded: 'If there was anything wrong in these figures I got them from official sources for which General Maurice himself is responsible and I think he might have said that in his letter when he was impugning the honour of Ministers.'

May I add that the Prime Minister's principal difficulty in refuting your allegations arose from the fact that your charges were made at perhaps the most critical moment of the war, when the Germans had met with a great initial success in their 1918 offensive, and were preparing to follow it up by further attacks. The Prime Minister was unable to meet this wholly unjustified attack—an attack which if it had been successful must have had the most serious results upon the confidence and morale of the Allied armies and nations at the most dangerous moment of the war—by quoting all the facts and figures of the case, for to have done so would have been to communicate information of vital importance to the enemy. Had he been able to do so he would have demolished completely your insinuations in regard to the strength of the British Army in France. The Government, however, went so far as to offer facilities for a judicial enquiry. Mr Asquith, however, refused this enquiry and preferred that the Prime Minister should make a public statement to the House of Commons. Accordingly on 9 May, the Prime Minister made as full a statement in reply to your accusations as it was possible to make at that time, a statement which completely satisfied the House of Commons. In view of these circumstances I do not think it will serve any public interest to enter upon any further discussion of the matter raised in your letter.

Yours sincerely,
P. H. Kerr

General Maurice drafted a further letter to Kerr dated 4 February, this time making his challenge to Lloyd George more specific, and stating that he proposed to send the correspondence between himself and Kerr to the press, but decided not to send it but to write to Lloyd George instead.

5 March, 1920

The Rt. Hon. David Lloyd George, MP,
10 Downing Street,
S.W.1.
My dear Prime Minister,

You will probably have seen Mr Philip Kerr's letter to me of 3 February. That letter does not answer the question which I asked in my letter of 15 January. It repeats the statement made by you on 9 May, 1918, that you obtained your figures from official sources for which I was responsible.

I desire to state categorically that no figures for which I was responsible were given to Ministers justifying the statements made by them on 9 April, 1918, in regard to the strength of the British forces in France and in the East. Nine days later in April, owing to an error the cause of which I have explained, some incorrect figures were given and these were corrected as soon as the mistake was discovered.

I wish also to state categorically that my department specifically warned Ministers in writing of the decline of the fighting strength of the British Army in France in 1918 as compared with 1917.

Mr Kerr says that you felt yourself to be under a disability in replying to my letter of 6 May, 1918. You are no longer under that disability, and I suggest that you are now free 'to demolish completely my insinuations' in regard to the strength of the British Army in France by asking the War Office to publish the strength of the fighting forces under the command of Sir Douglas Haig upon the following dates:

January 1917	January 1918
March 1917 (eve of the battle of Arras)	March 1918 (eve of the German attack).

If, as is possible, you should also desire to publish the total strength of the British Army in France on those dates, may I suggest that the numbers of labourers, (white, Chinese and other coloured labourers) on those dates, should be shewn separately.

It would complete the effectiveness of the reply if the War Office were asked to publish the strength of the white and native troops in Palestine and Egypt in March 1918.

As regards my conduct in publishing my letter of 6 May, 1918, it is a matter of opinion whether the interests of the Allies were best served by challenging the assertion made at the time when the British army was fighting 'with its back to the wall', that the Western front was well equipped to look after itself before the battle began, or whether it was more important to preserve the reputation of politicians.

If I am proved to be wrong I will at once publicly withdraw and apologise for any mistake I may have made.

Mr Kerr's reference to Mr Asquith's action is not apposite as I had no communication with Mr Asquith nor with any of his followers. I may say however, that Mr Kerr's description of Mr Asquith's action is a travesty of the facts. Mr Asquith did not prefer that you should make a public statement in the House of Commons. He asked for a Parliamentary Enquiry. That request was refused by the House of Commons because the House was led to believe

1.   that before sending my letter to the papers I had not called the attention of any one in authority to the incorrectness of the statements of Ministers, whereas I had informed my late Chief, the Chief of the Imperial General Staff, as soon as I was aware of all the facts.

2.   because it was led to believe that I was not in a position to know what occurred in Versailles with regard to the extension of the British front at the conference of the Supreme War Council at Versailles which assembled on 1 February, whereas I was duly informed, and

3.   that the statements of Ministers made on 9 April were based on statements supplied by myself, which is not the case.

I am,
Yours sincerely,
(F. Maurice)

P.S. The despatch of this letter has been delayed first because I was laid up with an attack of influenza and secondly because I did not desire that it should reach you while the Peace Conference was in session.

On 16 March, Kerr replied:

Dear General Maurice,

The Prime Minister directs me to reply to your letter of 5 March that he does not think any useful purpose could be served by entering into a controversy in regard to the fresh points which you raise. He directs me, however, to forward you a copy of the statement which he received from the War Office on 8 May, 1918, the day before his speech was made which shows that the statements which he made on 9 April and again on 9 May to the effect that the British Army was stronger in January, 1918 than in

January, 1917, were absolutely supported by the official documents he received from the War Office at the time. You will observe from this statement that the total effectives of the British Army on 1 January, 1918, was greater than the total effectives on 1 January, 1917, by just over 275,000 men while the total effectives of the British and Dominion armies combined was greater by approximately 325,000 men. The statement shows a reduction in the number of men treated as fighting troops but this was partly due to the adoption of a different classification of the British Army in 1918 than in 1917, and partly to the policy of G.H.Q. in the use of the effectives supplied to it by the Government. It cannot alter the essential fact that in January 1918 Sir Douglas Haig had 325,000 more effectives at his disposal including 100,000 coloured men, than he had in January 1917.

Yours sincerely,

The importance of this letter is that it proves that before Lloyd George spoke on 9 May, he knew that the answer to the Baring question, of which he made such effective use in the debate, was wrong. The statement enclosed with Kerr's letter, the AG return of 7 May, shows that the fighting troops on 1 January, 1918, were 88,332 less than on 1 January, 1917.

But General Maurice did not receive the letter, for it was never sent.

Lloyd George apparently changed his mind and instructed Kerr not to send it. It rests now in the Lloyd George papers where it was filed sixty years ago.

General Maurice's papers contain nothing to show why, when he received no reply to his letter he did not send the correspondence to the press, but he took no further action until 1922.

3 Intrigues of the War

In 1922, General Maurice was commissioned by J. A. Spender to write a series of articles for the *Westminster Gazette* on Lloyd George's conduct of the war.*

There were six of these:
1) 6 May
    The position at the Fall of Mr Asquith's Administration
2) 13 May
    Lloyd George's Conduct of the War—His Policy and Methods
3) 20 May
    The Nivelle Affair and its Sequel
4) 27 May
    The Versailles Council
5) 3 June
    Troops kept in Palestine
    Sir W. Robertson's Protest
    Divided Forces and Command
6) 10 June
    How Victory was Missed in 1917
    Premier's Conduct of the War
    Fifth Army Disaster. Its cause and responsibility
    The Plan to remove Haig
    Revelations of Major General Sir Frederick Maurice

He sent these to the Duke of Northumberland, who wrote to him on 19 June.

Albury Park,
Guildford

My dear General,
    Very many thanks for letting me see these articles. I think they are excellent and I hope you will publish them in pamphlet form. They give

* See Part Five, p. 181.

the whole story of LG's war policy so clearly and briefly that they would be invaluable in enlightening public opinion if produced in the form of a little book or pamphlet. The only suggestion I have to make is that you might say something further regarding the figures given by the PM in the House in May, 1918. You may remember that a week or two previously the Under Sec of State asked for figures of the British troops in France to give the House. By mistake Kirke supplied him with figures which included the troops in Italy. We subsequently informed him of our mistake *and we gave the correct figures to the War Cabinet*! In spite of this LG repeated the erroneous figure in the Debate on your letter and said it had been supplied by your Department!

Yrs sincerely,
Northumberland

General Maurice accepted the Duke's suggestion of publishing the articles in a pamphlet, but before doing so they decided that a further attempt should be made to challenge Lloyd George about his misstatements in the Maurice debate; and that General Maurice's letter to Lloyd George and the reply should be published as an appendix to the pamphlet.

It was agreed that the Duke should take the responsibility for statements of fact which might involve offences under the Official Secrets Act, but that Kirke, who was responsible for supplying Macpherson with the wrong figures used by Lloyd George in the debate, would see what General Maurice proposed to write, and confirm or otherwise the accuracy of any statements for which the Duke would take responsibility.

Kirke was anxious to preserve his own position, but the Duke had no such reservations. If proceedings had been taken against him under the Official Secrets Act, he would have been tried by his peers in the House of Lords, which would have delighted him and greatly embarrassed Lloyd George.

General Maurice sent both Kirke and the Duke the draft of his proposed letter to Lloyd George.

The Duke sent his comments on 12 July, and suggested that if Lloyd George declined to write the letter General Maurice asked for, he (the Duke) should add a note to the following effect:

17 Prince's Gate,
S.W.7.

My dear General,

The Prime Minister's conduct in making his statement on 9 May and in declining to withdraw the imputation that you have supplied him with

incorrect information is the more outrageous in that the Military Operations Directorate had repeatedly drawn his attention to the decline of
the fighting strength of the Allies in France, and to the steady increase of
the enemy's forces on the Western front. These figures were continually
challenged by Mr Lloyd George, who insisted that the Allied strength was
greater than was represented. The figures showing the increase of the
German forces in the months preceding the great attack of 21 March
were given weekly in the Summary of Operations circulated to Ministers,
and in the same document during the same period the decline in our
fighting strength was more than once stressed.

The Prime Minister knew the figures sent in by the Operations
Directorate, and with this knowledge fresh in his mind made the utterly
false statement of 9 April, and one month later actually pretended that
if a too favourable estimate had been given, the fault lay with the Military
Operations Directorate, whose warnings he had consistently disregarded.

Yours sincerely,

Northumberland

Kirke also wrote on 12 July, correcting some statements the Duke
had been prepared to endorse, and, for the first time, admitting to
General Maurice by implication that he had not sent any correction
to the reply to the Baring question; and that it was only after the
Maurice debate that he had informed Macpherson; but he did not
admit that he had not discovered the mistake until 9 May.

General Maurice sent his letter to Lloyd George on 15 July, and
received on the 21st a reply signed by one of Lloyd George's
Secretaries, E. W. M. Grigg (later Lord Altrincham).

10 Downing Street,

Whitehall, S.W.1.

Dear Sir Frederick Maurice,

The Prime Minister has received your letter of the 15th, and directs
me to acknowledge it.

What he said in 1918, he said in good faith upon the information
supplied to him; and he does not think it will be injurious to the public
interest or unjust to you if he leaves your criticism, like much more of the
same character, to the unprejudiced judgment of posterity.

As regards your threat to publish, he would refer you with all courtesy
for answer to a short observation made in similar circumstances by the
Duke of Wellington.*

I am,

Yours very truly,

E. W. M. Grigg

* 'Dear Fanny—Peach and be D - - - - d!'

It will be remembered that General Maurice, Northumberland and Kirke all knew that Lloyd George had been informed officially that the answer to the Baring question was wrong, and that General Maurice had stated in his letter to Mr Balfour on 1 January, 1920, that he had evidence that Lloyd George had received returns giving the correct figures of the fighting strength of the Army on 1 January, 1918, before he made his speech on 9 May.

After receiving Grigg's letter, he sent this evidence to the Duke of Northumberland, suggesting that the Duke should put a question in the Lords asking for it to be produced.

The Duke replied on 31 July:

Albury Park,
Guildford

My dear General,

Thanks for your letter—I had not seen the enclosed return. I am afraid it is too late to ask for it in the House of Lords as it rises this week. I don't know whether you could get anyone in the Commons to do it.

But I don't see why we should not quote it without putting it to a question in Parliament. LG says that his statement was made in good faith upon the strength of figures supplied to him. Now we know that no figures were supplied to him before his speech of 9 April which would justify his statement in *that* speech, while as regards his speech of 9 May —in view of this return, the W.O. cannot have supplied figures to corroborate his statement nor can he have made enquiries—would it not be worth while writing another letter to the Press challenging LG's statement that the figures were given in good faith and quoting the return prepared by A.G.1?

Yours sincerely,
Northumberland

'The enclosed return' dated 7 May, 1918, had been sent to the Secretary of the War Cabinet on 7 May and, by the DMO, General Radcliffe, to Kerr on 8 May.* But this General Maurice did not know. He knew only that it had been sent to the Secretary of the War Cabinet on 7 May. How he came into possession of it is not known, but the source must have been so vulnerable that he could not publish it, or ask anyone in the House of Commons to put down a question on it; so when the Duke of Northumberland was

---

* Maurice sent a copy of the return, 'British Forces in France' to H. H. Asquith in December, 1919, at the latter's request. It is reproduced in J. A. Spender and Cyril Asquith's *Life of Lord Oxford and Asquith*, without reference to the source from which it was obtained. Maurice's letter to Asquith does not survive.

unable to ask for it in the Lords, he could make no use of it, and he could not prove that Lloyd George had received it.

So the pamphlet *Intrigues of the War*, was published without it in August, 1922. The Marquis of Crewe wrote the Preface, and General Maurice's letter to Lloyd George and the reply from the Prime Minister's Secretary were published in an Appendix.

The Appendix also included the letter which the Duke of Northumberland had suggested he should write if Lloyd George refused General Maurice's request to withdraw the false statements he had made in his speech on 9 May.

General Maurice sent *Intrigues of the War*, with the appendices, to Lord Balfour on 15 July, but received from him a letter dated 17 July, which was an even greater disappointment to him than Balfour's letter of January, 1920, had been.

4 Carlton Gardens,
Pall Mall,
17 July, 1922

Private
Dear General Maurice,
One line to acknowledge your letter of the 15th and its enclosure. As I have no independent knowledge of the facts my opinion is worth nothing.
Yours sincerely,
Balfour

The publication of *Intrigues of the War* only confirmed what had long been taken for granted both in the Army and in all informed quarters about *The Crisis of May* 1918: that General Maurice had told the truth, and that Lloyd George had got his vote of confidence in the Maurice debate by prevarication and special pleading.

When it was published, Lloyd George's Premiership was on the point of ending. In October, 1922, the Coalition broke up, and Lloyd George resigned. He never held office again.

4 The Lloyd George Memoirs

In 1936, the fifth volume of Lloyd George's *War Memoirs* was published, which included a chapter on the Maurice debate.

This attacked General Maurice on grounds which departed even further from the facts than had his speech in the debate on 9 May, 1918.

The references to General Maurice in the index show in Lloyd George an unusual capacity for employing even an index as a means of venting his spleen on the man who had dared to challenge his direction of the war.

MAURICE, SIR FREDERICK, supports Robertson against War Cabinet; as comfortably placed as any politician; subservient and unbalanced; reports appearance of Brandenburg Corps south of Lille; supplies figures showing comparative strengths of Allies and enemy; his astonishing arithmetical calculations; the instrument by which the Government was to be thrown out; man-power figures given by on 13/3/18; his estimates of 10/4/18; his astonishing *volte-face* of 22/4/18; Sir Henry Wilson substitutes General Radcliffe for; intrigues against the Government, his mind being apparently unhinged; false allegations against Lloyd George and Bonar Law published by; the tool of astuter men; his double-dealing denounced by Lloyd George; responsible for the statistics he questioned; not present, as he alleged at Versailles discussion; his grave breach of discipline condoned by Asquith; dismissed.

But on this occasion Lloyd George did not go unchallenged. In June, 1936, three months before the *Memoirs* were published, the *Daily Telegraph* published an extract from the chapter on the Maurice debate, which included a new charge against General Maurice of having cooked the figures of the allied and enemy forces in the weekly summary for 18 April, 1918 because 'his nose was out of joint'; and made the wholly untrue statement that when General

Maurice ceased to be DMO Haig had refused to give him an appointment in France and that General Maurice

had spent his unsought-for vacation in caballing against the Government with its enemies in Parliament and in the Press. Deprived of his responsible post on the Staff, he became for the time being completely unhinged.

The extract was published in the *Daily Telegraph* on 25 June, 1936.

In a letter published in the *Daily Telegraph* on 5 July, General Maurice dealt with Lloyd George's charge that he was responsible for the weekly summary of 18 April, which he had not even seen, since he had been in France from 14 to 17 April, and had handed over to his successor, General Radcliffe on the 18th. He explained how these summaries were prepared, and showed that the suggestion that any individual could have cooked up false figures was ridiculous.

He then went on to deal with the figures themselves. Since Lloyd George had used the summaries to attack General Maurice, the latter had been given permission by the Secretary of State for War to give the facts concerning them.

He wrote:

It was the practice to report weekly any important changes in Allied or enemy strength, and to summarise these changes in a monthly table. It is this table, which appeared in the memorandum of 18 April, to which Mr Lloyd George objected. This is the passage:
Our casualties since 21 March amount to over 220,000. On 31 March we had about 30,000 drafts in France, and up to 13 April we had sent out from home 183,000 men to replace losses. The numbers now at our disposal to replace wastage are insufficient to maintain all our divisions at full strength and to provide for future losses; we have been compelled in consequence to withdraw six of our divisions, using the men for drafts and keeping the cadres until they can be refilled.
In the summary dated 14 March a comparative statement was given showing Allied and enemy strengths on the Western Front. Since then the situation has been altered materially by the reduction of the above-mentioned six British divisions, the disappearance for fighting purposes of the Portuguese contingent, and the arrival of 18 more German divisions from Russia, Italy and the Balkans. The following figures show approximately what the present situation is:

Army	Divs.	Battns.	Rifle strength	Artillery Fd & Hvy
British	33	477	500,000	5,850
French	103	927	680,000*	9,795
American	4†	48	49,000	421
Belgian	6	108	55,000	604
Total Allies	166	1,560	1,284,000	16,670
Total enemy	205	1,881	1,617,450	16,739

It will be observed that four of the five American divisions which Mr Lloyd George says I wiped out are included in the return; the fifth, as stated, was not then complete. The arrival of successive German divisions on the Western Front, a reinforcement so unexpected by Mr Lloyd George, had been reported in the preceding summaries.

It is not surprising that Mr Lloyd George was horrified when he saw in black and white the effect of his refusal to reinforce the Western Front before the battle.

Apparently an enquiry was held into the correctness of the figures. Of this I knew nothing, having left the War Office, and no questions as to the correctness of the figure were ever put to me, but the following appears in the memorandum for the period ending 26 April:

The summary for week ending 18 April shows an Allied
inferiority in rifle strength of 333,450 as compared with that of
the enemy. Owing to the impossibility of obtaining accurate
figures while heavy fighting is in progress, these calculations
were based to a great extent on estimates.
In the light of returns since available this Allied inferiority appears
to have been overstated and should read 262,200.

Doubtless the estimates were revised by Sir Henry Wilson's direction to soothe Mr Lloyd George as far as was possible. But when actuals are compared with estimates the figures of 18 April are found to be the more correct of the two.

For example, the British casualties in the German March offensive and the battle of the Lys in *Statistics of the Military Effort of the British Empire in the Great War*, War Office, 1922, p. 328, are given as approximately 343,812. On 18 April the battle of the Lys was nearing its end, and our subsequent losses in that battle were comparatively small,

* The figure for French rifle strength given in the summary of 14 March was 764,000. This estimate, which was given by the French War Office, seems to have included machine-gun units. The figure given here excludes these units, as in the case of the other armies.
† There are five combatant American divisions in France, but one of these is not yet fit to fight.

French reinforcements having arrived in Flanders. The estimate of our losses in the summary of 18 April as over 220,000 men was definitely conservative.

Sir G. Macdonogh's estimate of the enemy strength was also somewhat conservative. In the summary of 21 March he put the number of German divisions on the Western Front as 190. We now know it was actually 192 and three brigades (*Official History of the War, France and Belgium, 1918*, p. 142). In the summaries between 14 March and 18 April he reported the arrival in succession of 18 more German divisions. The fact that the Portuguese contingent was out of action and that we had had to reduce six of our divisions to cadres was well known to 'our poor harassed infantry in France'. In the following week four more divisions were also reduced to maintain the remainder at strength.

F. Maurice

4 July

With regard to Lloyd George's statement that Haig had refused to employ General Maurice, and that 'he had spent his unsought vacation caballing against the Government', it will be remembered that Sir Henry Wilson had informed General Maurice on 20 February, 1918, that he wished to bring General Radcliffe from France to succeed him as DMO; and that Haig had promised him command of a division.

In a letter to the *Daily Telegraph* published on 1 July, General Maurice revealed for the first time what post he had been promised by Sir Douglas Haig.

I saw Sir Douglas Haig on 14 April, and he then told me that he hoped to reconstitute the 5th Army, and instead of appointing me to a division wanted me to be Major-General of the General Staff of that army.

The suggestion that I became 'suddenly unhinged' by Gen Radcliffe's arrival, of which I had known for seven weeks, is therefore rubbish.

As Mr Lloyd George sees fit to use secret memoranda to attack me, which I cannot use to reply, I am unable to say more, except to repeat that at no time prior to my letter to the Press on 6 May, 1918, did I ever give any information to the Press or to the Opposition enabling either to attack the Government, nor was my letter inspired by any member of the Press or of the Opposition. Yours,

F. Maurice

When Volume V of the Lloyd George *War Memoirs* was published in September, 1936, it was found to contain even more inaccurate statements than those which had been confuted when the extract was published in the *Daily Telegraph*.

March 31st 1919
Jan 1st 1920.

Dear Mr Balfour

I want you to be good enough to give me some advice on a matter of some public importance. You will remember that the Prime Minister replied on May 9th 1918 in the House to the letter which I wrote to the papers on May 6th challenging, amongst other statements made by Ministers, statements which he had made on April 9th. In his speech on May 9th, you will find the passage in Hansard vol 105 n° 44 pp 2352-2353, the Prime Minister produced an answer which had been prepared in my department with to a question put by Sir Godfrey Baring on April 18th. That answer stated that the combatant strength of the British army was greater on 1st January 1918 than on 1st January 1917. Mr Lloyd George specifically stated that this was proof that a similar statement made by him on April 9th was correct.

Now in fact I knew nothing of either question or answer until I read Mr Lloyd George's speech of May 9th. I had been in France from April 13th to 16th, my successor had arrived in the War Office & I was occupied from the 17th to 19th in winding up & handing over to him. I left the War Office on the morning of the 20th. My deputy did not therefore think it necessary to trouble me with Sir G. Baring's question & I only found out what happened some time afterwards.

Private notice had been given of the question & the answer was required in a hurry. The figures asked for were not there with which my deputy usually dealt & he asked another department for them. The figures submitted to my deputy showed an increase in the combatant strength in January 1918 as compared with January 1917 & he endorsed the answer accordingly. Some days later it was discovered that in the hurry of typing out the figures a clerk had included in the strength of our forces in Italy, which then amounted to 5 divisions & a considerable force of artillery. On finding out the mistake my deputy informed Mr McPherson, then Under Secretary of State for War who had prepared the answer and Mr Philip Kerr. Both were informed of the facts before the Prime Minister spoke on

8 *Mr Lloyd George and Lord Derby in the garden at 10 Downing Street.*

In his attack on General Maurice for 'cooking the figures', Lloyd George quoted from the summary of 23 March to justify his surprise and indignation at the statement that according to the summary of 18 April 'an Allied superiority of 86,000 rifles had been converted into a German superiority of 330,000'.

He wrote:

On 23 March, the third day of the great battle we were given fresh figures. ... Here they are as they were given to the Cabinet by Sir Frederick Maurice, this time corroborated by a less mercurial arithmetician, General Macdonogh, the Director of Military Intelligence: German rifle strength 1,402,800; Allies 1,418,000: a superiority still which was the equivalent of two German divisions.

Lloyd George was quoting from the War Cabinet Minutes of 23 March, one of the secret memoranda to which he had access and General Maurice had not.

The whole passage in the War Cabinet Minute is as follows:

From figures given by the Director of Military Intelligence and Director of Military Operations it appeared that the comparison of enemy and Allied forces was as follows:

Germany
Divisions	191
Rifle strength	1,402,800

Allies   *Divisions*

French	99
British	58
Portuguese	2
Belgian	6
American	—

(None as yet available for heavy fighting)

165

Rifle strength	1,418,000

It was pointed out that the rifle strength of the Allies included 40,000 Americans, 58,000 Belgians, and 26,000 Portuguese. The Chief of the Imperial General Staff considered that for purposes of calculation, the present forces might be reckoned as approximately equal.*

It will be seen that General Maurice and General Macdonogh estimated that the Germans had 191 divisions to the Allies' 165.

---

* War Cabinet Minutes, W.C. 371.

Lloyd George made no mention of the numbers of divisions when he wrote in his *Memoirs* that the Allied superiority 'was the equivalent of two German divisions'. Nor did he refer to the statement by the DMO and the DMI that for purposes of calculating the comparative rifle strength of the German and Allied forces on the third day of the German attack, the Americans, the Belgians and the Portuguese should be excluded, which converted an Allied superiority of 16,400 into a German superiority of 117,600 in effective rifle strength.

Sir Henry Wilson's statement that 'for purposes of calculation the present forces might be reckoned as approximately equal' was no doubt made for the same reason as his revision of the figures Lloyd George was so enraged by in the summary of 18 April, that is 'to soothe Mr Lloyd George as far as was possible', but it shows him to be both irresponsible and incapable in the role of principal military adviser to the Government, a role into which he had manoeuvred himself to replace General Sir William Robertson, who, unlike Sir Henry Wilson, always told the truth, even if it was unpalatable.

In the *Memoirs*, Lloyd George repeated the assertion he had made in the Maurice debate that the figures he had given in his statement on manpower on 9 April, which General Maurice had challenged, had been supplied to him by General Maurice's department, and that 'if there were in fact anything inaccurate in the statement made by me Maurice would himself have been responsible for misleading the Premier and through him the public'.

Lloyd George was well aware that this statement was untrue, since he had informed the War Cabinet on 8 May that for his speech on 9 April he had used the figures in the War Office statistical abstract. These came from the Adjutant-General's department, not from General Maurice or his staff, and it was Lloyd George's analysis of them, not the figures themselves, which was inaccurate.

A year before Volume V of the *Memoirs* was published, the *Official History of the War, Military Operations, France and Belgium, 1918*, published the correct figures of the British forces in France in January, 1917, and January, 1918, in a memorandum from the Adjutant-General dated 4 February, 1918, which showed that the only correct figure Lloyd George had used was the ration strength in January, 1918, compared to January, 1917 (1,949,000 compared to 1,646,600). It was this return which Lloyd George had used for his speech on 9 April.

The official historian added the following note:

It will be noticed that the total of the fighting troops, after rising to what was its maximum in June, fell so that in January, 1918, it was less than in January, 1917, the infantry in particular being some 70,000 less—and there was a faster fall between 1 January, 1918, and the date of the German attack. That the total strength was more is mainly accounted for by wounded and sick, by labour rising from 80,524 to 302,904 and by a small increase due to the formation of the Transportation service.

When Lloyd George's attention was drawn to this by letters in the *Daily Telegraph* from Air Marshal Trenchard, General Sir Noel Birch, Major-General Sir John Davidson and M. Boyland, Lloyd George replied that *'he was not concerned what figures the official Historian chooses to publish in 1935'* and added:

The figures which the Government had to accept in 1918, and use as the basis for its statements in Parliament were those furnished at the time by Sir F. Maurice himself on behalf of the War Office Staff.

But if Lloyd George had been unscrupulous in charging General Maurice with supplying him with inaccurate figures which he himself had cooked, he laid himself open to an even more serious charge in his use of the reply to the Baring question. He wrote:

The figures given me by General Maurice's Department on 18 April, showing Combatant strength only in the B.E.F. France were

January, 1917	1,253,000
January, 1918	1,298,000

I quoted to the House (on 9 May) the conclusion of the covering Note from General Sir Frederick Maurice's Department which ran:
From the statement included, it will be seen that the combatant strength of the British Army was greater on 1 January, 1918, than on 1 January, 1917.

It will be remembered that Lloyd George had received the correct figures from the War Office on 8 May and that Lord Milner had informed him officially on 15 May, that, owing to Kirke's mistake, the 1918 figures had included 86,000 men in the forces in Italy.

And he had known since March, 1920, that General Maurice had had no responsibility for or knowledge of these figures.

That, in what he claimed to be a serious contribution to history 'of lasting value and enlightenment', he should deny these facts is all the more strange in that by the time Volume V of the *Memoirs* was published, the truth was a matter of public record.*

But if Lloyd George continued to deny the truth and to justify his statements of 9 April and 9 May, the evidence against him, with himself as chief witness, was formidable. General Maurice had charged him with so misdirecting the conduct of the war that only the fighting qualities of the troops had averted defeat. The Prime Minister had stated that he was content to leave General Maurice's criticism 'to the unprejudiced judgment of posterity'. With the publication of the *Memoirs*, and the evidence of the Official Historian, all the facts which General Maurice had sought to elicit were available. He had every reason to believe that 'the unprejudiced judgment of posterity' would endorse the Maurice case against Lloyd George.

---

* To justify his statement on 9 April Lloyd George quoted from the *Statistics of the Military Effort of the British Empire* the figures for 1 January, 1917, as being 1,591,745, and on 1 January, 1918, as being 1,828,616 excluding 'certain non-military labour units, Chinese, Indian, etc.' But he included in the 1918 figure 270,000 non-combatants.

The actual total of non-combatants was 410,897, of whom some 300,000 were Chinese coolies and unarmed British labourers.

Lloyd George only deducted 141,384 of these from the total, in an endeavour to justify his statement on 9 April that the Army was stronger in January, 1918, than in 1917.

As the Official History put it:

> 'On 9 April, 1918, Mr Lloyd George stated in the House of Commons that the fighting strength of the Army in France, in spite of its heavy casualties, was considerably greater on 1 January, 1918, than on 1 January, 1917. This statement he was able to defend on 16 April on the authority of figures supplied to the Parliamentary Secretary of the War Office by the Directorate of Military Operations, War Office, on 18 April, in the absence of the Director, Major-General Sir Frederick Maurice, in France. The figures sent were: January, 1917, 1,253,000 all ranks, and January, 1918, 1,298,000; but by a mistake 86,000 men of the British Army in Italy had been included in the latter total, and labour units (R.E., Infantry, and some A.S.C.) added in both totals.'

The Appendix's reference to Lloyd George's defence 'on the 16 April' is an obvious error, since Lloyd George made no statement on 16 April and the answer to the Baring question was only given on 18 April. The correct date is 9 May. (*Military Operations, France and Belgium*, 1918, Appendix 7, p. 34.)

5 The Burnt Paper

Five years after General Maurice's death, Lord Beaverbrook published in *Men and Power* an extract from the diaries of Frances Stevenson, Lloyd George's Secretary in 1918, who is now Countess Lloyd George of Dwyfor.

This extract was dated 5 October, 1934, 16 years after the events to which it referred, and was as follows:

Have been reading up the events concerned with the Maurice Debate in order to help Ll.G. with this Chapter in Vol. V, and am uneasy in my mind about an incident which occurred at the time and which is known only to J. T. Davies and myself. Ll.G. obtained from the W.O. the figures which he used in his statement on 9 April in the House of Commons on the subject of man-power. These figures were afterwards stated by Gen Maurice to be inaccurate.

I was in J. T. Davies' room a few days after the statement, and J.T. was sorting out red dispatch boxes to be returned to the Departments. As was his wont, he looked in them before locking them up and sending them out to the Messengers. Pulling out a W.O. box, he found in it, to his great astonishment, a paper from the DMO containing modifications and corrections of the first figures they had sent, and by some mischance the box had remained unopened. J.T. and I examined it in dismay, and then J.T. put it in the fire, remarking, 'Only you and I, Frances, know of the existence of this paper.'

There is no doubt that this is what Maurice had in mind when he accused L.G. of mis-statement. But the amazing thing was that the document was never fixed upon. How was it that the matter was never clinched, and Maurice or someone never actually said: 'The figures supplied by us were so and so'? They argued round and over the point, but never did one of them put any finger on it. I was waiting for the matter to be raised, and for the question to be asked: Why did L.G. not receive these supplementary figures? Or did he? But the questions never came and I could not voluntarily break faith with J.T., perhaps put L.G. in a fix, and who knows, have brought down the Government!

The only explanation is that Maurice and Co., were relying on getting their Judicial Committee, where every point would have been thrashed out in detail. When the Judicial Committee was turned down, it was by that time too late to bring up details again, and by that time also Maurice was beaten.

I suppose it is too late now for the matter to be cleared up and I had better keep silent. But I will talk it over with J.T. In any event, no good could come of any revelation made now, but the amazing thing to me still, is that in all these years no one has fastened on this particular point. There is a slight allusion in Colonel Repington's book about a discrepancy in figures, but this also seems to have escaped attention. And as the Official Statistics since compiled seem to justify L.G.'s statement at the time, it were better perhaps to let sleeping dogs lie.

When *Men and Power* was published in 1956, it caused only less of a sensation than had the Maurice letter itself. A review by Lord Templewood in *The Spectator* led to correspondence as to what 'The Burnt Paper' was, and on what date Davies burnt it. In her diary Lady Lloyd George had said that the document was 'corrections from the DMO to the first figures they had sent', which Lloyd George had used in his statement on 9 April in the House of Commons on the subject of manpower; she gave the date of its destruction as 'a few days after' Lloyd George's speech on 9 April. But in a letter to *The Spectator* published on 23 November, 1956, she wrote:

Sir, I would like to correct the assumption in Miss Maurice's letter (in your issue of 16 November) that the War Office document containing supplementary figures was discovered *before* the Maurice Debate on 9 May, 1918. In fact, the paper was only found *some time afterwards*. This, I think you will agree, materially alters the case.

The facts are plainly stated in Lord Beaverbrook's book. Your reviewer, Lord Templewood, preferred to ignore them and to give his own version, and it is upon his review, that Miss Maurice appears to base her statements.

I am not seeking to exonerate the destroying of the paper, nor my own silence in the matter. But I feel that I should correct a false statement before it is in danger of becoming an accepted historical fact. Yours faithfully,

FRANCES LLOYD GEORGE

Avalon, Churt, Surrey

Lord Templewood commented:

Of course I unreservedly accept Lady Lloyd George's statement that the box was not opened and the paper burnt until after the Maurice debate of 8 May [sic]. If there has been any confusion on the point it has arisen from her own words that the box was opened 'a few days after the statement' [the Prime Minister's statement of 9 April]. In any case, the date does not affect the three conclusions of my review. First, that it was a surprising lapse on the part of the Prime Minister's secretaries to leave a War Office box unopened at a critical moment of the war; secondly, that it was much worse than a lapse to burn the very important paper that the box contained; and, thirdly, that the suppression of the correct figures proved of great value to the Prime Minister and his plans for the Coupon Election.

In her autobiography *The Years that are Past*, Lady Lloyd George has devoted a chapter to this affair, which has clearly lain heavily on her conscience. Having reproduced the extract from her diary quoted by Lord Beaverbrook, she adds:

When L.G. was writing his account of the Maurice debate in his memoirs (when I made the entry in my diary) I telephoned to J. T. Davies in London and said I thought we ought to tell him of the incident of the burnt paper. J.T.'s reply was that he had no recollection of the incident. So L.G. never knew what had happened.

But in her book she does not correct the statement in her diary that the document was burnt 'a few days after' 9 April; and she does not repeat what she wrote in her letter to *The Spectator* that it was destroyed 'after the Maurice debate on 9 May'.

Writing from memory sixteen years after the event, she has got almost all her facts wrong.

Lloyd George did not 'obtain from the War Office the figures which he used in his statement on 9 April in the House of Commons on the subject of man-power'. He made his own analysis of an Adjutant-General's return. It was this statement which General Maurice challenged.

The DMO's department sent no paper, 'a few days after 9 April,' or subsequently, 'containing modifications and corrections of the first figures they had sent', since they had not sent the figures Lloyd George used on 9 April.

So, whatever paper it was that Davies burnt, it did not come from the DMO's department.

Nor can it have been a correction to the reply to the Baring question on 18 April, since Kirke sent no correction either to 10 Downing Street or anywhere else before the Maurice debate.

What, then, was the burnt paper?

I have no doubt that it was the AG return headed 'British Forces in France', addressed to the Secretary of the War Cabinet, which General Maurice referred to in his letter of 1 January, 1920, to Mr Balfour as 'evidence that on the appearance of my letter in the papers the War Cabinet asked the War Office for the correct figures which were furnished in a statement dated 7 May', and which he sent to the Duke of Northumberland in July, 1922.

When Lady Lloyd George writes in her diary, 'The amazing thing was that the document was never fixed upon. How was it that the matter was never clinched, and Maurice or someone never actually said: "The figures supplied by us were so and so"? They argued round and over the point, but never did one of them put any finger on it', she is of course mistaken. The only 'wrong' figures which the DMO's department supplied, which Lloyd George used in the Maurice debate, *were* 'fixed on' on the morning of 9 May, and Lloyd George had the correct figures before he spoke. After the debate Macpherson, Lord Milner and Lloyd George himself were informed officially of the mistake.

As regards Davies himself, what happened will never be known, but I believe that the most probable explanation is that he staged the discovery of the War Office document he destroyed, and made Frances Stevenson his innocent accomplice, knowing how inconvenient it would be to the Prime Minister to receive from the War Office on 7 May 'modifications and corrections' to the figures he had used on 9 April.

Davies's statement to Miss Stevenson on 5 October, 1934, when she telephoned him to ask his permission to tell Lloyd George about the burnt paper 'that he had no recollection of the incident' reinforces this view. For even Davies can hardly have been so in the habit of destroying official documents which it would have been inconvenient to the Prime Minister to receive that he could not remember what one must hope was an isolated act of villainy.

Moreover, the account given by Miss Stevenson does not make sense. Supposing the War Office box was not opened and its contents read before its 'discovery' in the Secretaries' room, how would Davies know at a glance that it contained 'corrections' to the figures given by Lloyd George on 9 April? The reproduction on

p. 139 shows that it is a straightforward return of the British Forces in France in January, 1917, and January, 1918. It bears no relation to the statement made by Lloyd George on 9 April, except that it was accurate and Lloyd George's statement was not.

My own hypothesis is that Davies opened the box on 7 May as soon as it arrived, and reversed or removed the 'Urgent' pink label which it bore, before putting it into the Secretaries' room with the document still inside.* Some time later, in the presence of Miss Stevenson, probably after the Maurice debate, he enacted the scene she describes to give himself an alibi for having, in his ardour to assist Lloyd George in discrediting General Maurice, suppressed the paper before the Prime Minister spoke on 9 May. It was the same ardour that caused Sutherland to tell Lobby correspondents that he had personally taken General Maurice to hear Lloyd George's speech on 9 April.

What Davies did not know was that another copy of the AG return had been sent by the War Office to 10 Downing Street on 8 May addressed to Philip Kerr. This is included in the Lloyd George papers in the Beaverbrook Library.

It was the conviction that this return had been received by Lloyd George before he spoke in the Maurice debate that caused General Maurice to write in his letters to Balfour, Kerr and Lloyd George that when Lloyd George used 'the accidentally incorrect return made on 18 April to justify what he said on 9 April, he had at his disposal a return showing that the note of 18 April was incorrect'; and in his letter to Balfour that he found it hard to believe 'that a man who can act as Mr Lloyd George appears to have acted is a fit person to be Prime Minister'. He never knew that Davies had destroyed the return of which he had a copy, since *Men and Power* was only published after his death, or that another copy of it had been sent to 10 Downing Street on 8 May; but as Lloyd George got his vote of confidence in the Maurice debate by using the wrong answer to the Baring question and ignoring the correct figures which were in his possession before he spoke, he did in fact show himself as unfit to be Prime Minister, as General Maurice had contended.

* The normal procedure when a War Office box bearing an 'Urgent' label was received at 10 Downing Street was that it was opened immediately by one of the Secretaries, the contents were removed and handed to the person to whom it was addressed (in this case the Secretary to the War Cabinet), that the 'Urgent' label was reversed, and the box was put into the Secretaries' room to be returned to the War Office, to which the label was addressed.

Coda

You are contemplating a great thing, to your undying credit.

SIR WILLIAM ROBERTSON

I am persuaded that I am doing what is right, and once that is so, nothing else matters to a man.

(FROM THE LETTER TO HIS CHILDREN)

General Maurice's decision to write his letter to the press was an act of desperation. Both he and Sir William Robertson were convinced that if Lloyd George continued the policy and methods which had resulted in the German breakthrough on 21 March, the war would be lost. He saw no other way to save the Army and the nation than to sacrifice his career in the Army by taking the action he did.

He never regretted his decision, and on the ashes of his sacrifice he built a new career of great distinction: Principal of the Working Men's College, founded by his grandfather, Frederick Denison Maurice, from 1922 to 1944; Professor of Military Studies, London University, in 1927; Principal of Queen Mary College from 1938 to 1944; President of the British Legion in succession to Earl Haig from 1932 to 1947; and the most distinguished military historian of his time. *

Queen Mary College was evacuated to Cambridge on the outbreak of war in 1939, and when he resigned as Principal in 1944, to his great pride he was made an Honorary Fellow of King's College, which had been host to Queen Mary College until it returned to London.

He spent the last years of his life in Cambridge. From 1949, failing health confined him to the University City he loved. He greatly enjoyed his 80th birthday, and the telegrams and letters from the many who loved, respected and admired him. Every year, he made Christmas a feast for his children and grandchildren.

On the evening before he died, he talked for a long time with his youngest daughter Phyllis, remembering all the famous men he had

* See Biography, p. 237.

176

known, from Ruskin to Churchill. Of those he had known intimately, he said that Asquith had the most brilliant mind, but he
lacked the common touch—he could not communicate. Of Lloyd
George he spoke without rancour, saying that unlike Asquith he
was at pains to keep in close touch with popular opinion; he read
every newspaper every day; he was at his best in a crisis, but he was
incapable of straightforward dealing; even when deviousness was
unnecessary, he used no other method.

In the morning, General Maurice was dead.

This book is his memorial.

NANCY MAURICE
London, May, 1968

Part 5

1 Intrigues of the War
by Major-General Sir Frederick Maurice

MR LLOYD GEORGE'S CONDUCT OF THE WAR

It is customary for soldiers to damn politicians. While this is very natural, it has never seemed to me to be a very useful practice, for no soldier has yet invented an efficient substitute for the politician. It is more profitable, therefore, to try to make politicians better than to condemn them to perdition. As in this pamphlet I shall be very critical of some politicians, I wish to make it clear at once that my criticism will be no vague abuse, but an attempt to get at the truth for the guidance of ourselves and posterity.

I
The Position at the Fall of Mr Asquith's Administration

The general opinion to-day, perhaps less strongly held than it was a year ago, but still very prevalent, is that Mr Asquith's Administration had brought us at the end of 1916 to the verge of ruin, from which we were saved by Mr Lloyd George's advent to power; that Mr Asquith's methods of conducting the war were all wrong and Mr Lloyd George's generally right. This opinion I hold to be erroneous, and so much relating to the conduct of the war has now been published in the countries of all the belligerents that it is possible at length to support my opinion with chapter and verse.

Mr Lloyd George has repeatedly told us that he was called to office at a time when our fortunes were at a very low ebb. From the correspondence which passed between him and Mr Asquith in December, 1916,* we learn that he had a conversation with Mr Asquith on 1 December, and that Mr Asquith wrote to him on that day:

My dear Lloyd George, I have now had time to reflect on our conversation this morning and to study your memorandum. Though I do not

* Published in *Atlantic Monthly*, February, 1919.

altogether share your dark estimate and forecast of the situation, actual and perspective, I am in complete agreement that we have reached a critical situation in the war.

WRONG ASSUMPTIONS

There is therefore no doubt that Mr Lloyd George believed the situation to be desperate, and to require drastic changes in the methods of administration. It was upon that assumption that he made his plans. It was upon that assumption that his methods of conducting the war were based. There is no difficulty now in proving that the assumption had no foundation in fact. Where did Mr Lloyd George get the information on which he based his 'dark estimate and forecast of the situation, actual and perspective'? Not from the naval and military chiefs of the Alliance. On 16 November, 1916, Joffre held a conference at his headquarters at Chantilly to decide upon the plan of campaign for 1917. That conference was attended by Haig and Robertson, by the chiefs of the Russian, Serbian and Roumanian military missions. Of that conference Sir William Robertson says:

The exhausted condition of the German armies was not then as well known to us as it has since become, but we knew sufficient about it to realise the wisdom of taking full advantage of the successes gained in the Verdun and Somme campaigns, first by continuing to exert pressure on the Somme front as far as the winter season would permit, and secondly by preparing to attack the enemy early in 1917 with all the resources that could be made available, before he had time to recover from his difficulties. The Conference decided on a plan of this nature, but it was not carried out.*

Why? That I must leave to the next chapter. I am now concerned with Mr Lloyd George's 'dark estimate and forecast'.

ALLIED GENERALS AGREE

The Allied Generals were thus agreed that the situation was good. What of the enemy generals? Their opinion was even more definite. It will, I think, be conceded that where Hindenburg, Ludendorff, Falkenhayn and Tirpitz are agreed upon a German military problem

* *From Private to Field-Marshal*, Sir W. Robertson, p. 285.

there is little margin for doubt. Hindenburg says of the position at the end of 1916:

There was no doubt that the relative strength of our own and of the enemies' force had changed still more to our disadvantage at the end of 1916 than had been the case at the beginning of the year. Roumania had joined our enemies, and despite her severe defeat she remained an important factor with which we had to reckon. The beaten army found refuge behind the Russian lines, where it gained time to recover and was certain of receiving a large measure of help from the Entente.[*]

Ludendorff is more definite:

We were completely exhausted on the Western front . . . . We now urgently needed a rest. The army had been fought to a standstill and was utterly worn out.

G.H.Q. had to bear in mind that the enemy's great superiority in men and material would be even more painfully felt in 1917 than in 1916. They had to face the danger that 'Somme Fighting' would soon break out at various points on our fronts, and that even our troops would not be able to withstand such attacks indefinitely, especially if the enemy gave us no time for rest and for the accumulation of material.[†]

Ludendorff's chief fear, then, was that the Chantilly plan should be carried out. Tirpitz says of the German situation at the end of 1916:

G.H.Q. doubted seriously whether we could hold out for another year (1917–1918).

It is difficult to say whether if I had been the responsible statesman, knowing all the details then available, I should still have begun the campaign at the beginning of 1917. Our desperate position, of course, hardly left us any other way of escape from complete ruin.[‡]

The 'campaign' to which Tirpitz refers is unlimited U-boat warfare (Germany's last desperate coup), which brought America into the war. Falkenhayn was responsible for planning the battle of Verdun, and he resigned in the middle of the battle of the Somme, because of the failure of his plans. Naturally, therefore, he is on the defensive, and in his book paints the situation in the most

[*] *Ausmeinem Leben*, Hindenburg, p. 220.
[†] *My War Memories*, Ludendorff, Vol. I, p. 307.
[‡] *General Headquarters and its Critical Decisions*, Falkenhayn, p. 289.

favourable light. Yet the best he is able to say of the German position at the end of 1916 is:

The survey of the situation at that time revealed little that was inviting, as well as much that was serious. But there was no grounds for describing it as desperate.

Lastly, Haig in February, 1917, gave an interview to certain French pressmen, in which he described the prospects of victory in 1917 as rosy. This interview, expressing opinions so contrary to his own, so annoyed Mr Lloyd George that he endeavoured to use it as a pretext for getting rid of Haig, but was opposed by the rest of the Cabinet.* There was then amongst the naval and military chiefs on both sides complete agreement that the position of the Allies, at the time when Mr Lloyd George became Prime Minister, was very favourable, and the position of the Germans very serious.

MR LLOYD GEORGE LACKS COURAGE

Why did Mr Lloyd George think otherwise? Because he hadn't the Duke of Wellington's 'One o'clock in the morning courage', the courage which in the midst of troubles and difficulties sees also the enemy's troubles and difficulties. Unrivalled in a sudden crisis, he had not the temperament to endure a long-drawn-out battle, and to give at its end just that extra push which means victory. He was swayed by sentiment. His sentimental affection for small nations caused him to exaggerate the effect of Roumania's defeat and to exaggerate still more the German forces which had brought that defeat about. His views about Roumania were unstable. On 5 December, 1916, he wrote to Mr Asquith:

There has been delay, hesitation, lack of foresight and vision. I have endeavoured repeatedly to warn the Government of the dangers, both verbally and in written memoranda and letters, which I crave your leave to publish if my action is challenged, but I have failed to secure decisions or I have secured them when it was too late to avert the evils. The latest illustration is our lamentable failure to give timely support to Roumania.

Now, early in August, 1916, Mr Lloyd George went to Paris on behalf of Mr Asquith's Government to negotiate with M Briand the agreement which was to bring Roumania into the war. Then was the time for 'forethought and vision', and to arrange for

* *The Press and the General Staff*, Lytton, p. 70.

184

'timely support', but the agreement was concluded with Mr Lloyd George's active assistance, and not until September, when it was too late to save Roumania from her blunders did he, in a Cabinet paper, which found its way somewhat strangely into the *Atlantic Monthly* correspondence, call upon the General Staff to give Roumania succour which he must have known could not have been given in time.

THROWING AWAY VICTORY IN 1917

His early aversion to seeking a decision on the Western Front was strengthened tenfold by the 'bloody assaults of the Somme',* and with his uncanny instinct for divining the trend of public opinion he sensed the effect of that terrible struggle. The Somme was the first great battle of the national armies of the Empire. It first brought the real horrors of war into the homes of the people, and we British hold curious views about war. We are prepared to stand and even to glory in any hammering in defence, but we shudder at any attack which does not bring immediate and visible results. So in his 'dark estimate and forecast' Mr Lloyd George had public opinion with him. Both were wrong. Public opinion needed to be led forward with courage to garner the fruits of the sacrifices of the Somme. Believing there were no fruits Mr Lloyd George threw away the chance of victory in 1917.

II

His Policy and Methods

In December, 1915, Mr Asquith had made a drastic change in the methods of conducting the war. He brought Sir William Robertson home from France, appointed him Chief of the Imperial General Staff, gave him increased powers, and made him directly responsible to the War Committee of the Cabinet for military operations.† The system thus established, together with the reconstruction of the General Staff, which Robertson undertook, brought about a great change in our fortunes. Under this system the respective functions of Ministers and of their military advisers were for the first time

---

* *Mr Lloyd George's Speech in Paris*, 13 November, 1917.
† *From Private to Field-Marshal*, p. 237 *et seq.*

clearly defined, and under this system a situation which in December 1915, after the failures of Gallipoli and Mesopotamia, was indeed gloomy, was changed to one which as I showed in my last chapter was, in December, 1916, full of promise. It took many months before decisions reached in London could become effective on the fighting fronts. Normally, it was six months before a measure passed in Parliament for increasing our manpower could add to our military strength even in the nearest theatre of war, France. So the results of Mr Asquith's system did not end with his term of office. The plans and preparations which brought Maude to Baghdad and wiped out the memory of Kut-el-Amara were all completed before Mr Lloyd George became Prime Minister, and it was preparations similarly made which brought our fighting strength in France at the end of May, 1917, up to the highest point which it ever attained in the course of the war. The vigorous impulse which Mr Lloyd George appeared to give to military affairs in the spring of 1917 had, in fact, been arranged before he became Prime Minister.

HIS INSTINCTIVE DISTRUST

On the false assumption that our affairs were at the end of 1916 going from bad to worse, Mr Lloyd George, on becoming Prime Minister, proceeded to change the system. He had an instinctive distrust of military opinion. He regarded the great influence which Kitchener wielded during the first year of the war as one of the prime causes of our early failure, and believing the situation after a year of Robertson's direction of military affairs to be dark, he would have liked to have curtailed the powers conferred on the Chief of the Imperial General Staff by Mr Asquith, and to have got rid of Haig, but he did not feel strong enough at first to do either of these things. He therefore proceeded to gain his end in other ways. His end was greater control over the conduct of the war. He had been in communication with his friends in France on this subject, and had come to an agreement with them.

M. Painlevé, the forceful man of France, was in communication with Mr Lloyd George, and both were disturbed about the direction of the war particularly in the East. Their point of view was not dissimilar, inasmuch as both wanted to use political machinery to bring about a sort of military revolution in the way of a more vigorous direction of the war.*

* *Mr Lloyd George and the War*, by an Independent Liberal.

The 'sort of military revolution' took place in France first. Joffre was deposed on 12 December, 1916, and Nivelle reigned in his stead.

A COLD DOUCHE

Mr Lloyd George's attempt to put the soldiers in their place followed quickly. Early in January, 1917, a Conference of the Allies produced a plan for transferring from France to the Italian front 300 to 400 medium and heavy guns and several divisions with the object of knocking out Austria.* This was the famous Laibach campaign, to which Mr Lloyd George referred with pride in his speech in Paris on 12 November, 1917. Of this plan none of the Allied military chiefs had any inkling before it was produced at the Conference. Doubtless Mr Lloyd George expected that it would be received in Italy with such enthusiasm as would sweep away the opposition which he anticipated from his own military advisers. But neither the French nor the Italian Ministers were accustomed to making military plans in that way, and his scheme was referred by the Conference to the soldiers for examination and report. This procedure came as a cold douche upon Mr Lloyd George's zeal for the Italian enterprise, and on the return journey from Rome he was caught on the rebound by his French friends, who assured him that they had found in Nivelle the man who could win the war, and that Nivelle had a plan for breaking through on the Western front in a battle which after a short preliminary struggle would be decided one way or the other in forty-eight hours. This plan attracted Mr Lloyd George as offering an alternative to another battle of the Somme. Nivelle was invited to London, where he met the War Cabinet on 14 January, and was promised the whole-hearted support of the British Government.† Two days later Cadorna presented his report on the Italian scheme, warmly approving Mr Lloyd George's plan, and asking alternatively either for at least 300 medium and heavy guns or, to enable a more imposing enterprise to be undertaken, for at least eight Allied divisions.‡

As we were then fully committed to the support of the Nivelle plan, the Laibach scheme was temporarily interred to rise again.

* *La Verité sur l'Offensive du 16 Avril, 1917*, Painlevé, p. 18.
† Ibid.
‡ *La Guerra alla Fronte Italiana*, Cadorna, Vol. II, pp. 36–38.

Just what Cadorna thought when he learned that within a fortnight Mr Lloyd George was backing another plan to that which he had proposed at Rome the Italian general does not say. So within the first six weeks of Mr Lloyd George's administration the Chantilly plan had been thrown over, the Italian plan had been advocated and abandoned, and the Nivelle plan finally adopted, at a time when all discussions as to plans should long have ceased and preparations for the campaign of 1917 been well advanced. Such was 'the more vigorous direction of the war'.

CONFERENCE SECRECY

Having failed at Rome to impose his military ideas on the soldiers, Mr Lloyd George began another attempt to achieve his object. On 1 February he met Major Bértier de Sauvigny, a French officer attached to my staff at the War Office as a liaison officer, and told him that he had complete confidence in Nivelle, and thought that the British forces in France should be placed under his command. 'Doubtless,' he went on,

the prestige which Field-Marshal Haig enjoys with the British public and Army will make it difficult to subordinate him completely to the French command, but if the War Cabinet recognises that such a measure is indispensable it will not hesitate to give Field-Marshal Haig secret instructions in that sense.*

Mr Lloyd George accordingly arranged secretly for a Conference with the French Ministers at Calais at the end of February to discuss the placing of the British Army under Nivelle. It was given out to the British soldiers that the Conference was called to deal with transport difficulties which had arisen on the French railways, and it was attended for that purpose by Sir Eric Geddes, then in charge of railway transport at the War Office. Neither Haig nor Robertson had the least idea of what was afoot, and the proposal to give Nivelle control of the British Army was suddenly sprung upon them in the middle of the Conference and in the presence of our Allies, a situation as embarrassing to Nivelle, who was fully prepared for it, as it was to Haig, who had been kept in complete ignorance.†

* M. Berenger's Report to the French Senate on the Offensive of 1917.
† *From Private to Field-Marshal*, p. 307.

The first French proposal was, from our point of view, unworkable, and had to be modified in a great hurry during the Conference. But a vital measure of this kind required the most careful consideration, and Mr Lloyd George's method of conducting the business of the war made such consideration impossible. As the event proved, the plan was fundamentally defective, for it placed the Commander-in-Chief of one army, who was already fully occupied with the cares and responsibilities of his own front, in control of the Commander-in-Chief of another army. What was required was that one man, provided that the right man could be found, should be placed in general control of the whole front, and relieved of specific responsibility for any one part of it. This was a technical problem of military organisation, but Mr Lloyd George was determined to be his own expert, and the result was a failure. His general idea at this time appears to have been that he should be the modern Pitt. But his historical studies had not taken him sufficiently far to allow him to distinguish between the methods of the elder and the younger Pitt. He does not seem to have known that the strategical methods of William Pitt were disastrous, or that the methods of Chatham needed modification before they were applied to the modern nation in arms. His ruling passion was to get control, which might have worked if he had trusted his generals and they him. Things being as they were, he fell back on the method of trying to gain his ends behind their backs, and the experiences of Rome and Calais did not tend to harmony. In this atmosphere, the fateful campaign of 1917 started.

III
The Nivelle Affair and Its Sequel

The first effect of the 'sort of military revolution in the way of a more vigorous direction of the war', which Mr Lloyd George and his French colleagues had brought about in December, 1916, was the escape of the Germans from their very difficult position on the Somme battlefield, an escape for which Haig was freely blamed at the time. Joffre and Haig had agreed at Chantilly in November, 1916, to press the Germans on the Somme during the winter, and to be ready to resume the offensive on a large scale early in February, 1917.

Unfortunately, Joffre said that the French Army, owing to its heavy losses, would only be able to take the chief part in one more great battle, and that thereafter the burden must fall more and more upon the British Army. He was quite right, as the events, showed, but he was most unwise to give expression to his views. The consequence was that many French soldiers, who viewed with horror the idea of France standing at the end of the war in a secondary position to Great Britain and wanted their army to play a greater part in the campaign of 1917, threw in their lot with the politicians who desired more complete civilian control, and together they brought about Joffre's downfall.

The essence of Nivelle's plan was that the French Army should do more and the British Army less than had been proposed by Joffre. He said to the British War Cabinet on 14 January, 1917,

In proposing this plan of action the French Army, which had already made proportionately far larger sacrifices than any other of the Allied Armies, again assumes the largest share.*

HIS DOMINANT IDEA

It was this, together with the promise that the forthcoming battle should be short, sharp, and decisive, which commended Nivelle's plan to Mr Lloyd George despite Haig's expression of opinion that a decision could not be gained without prolonged and severe preliminary fighting.† At this time Mr Lloyd George's dominant idea was to spare the British Army the losses of another Somme, but, as the experience of war shows, the attempt to save losses by finding a way round or by shifting the burden on to other shoulders often results in greater losses. So it was in this case. To make the French Army stronger in the battle Nivelle required the British Army to take over a longer front during the winter and early spring. This had the result of preventing the British Army from maintaining the pressure on the Germans on the Somme battlefield to the extent which had been agreed upon by Haig and Joffre and of prolonging the necessary preparations. The campaign which Joffre had hoped to begin early in February actually began early in April. A fateful delay of two months. This delay gave the Germans a respite they had not expected, and one of which they took the fullest advantage.

* *La Verité sur l'Offensive du 16 Avril, 1917*, Painlevé, p. 18.
† Ibid, p. 19.

190

The German retreat to the Hindenburg Line began on the British front while the Calais Conference was actually in session, and was discovered and reported by General Gough.* Nivelle, fully occupied with his own concerns, and not in a position to appreciate fully the importance of events on the British front, did not believe in the retreat until the Germans had escaped,† and then, though the data upon which his plan had been formed were no longer applicable, he obstinately adhered to his programme and failed disastrously.

POLITICAL INTERVENTION

But for the political intervention in the conduct of the war in France and Great Britain at the end of 1916, there is every reason to believe that the Germans would have been made to suffer as severely during their retreat in the spring of 1917 as they suffered when retreating over the same ground in September, 1918, the whole programme of the year's campaign would have been antedated by two months, the Germans would have been heavily punished before the untimely break in the weather of August, 1917, which involved us in the muddy horror of Passchendaele, we should have left the Germans no leisure to prepare the attack upon Italy, we might have prevented the complete collapse of the Russian Armies, which did not take place until July, 1917, and the victory in 1917 which Kitchener had promised might well have been realised.‡ Such were the fatal consequences of Mr Lloyd George's mistaken assumption that the situation in December, 1916, was dark and could only be brightened by his personal direction of our strategy.

The collapse of Nivelle's offensive had the most disastrous consequences in France. It was followed by a period of deep depression, both amongst the French public and in the Army. A series of mutinies broke out on the front which crippled the military power of France for many months, and Pétain, who had succeeded Nivelle, had to call upon Haig to keep the Germans occupied while he restored the *morale* of his troops. Soon after the collapse of the Russian Army became certain, while the unlimited U-boat warfare produced a crisis in our maritime communications. The situation had indeed become dark, and was relieved only by America's entry

* *From Private to Field-Marshal*, p. 308.
† *La Verité sur l'Offensive du 16 Avril, 1917*, Painlevé, p. 23.
‡ *From Private to Field-Marshal*, p. 264.

into the war. It was clear that America's military aid would not be considerable until the summer of 1918, and that till then the *Entente* Powers would have to face a period of danger. In these circumstances the Allied Commanders-in-Chief and Chiefs of Staff agreed in July, 1917, that it was necessary to reduce all commitments in secondary theatres of war to a minimum, and to strengthen the Western Front as much as possible. We could play our part in this programme by relieving British troops in Palestine, Mesopotamia, and in Salonika by Indian troops, who, as experience had shown, could not be employed effectively on the Western Front, and by keeping our forces in France up to strength by means of drafts from home. I will leave to a later chapter the question of secondary theatres of war, but must now say a word on the question of manpower, one of the prime concerns of the War Cabinet.

DECLINING FIGHTING POWER

Mr Lloyd George had come into power to give a more energetic impulse to the conduct of the war, and it was expected that he would at once proceed to develop to the fullest extent our military resources. The contrary proved to be the case. I have already pointed out that it took about six months for a measure affecting manpower to produce rifles in the trenches in France. The Military Service Act of 1916 enabled our fighting strength in France to be brought to its highest point in June, 1917, and from then it steadily declined. As early as November, 1916, the General Staff had foreseen that this would be so, and Sir William Robertson had then asked for an extension of the age of military service.*

Owing to the change of Government in the following December nothing was done at the time, and the measures which Mr Lloyd George took on becoming Prime Minister were wholly inadequate.

The difficulty of providing drafts in 1917 can be understood when I say that while we then had on the West Front a greater number of divisions than before, the fighting being prolonged and severe, we took into the Army only 820,000 men, as against 1,200,000 in the previous year,†

and the greater part of these 820,000 men were provided by measures taken before Mr Lloyd George became Prime Minister.

* Ibid, p. 303.   † Ibid., p. 301.

In the summer of 1917, when it had become obvious that it was necessary to provide more men for the danger period, the Army Council pressed the War Cabinet to extend the military age.* Nothing effective was done until January, 1918, when minor amendments to the Military Service Act of 1916 were introduced. These gave the Army 100,000 'A' men, a number absurdly less than the Army Council had asked for, and not one of these men was trained in time to go into the trenches to meet the great German attack of March, 1918. Sir Auckland Geddes, in introducing this measure, said that the Cabinet was satisfied that no extension of the age for military service was necessary.† On 9 April, 1918, after the German attack had taken place, after it had become necessary to break up 25% of the British battalions in France to provide drafts for the remainder, and after we had suffered enormous losses which we need not have suffered had timely provision been made, the Prime Minister brought forward the proposals for increasing the age of service which Robertson had asked for in November, 1916. Determined to run the war in his own way, Mr Lloyd George was alternately quarrelling with and disregarding his military advisers, and the result was that throughout 1917 he was too late. With strange prescience, he at the end of 1915 foretold the fatal error of his own conduct of the war.

Too late in moving here! Too late in arriving there! Too late in coming to a decision! Too late in starting with enterprises! Too late in preparing! In this war the footsteps of the Allied forces have been dogged by the mocking spectre of Too Late!‡

IV
The Versailles Council

For a brief moment after the failure of Nivelle's attack, Mr Lloyd George was in agreement with his soldiers. Haig and Robertson were clear that if the Germans were given a respite they would be free to crush the Russian armies which Kerensky was endeavouring to rally

* *Experiences of a Dug-Out*, Callwell.
† House of Commons, 14 January, 1918.
‡ House of Commons, 20 December, 1915.

for an offensive, or to attack Italy, and early in May, 1917, at a conference in Paris, the Prime Minister stoutly pressed the French to continue the fight on the Western front. But very soon after this conference the French army became incapable for a time of taking an equal share in the struggle, and Mr Lloyd George again changed his mind. Fresh plans followed one upon the other. It is not my purpose to enlarge upon the evils which accompany the tendency to change from one plan to another, at bewilderingly short intervals and without sufficient military reason, beyond observing that it has an unsettling effect on the troops, and monopolises much of the time of commanders and their staffs which ought to be given to other matters. At a guess I would say that in 1917 at least 20% of the time of the General Staff at the War Office was occupied in explaining either verbally or in writing that the alternative projects put forward were either strategically unsound or were wholly impracticable.*

'SO EASY!'

The proposal to send troops to Italy in order to crush Austria reappeared, and a new plan for a landing at Alexandretta in rear of the Turkish army in Palestine was proposed.† It is so easy to pick up a pin from a map and to move it from one continent to another; it is so difficult to foresee what the enemy may do while the troops, who cannot fight when they are on the move, are getting to their places. I have said that Mr Lloyd George, full of courage when his blood was hot in a crisis, lacked 'one o'clock in the morning courage'. Full of imagination of a kind, he lacked that particular kind of imagination which is needed to guess what is happening or may happen 'on the other side of the hill'. Great on a small-scale map, which showed the world with the surface of a billiard ball, he examined large-scale maps, which displayed the features of the ground and those obstacles of terrain which mean so much to military movement, with equal interest both upside down and right way up. None of this would have mattered in the least had he been satisfied to choose his expert and to rely upon that expert's advice in technical matters, but it was the very devil when he sought to be his own expert.

* *From Private to Field-Marshal*, p. 319.
† Ibid, p. 315.

When all hope of wringing success from Nivelle's plans disappeared, Mr Lloyd George's temporary devotion to the Western Front disappeared too. It is notorious that he was bitterly opposed to Haig's campaign in Flanders, which culminated in the battle of Passchendaele. But the risks of leaving the Germans free to attack the French, while Pétain was in need of breathing space in order to restore the fighting spirit of his army, were so obvious that Mr Lloyd George's plans for finding a way round either through Laibach or Constantinople were overruled. Evidently he felt that deeply, for in Paris, on 12 November, 1917, he said:

But when the military power of Russia collapsed in March, what took place? If Europe had been treated as one battlefield you might have thought that when it was clear that a great army which was operating on one flank could not come up in time, or even come into action at all, there would have been a change in strategy. Not in the least.

His plans had been thwarted, and he pointed with accusing finger to the consequences. 'Look at the horrible slaughter of Passchendaele. Look at the disaster on the Italian front.' He was able to say to those who opposed him, 'If only my advice had been followed, and we had sent troops to fight in the mountains of Italy, instead of in the mud of Flanders.' The opportunities for rhetorical argument were unlimited, and the soldiers' 'Think what might have happened if we had weakened the Western Front at this time, when the French Army is temporarily *hors de combat*', was in the face of apparent failure an ineffective reply. So early in November Mr Lloyd George saw his way clear to a further step towards obtaining control, and at the height of the crisis on the Italian front he rushed off to Rapallo, and there instituted the Supreme War Council.

It has been generally assumed that this Council was created in the teeth of bitter opposition from the soldiers. This is pure fiction. It had long been felt that some such body was needed for the better co-ordination of Allied policy and plans. I was the General Staff Officer referred to by Mr Lloyd George as having assisted him in drafting the constitution of the Council,* and I was able to do the work very quickly, for some such plan had been considered for months previously.

* House of Commons, 19 November, 1917.

'It was proposed,' said Mr Lloyd George, speaking in the House on 19 November, 'in July this year, at a meeting of the Commanders-in-Chief. I forget whether all were there, but the Chiefs of Staff were. At any rate Sir William Robertson, General Pershing, General Cadorna, and General Foch were there. They recommended, as a means of dealing with the situation, the setting up of an inter-Allied Council.'

Why was the Council not set up before? The soldiers wanted it, the French Government was eager to have it. Because Mr Lloyd George wanted a particular form of Council, and not until Passchendaele had brought discredit on the soldiers' strategy and credit upon his strategical vision and foresight was he able to get his way. He had found it hard to get his way when his strategy was opposed by Haig and Robertson, so he bethought him of the old political maxim. '*Divide et impera*,' said the Roman, and he wanted to rule. He therefore insisted that the British Military representative on the Versailles Council should be entirely independent of the Chief of the Imperial General Staff, and should give his advice directly to the War Cabinet. With two advisers, Mr Lloyd George did not need to make a large draft upon his skill in order to play off one against the other, and so get his way.

POLITICAL CONTROL

It seems clear that, in setting up the Council, the real object of Ministers was not so much to provide effective unity of military command as to acquire for themselves a greater control over the military chiefs. That there was no intention of unifying the command by the appointment of an Allied Commander-in-Chief seems equally evident, not only from the constitution of the Council itself, but also from the fact that a few days later the Prime Minister stated in the House of Commons* that he was 'utterly opposed' to the appointment of a Generalissimo, as it 'would produce real friction and might create prejudice not merely between the armies but between the nations and Government'.† The Versailles Council was an admirable institution, and it did excellent work. It systematised the business and methods of the frequent conferences of Allied Ministers, and provided a much-needed clearing house for the affairs of the Entente Powers. It never was and never could be

* House of Commons, 19 November, 1917.
† *From Private to Field-Marshal*, p. 320.

an effective means of exercising command over the Allied forces. That was a problem which, at the end of 1917, remained to be solved, and with Germany rapidly transferring troops from her Eastern to her Western front it became increasingly urgent that it should be solved. The story of its solution I must leave to another chapter.

Tacked on to the constitution of the Versailles Council was the purely British condition which supplied the British Government with a new and independent adviser, and more particularly supplied Mr Lloyd George with the bit for which he had long been seeking, the bit which he hoped would enable him to control the unruly soldiery which would not accept his views on strategy at the value placed upon them by himself and his friends. There is much to be said for a dictatorship in time of war, provided that the dictator has the knowledge to direct both strategy and policy, or knows how to use his experts, and trusts them. There is nothing to be said for a system under which a Prime Minister and his experts seek to win a war by different methods. Circumstances prevented Mr Lloyd George from working openly for his end. The prestige which Field-Marshal Haig enjoyed with the British public and Army* made this difficult, and he had to resort to the manoeuvres of Calais and Rapallo. But, as he gradually saw his way more clearly, Mr Lloyd George took less and less pains to conceal his distrust of Haig and Robertson. 'You must either succour or sack,' said to him one of his colleagues given to epigram and alliteration. He would not succour and he dared not sack, and with this deadweight of disagreement as to the higher direction of the war on his shoulders he drifted into the dangers of the spring of 1918.

V
Troops Kept in Palestine

In January, 1918, the paramount fact in the military situation was that the Germans were bringing divisions from the Russian Front into France and Belgium as fast as their railways could transport

* Mr Lloyd George's statement to Major Berthier—*Berenger Report*.

the troops. To meet this situation the British General Staff continued to press the Government to give effect to the recommendations made by the Allied Commanders-in-Chief and Chiefs-of-Staff in Paris, including Foch, in July, 1917, that we should act defensively in the secondary theatres of war and bring back as many British troops as possible to France. We had at the end of 1917 not less than 1,200,000 men in distant parts, and a large number of British troops could have been sent from the East to help Haig to meet the expected German attack without the smallest risk to our Oriental interests.* But Mr Lloyd George was, after Passchendaele, more than ever convinced that the barrier in the West was impenetrable alike by ourselves and by the Germans, and was therefore opposed to sending more men to France. He foresaw a period of anxious defensive struggle on the Western front, and was eager for political reasons to compensate for this by success in the East. Therefore he urged that Allenby should attack and drive the Turks out of Palestine, and forbade the transfer to Haig of any of the 100,000 British troops in that theatre of war. There was thus a direct conflict of opinion between the Prime Minister and the Allied soldiers.†

OPPOSED TO GENERALISSIMO

Was the barrier in the West impenetrable? Was the Western Front safe? These were the questions that went to the root of the matter, and Mr Lloyd George believed he could answer them. The Germans would certainly be able to attack in the early spring, and it was to be expected that while threatening various parts of the Allied Front they would make a great effort against one part, but they would not have any marked superiority of numbers on the whole front, and it was clear that the right answer for the defence was it should be under one authority, able to decide at once as to the point of danger, and controlling ample reserves. It was now evident to the statesmen that the Versailles Council was not such an authority. Something more was necessary. What form should this something more take? The idea still very prevalent that Mr Lloyd George had to struggle for unity of command against a narrow-minded soldiery is absurdly wide of the truth. The soldiers wanted a workable scheme of military command, but Mr Lloyd George had expressed

* *From Private to Field-Marshal*, p. 324.
† Ibid, p. 317.

himself in the strongest terms as opposed to the creation of a generalissimo; therefore some other solution had to be found.* The Versailles Council met at the end of January, 1918, to find this solution and to agree upon the main lines of the campaign for 1918. At this meeting of the council Mr Lloyd George propounded his Palestine plan, which was opposed by M Clemenceau. Eventually it was agreed as a compromise that Allenby should attack, provided that no reinforcements were diverted from the Western Front to Palestine. Robertson protested, as he wanted to bring troops from Palestine to France, but was overruled. Then came the question of command. After a prolonged discussion Mr Lloyd George's proposal to form a strategic reserve for the Western Front, and to place this reserve under an Executive Committee of the Versailles Council composed of the military representatives at Versailles of the Allies, with General Foch as chairman, was accepted, and he came home satisfied that the Western Front was safe. Robertson again protested, after putting forward an alternative plan, and was removed from his position as Chief of the Imperial General Staff.

NO STRATEGIC RESERVE

Now, in fact, the strategic reserve was never formed, and the Executive Committee never exercised any real functions, for reasons which I will explain. It is upon this hangs the defence of Mr Lloyd George's policy. If, argue his friends, the Committee had been allowed to work and the reserve had been formed, the disaster to the Fifth Army would never have occurred, but the Committee was torpedoed by Pétain, Haig and Robertson. What happened? The Committee met and called upon the Commanders-in-Chief to provide contingents for the strategic reserve. Haig was asked to supply eight divisions, and replied on 3 March that he could not furnish them. The British Commander-in-Chief was extraordinarily well served by his intelligence department, and by the end of February he had come to the conclusion that the main German attack would be made against the Third and Fifth Armies.† Owing to the political pressure which the French Government had brought to bear upon the British Government he had been compelled to make a large extension of the front of the Fifth Army in relief of French

* House of Commons, 19 November, 1917.
† Sir Douglas Haig's Despatches, p. 182.

troops. He had had to send five divisions to Italy in November, and had received none in return, nor had the losses of Passchendaele been made good. In default of drafts from home he had had to break up 25% of his British infantry battalions in order to find men for the remainder. In these circumstances he could not garnish his whole front to meet the coming attack, and he decided that he could best take risks on the front of the Fifth Army, which was nearer to the French and had more room to give ground than had the armies further north.* Had he furnished the reserves which the Executive Committee asked for, these reserves must in the main have come from the troops which in the event supported the Third Army in the battle. Now Ludendorff tells us that his plan was to break through north of the Somme—that is, on the Third Army front—and to use the Somme to hold off the French while he rolled up the British Army. It was only when he found that he was not succeeding as he had hoped north of the Somme that he agreed to let the Crown Prince follow up south of the river against the Fifth Army what seemed to be an easily won success, towards Amiens.† If Haig had let the reserves go Ludendorff's plan would almost certainly have succeeded, for the Executive Committee at Versailles, not in as close touch with events as were the Commanders-in-Chief, after such debate as always takes place in committee, after satisfying itself that the main attack was really against Haig, a fact of which Pétain was still doubtful on the sixth day of the battle, would only have released the reserves much later than did Haig, and they could not have arrived in time to save the Third Army, which would have been involved in the disaster of the Fifth Army, with consequences far more serious. Be it remembered that the Committee controlled only the reserves, and left the Commanders-in-Chief entirely responsible for their armies. The Versailles decision did not give Foch any voice whatever in the disposition of the troops on the front. Had Haig sent the reserves away, he would have endangered his army, the safety of the Channel ports, and the whole Allied cause. His refusal was completely justified, and was upheld at an Allied Conference held in London on 14 March, which in effect put an end to the Executive Committee on the eve of the battle.‡

* Sir Douglas Haig's Despatches, p. 183.
† *My War Memoirs*, Ludendorff, Vol. II, p. 590.
‡ *Comment finir la Guerre*, Général Mangin, p. 167.

Mr Lloyd George repeated at Versailles the blunder he had made at Calais eleven months before. His object was to obtain unity of direction, but he desired to do this without sacrificing his own influence upon the strategy of the war. He therefore, knowing how eager the French were to take any step which would lead to control by themselves of the operations on the Western Front, forced through a plan which his experience of conferences led him to think would be accepted, without giving Haig and Robertson time to work out the military effect of the proposal. This plan divided the forces in France still more than they had been divided before. A portion was left under the control of the Commanders-in-Chief, another portion was placed under a committee, and command by committee has always failed in war. In this instance the Committee, being composed of representatives of different nations, was doubly defective. It proceeded to bargain. The French would produce so many divisions for the reserve, the Italians so many, if the British provided so many more. The right way to approach the problem was to regard the front as a whole, without consideration of the nationality of the troops on the front, and to decide what parts of the front could afford to give up reserves for the benefits of those parts which might need support, but to such a committee this was impossible. These matters and the more technical problems of the rate at which reserves could be delivered at the front were beyond Mr Lloyd George's competence, but he gave the soldiers no chance of considering them before the Committee was formed. He succeeded however, in preserving the position he had won at Rapallo. The British representative on the Committee was to be entirely free and independent of the British Commander-in-Chief and the British Chief of the General Staff, and was to have power to issue orders to the British portion of the reserve. The Prime Minister was thus sure of being able, if need were, to play off one soldier against another and preserve his own influence. A curious form of unity. Divided forces and divided command.

ABSURD INTRIGUE RUMOURS

The absurd charge has been made that Haig and Pétain engaged in an intrigue to prevent Foch from controlling the reserves. In fact,

Haig, on studying the effect of the Versailles decisions, found them to be unworkable, and at once proceeded to concert with Pétain arrangements for mutual support. Foch was fully informed of the results of the conferences which ensued between the two Commanders-in-Chief, and his representatives were present at the more detailed discussions between the two Staffs. It was on Haig's initiative that the Conference at Doullens, which placed Foch in control, was held; it was he, not Mr Lloyd George, who supported enthusiastically the creation of a generalissimo, and it was he who proposed that Foch should be nominated.* With that nomination unity of command on military instead of political principles was established, and with it passed away Mr Lloyd George's influence on strategy. The German attack was stayed, but only after we had suffered losses more terrible than we had endured in any corresponding period of the war, and, after the blow had fallen, all those measures were taken which Mr Lloyd George had resolutely opposed throughout the summer and autumn of 1917. It is, of course, true that Mr Lloyd George accepted Foch's appointment when it was notified to him, and as long as Foch was sending troops to help us the generalissimo naturally enough received the fullest support from our Government; but on the first occasion on which the process was reversed, when Foch called upon Haig to supply eight British divisions to help him make the counter-attack of 18 July, 1918, which resulted in the victory of the second battle of the Marne and turned the tide of war in our favour, the Government threw the entire responsibility for weakening the British front upon Haig, who insisted that, having appointed Foch generalissimo, it was our duty to support him in his plans. In a small book which I wrote in 1919 I applauded that decision as a mark of Mr Lloyd George's courage and readiness to take risks.† I have since learned that the courage was Haig's alone. The initiative, both in the appointment of Foch and in supporting him when appointed, came from the British Commander-in-Chief, not from the British Prime Minister.

* 'Lord Milner's report on the Doullens Conference', *New Statesman*, 23 April, 1921.
† *The Last Four Months*, Maurice, p. 70.

VI
Plan to Remove Haig

When the crisis came Mr Lloyd George was splendid. While others wavered and began to give us hope, he never lost his faith in victory, and with rare energy he repaired in a few weeks all the errors of omission of the previous year. His vigour and courage in the dark days of the spring of 1918 won for him the admiration and the devotion of his colleagues, of whom few knew the full story of the events which I have narrated in previous chapters.

We all of us admire the man who risks his life to save the occupants of the house which he has set on fire, and our admiration is the greater when we do not know the cause of the conflagration. It is only on reflection that we realise that the man who takes precautions to prevent fire is the more useful citizen. The sole precaution which had been taken to meet the German attack was the establishment of the futile Executive Committee, agreed to by M. Clemenceau because of Mr Lloyd George's assurance that the British Government would go no further towards unity of command, but after the event everything that was possible was done.

In January, 1918, the Government had decided that an additional 100,000 men would meet the needs of the Army. In April 400,000 more were provided, and so the 500,000 men whom Robertson had asked for in July, 1917, were found. One complete British division was brought to France from Italy and two more from Palestine. Indian battalions took the place of British battalions in four other divisions in Palestine, and the British battalions so released were used to reconstitute four shattered British divisions in France.

THE VITAL FRONT

The Western Front had suddenly become, even in the eyes of the War Cabinet, the vital front, and, be it noted, these measures did not prevent the overthrow of the Turk or the defeat of the Bulgar. Wisdom after the event is better than no wisdom at all, but it is a costly commodity, and we had to buy it at the price of 300,000 casualties within the space of five short weeks—that is, nearly 70,000 more than we suffered in the fourteen weeks of the battle of Passchendaele. We lost 1,000 guns, vast quantities of stores, and were brought to the brink of defeat.

We were saved by Haig's cool leadership, by the stubborn valour of the British soldiery, by the fierce energy with which Foch filled the gap between the British and the French armies, and by Mr Lloyd George's power of rising to heights in an emergency.

Unfortunately, immediately the first crisis was passed Mr Lloyd George reverted to his former methods. He had rid himself of Robertson, and he now saw a chance of ridding himself of Haig.

I come now to the events which caused me to intervene.

On 9 April, on introducing the measure to extend the age of military service to 51, Mr Lloyd George stated that our Armies in France were stronger than they had been in the former year, and denied that forces which might have been in France had been kept in the East. Lord Curzon, coached by the Prime Minister, made similar statements simultaneously in the House of Lords.

FEELING IN FRANCE

I did not know of these statements at the time when they were made, for the German offensive in Flanders began on 9 April, and I was much too occupied to read speeches. On 13 April I went to France, and I there heard that the Prime Minister's statements on 9 April had aroused great indignation as tending to throw the whole responsibility for failure unfairly upon Haig, at a time when he required all the support, both moral and physical, which the Government could give him.

I promised to go into the matter on my return to London, and on 20 April, I procured copies of Hansard, and then for the first time realised how misleading the statements of Ministers were. While I was still considering the best course to take, I read on 24 April a statement made by Mr Bonar Law in reply to a question in the House that the arrangement for the extension of the front of the Fifth Army before the battle was purely a military one, that is to say that the responsibility for the extension was again Haig's alone.

Simultaneously I learned that a scheme for removing Haig from the supreme command in France was coming rapidly to a head. I had then handed over my work in the War Office to my successor and was awaiting appointment to a command in France. Being free, I went away for a week to the country to think quietly. I say this to show that I acted on no sudden impulse. On 30 April I wrote to the Chief of the Imperial General Staff calling his attention to the incorrect statements of Ministers and to their effect in France.

Getting no reply and believing the matter to be one of extreme urgency, I decided to take the grave step of challenging publicly the statement of Ministers.

I had made up my mind that I must act alone, as I could not brief anyone without disclosing confidential information, which I would not do. I therefore communicated with no one even remotely connected with the Press, and the only person in any way connected with politics whom I consulted was Lord Salisbury, to whom I told only what I had heard in France.

JUSTICE IN OUR CAUSE

I repeat this because it is still said that I was concerned in a political conspiracy. I was concerned to prevent what appeared to me to be action fatal to our cause. I believed the moral strength which the justice of our cause gave us was our chief asset, and that we should impair and even destroy altogether that moral strength if the Government, after refusing throughout the latter half of 1917 to take the steps which the soldiers had urged upon them to meet the German attack, threw the blame for the March disaster upon the soldiers, and then removed Haig. I believed that a public challenge would have the effect of making known to the whole Cabinet the facts as to the strength of our armies in France and in the East, and would stop the attacks upon Haig.

I knew that I was sacrificing a career of some promise and giving up my means of livelihood, but I believed that I was acting rightly, and that if I was right I would not suffer materially. I had no political motive and took no part in the political events which followed my letter to the Press. It would have been easy for me to go to the House of Commons and coach those who were ready to attack Ministers. I stayed in the country.

The statements which I challenged were Mr Lloyd George's of 9 April that the strength of the Army in 1918 had been more than maintained as compared with 1917, that in Egypt and Palestine there was a very small proportion of British as compared with Indian troops, and Mr Bonar Law's of 23 April that the extension of the British front which took place before the battle was an arrangement made solely by the military authorities.

The facts are beyond dispute. The total strength of the Army in France on 1 January, 1917, was 1,299,000, and on 1 January, 1918, was 1,570,000, but in 1918 there were included in the total strength 300,000 unarmed British labourers and Chinese coolies who did not appear in the 1917 figures, while the fighting troops in 1918 were more than 100,000 weaker, and between 1 January and 21 March, when the Germans attacked, Haig had to disband 140 battalions for lack of men to replace the losses we had suffered. In Palestine and Egypt there were at the beginning of March 213,600 white troops and 37,300 native troops. The extension of the front of the Fifth Army was undertaken because of the pressure which M. Clemenceau brought to bear on our Government.

These being the facts, the case against Haig collapsed, though Mr Lloyd George, handling the facts as a juggler does a pack of cards, won a political triumph. His misstatements were, I believe, in part due to his disposition to interpret facts to suit conclusions already formed, and in part to the organisation with which he had surrounded himself. He had established a special Prime Minister's secretariat in the garden of No. 10 Downing Street, and this department, independent of all other Government departments, had a tendency, natural enough in the circumstances, to look for the information which the Prime Minister required, and to give to the information a colour suited to his views, a process which in military matters was easy, as the department had no one to tell them how to interpret figures supplied by the War Office, or to explain that unarmed Chinese coolies were not a valuable reinforcement for Gough's thin line. The Prime Minister's secretariat made it possible for him to be a dictator, but did not supply him with the means to dictate wisely.

PREMIER AND STRATEGY

As I have said in a previous chapter, with Foch at the helm Mr Lloyd George's influence upon strategy ceased. He was the Prime Minister when victory came, therefore he was the man who won the war. He still, if one may judge from his speeches, believes that his strategy was right and the soldiers' strategy all wrong. If we are ever to be engaged in another world war, which God forbid, it is vital that the facts should be known.

Mr Lloyd George's strength as a War Minister was his faith in victory and his power of keeping the confidence of the public. His weaknesses were his belief in his military judgment, his power of deceiving himself, his failure to understand that opportunism, sometimes successful in peace, is highly dangerous in war, and, above all, his misconception of the qualities which are required in a leader in war, and his lack of appreciation of the vital importance to a Commander-in-Chief in the field of support from the Government at home. He wanted soldiers quick of wit and clever in council, and had no sense of the importance of character and determination in the field.

He could never bring himself to encourage Haig in the way in which Mr Asquith encouraged his Commanders-in-Chief. He could never see the need for such a system of bringing the functions of the statesman and soldier into harmony as Mr Asquith adopted. The consequences were that he missed the chance of victory in 1917, and brought us nearer to defeat in the spring of 1918 than we had ever been, while the final triumph was won by methods which he had previously opposed with all the vigour at his command.

2 The Defeat of the Fifth Army
by Major-General Sir Frederick Maurice

At the end of 1917 there were few who believed that complete military victory over our chief enemy was possible. Had any one dared to prophesy that the following year would see the collapse of Germany's military power and our arms everywhere triumphant, he would have been regarded as an irresponsible optimist. The French Army had not fully recovered from the shock of the failure of General Nivelle's offensive in the spring. Our own Army was exhausted by the slow, bloody struggle through the mud of Flanders up the ridges from Ypres to Passchendaele, and was grievously disappointed that the brilliant promise of the tank attack at Cambrai in November had ended in one more failure. The Italian Army had met with all but overwhelming disaster, and both we and our French Allies had had to weaken materially our forces on the Western Front in order to bring help to our friends in the southern theatres of war. Worst of all, the collapse of Russia was definite and complete, and German divisions were streaming from the eastern to the western theatre of war. It had become a certainty that in 1918 Germany would be able for the first time in the war to concentrate in France and Flanders almost her full military strength. Speaking in the House of Commons on 14 January, 1918, Sir Auckland Geddes stated that the secession of Russia from the Allies had added to the potential enemy strength on the Western front, including Italy, as many as 1,600,000 men, without taking into consideration the reserves which would otherwise have been required for service on the Russian front. By that time it was evident that the Germans were moving this great mass of troops westwards as fast as the capacity of an excellent network of railways would admit, and it had long been obvious that the most careful preparation was necessary to meet the eventuality of a great enemy offensive delivered against us or against the French or against both.

While we were attacking, and could choose our own time and place for giving battle, it was possible for the Allied Commanders-in-Chief to draw up their plans in unison. That unison had not always been complete, and there had been waste of power and of opportunity, but it had passed muster, and the weakness of the system of divided command had not been sufficient to outweigh the political objections to placing the army of one nation under the control of the general of another. The disaster which the Italian Army suffered at Caporetto frightened the Allied Governments into action, and they agreed at a conference held in November, 1917, at Rapallo, on the Franco-Italian Frontier, to establish at Versailles a Supreme War Council, with a permanent military and political secretariat. This Versailles Council provided a permanent and efficient organisation for the preparation of the business of the Conference of Allied statesmen, which had till then been somewhat irregular and lacking in method. It also furnished useful machinery for collecting, sifting, and co-ordinating, information obtained from each of the Allied Armies and for formulating general military policy; but it was not, and could not be an effective instrument of military command. The Versailles secretariat, as established at Rapallo, had authority to advise the Allied Governments as to military plans, but it had no authority to issue orders to the Allied Armies. Military command, to be effective, must have both power and the capacity to issue prompt orders in accordance with daily or even hourly changes in the situation, and to be able to supervise the execution of the orders issued. The Versailles Council could not do this, and therefore its institution was but a small step forward towards unity of command.

While we were wrangling about this vital question, the German Armies on the Western front were steadily growing in strength, and effective measures to meet the menace they presented became more and more urgent. When there are two commanders-in-chief in charge of armies side by side upon one front, each naturally and properly looks first to the safety of his own army, and to the protection of the vital interests which are in his charge. As long as there remains any doubt as to where the enemy means to attack, each is disposed to believe that the blow will fall upon him, and, as in duty bound, he takes measures accordingly. This is a position which any skilful enemy will turn to his own advantage, and it is a commonplace of war that in it lies one of the main sources of strength of a single homogeneous army fighting against an alliance. Napoleon owed many of his greatest triumphs to his appreciation of this weak point in the armour of any confederacy. Something better than a Versailles Council was needed, and at the end of January, 1918, the Supreme War Council met at Versailles for the express purpose of finding this something better. Another compromise between political exigencies and military necessities was the result. No one general in the Allied ranks had then established a reputation which entitled him to a position of supreme and unfettered control, and, failing this, no one had the courage to brush aside national *amour-propre* and professional prejudice; each army and each nation had to be represented in the supreme command. An executive military committee of the Versailles Council was established under the chairmanship of General Foch, composed of distinguished generals from the British, French, Italian, and American Armies, and was given somewhat limited powers to prepare plans and issue orders for their execution. Never in the history of war has a committee, though it has been tried again and again, been able to command successfully. A committee almost invariably results in compromise and delay, both of which are fatal in war. A polyglot committee, composed of generals each responsible to a separate government, was bound to be slow and hesitating in action, for each general, when a decision was proposed which involved risks to the army or to the national interests represented by him, would almost certainly refer the matter to his Government. Unfortunately, democratic statesmen do not study the history of war, and they returned home from Versailles convinced that they had provided a combination able to challenge Hindenburg and Ludendorff.

Apart altogether from the question of command, the certainty that Germany was about to make a final effort to win the war in the West made it prudent that everything possible should be done to strengthen our forces there. General Allenby's victories in Palestine and the capture of Jerusalem had removed all danger to Mesopotamia and to Egypt, and we had around Jerusalem and Baghdad many more troops than were necessary to secure our position in the East. Not a man, however, was moved to reinforce Sir Douglas Haig until after the German blow had fallen, and our armies had suffered the most serious reverse which befell us during the whole course of the war. It was even more necessary that the heavy losses incurred in the fierce fighting which took place during the autumn and early winter of 1917 should be made good. Our troops were wearied with their efforts, and it was of the first importance that as many of them as possible should be taken out of the line for rest and training, but the ranks were so depleted, that it was not possible to spare from the front anything like the full proportion of divisions which should have been in training areas behind.

The natural and normal experience on the Western front during the war was that at the end of the year's campaign the losses in battle had greatly exceeded the flow of drafts from home, with the result that the fighting troops had not at the end of the year their full complement of men. During the winter the conditions of weather and of ground put a stop to operations on a grand scale, and the losses were comparatively small. This, then, was the time to bring the army up to strength in preparation for the campaign which might be expected in the spring. Thus in December, 1916 the ranks of the fighting troops had been heavily depleted by the long and bitter struggle on the Somme and on the Aisne, but by April, 1917, that is to say, on the eve of the battle of Arras, the ranks were again full, and Sir Douglas Haig had been provided with considerable additional reinforcements. Yet, despite the danger which threatened us, no corresponding measures were taken during the early months of 1918, and in fact during those months the shortage of men became so acute that it was impossible for Sir Douglas Haig to maintain his army any longer at the strength at which it had been during the previous autumn. Between the middle of January and the middle of February, three battalions out of the thirteen of each of the British divisions were broken up, and the men in them used to take the place of drafts from home and to fill up the ranks of the remaining battalions. Worse still, the French Army was also declining in strength, and the French Government became more and more insistent that we should take over a longer stretch of the front. General Pétain at this time thought it extremely probable that the German attack would be made upon him, and he did not feel himself able to meet such an attack unless we relieved some of his troops. Accordingly, in December and January, Sir Douglas Haig had to take over an additional twenty-eight miles of front and to extend his line south of the Somme as far as the River Oise. This new front fell to our 5th Army, which had borne the brunt of the fighting at Passchendaele. The discussion as to the extension of the front had gone on for some time, and the French troops holding this section had become aware that they would be relieved. Therefore, human nature being what it is, they had left it to us to complete the defensive arrangements necessary to meet a great German attack. So it came about that General Gough's 5th Army, which was urgently in need of rest, had in the few weeks which preceded the German attack to familiarise itself with new ground and to work incessantly at the erection of new defences. Actually then, our preparations for meeting the threat which Ludendorff held over us were that we had agreed with our Allies to vest the supreme command in the hands of an executive committee, we had reduced the number of infantry battalions at Haig's disposal by close on 25%, and had at the same time increased our liabilities by taking over twenty-eight miles of new front, this new front being one of the most important sectors of the whole long line, for it covered the roads leading to Amiens and to Paris. Against this important reduction in the strength of the army we could set an increase in the number of tanks, guns, and machine guns, due to the steady increase in the output of our munition factories; but, as events turned out, the defensive power of these weapons was to a great extent neutralised by an accident of war. The one bright spot in the picture was the entry of America into the war, and the arrival of American troops in France. But America had to create her army almost from the beginning. Her standing army was very small, and she decided to use her trained officers and men to leaven the ranks of her new forces. It would therefore take time before she could intervene effectively, and she could not be expected to take any large part in the spring campaign.

It will naturally be asked how it came about that we did not do more to prepare for the great German attack which was expected long before it took place. Throughout 1917 the fighting strength of the Allies on the Western front had been considerably greater than that of the Germans. We had made repeated efforts to break through the vast network of enemy trenches, and none of our attempts had given us any gain of ground which materially altered the situation or appeared to have brought the prospect of final victory any nearer. Our statesmen were therefore sincerely convinced that the barrier in the west was impenetrable alike by us and by the Germans. Though the procession of German troops from east to west had begun in November, and continued steadily throughout the winter and spring, it was not until March that the balance of fighting strength began to turn in the enemy's favour.

Ministers believed that they had in their Executive Council found the means of overcoming the weaknesses which are inherent in a group of allied armies opposed to one foe. They also believed that the whole experience of the war on the Western front had shown them that the Germans would require far greater numerical superiority than they appeared to possess in order to endanger our position. It is, however, not possible to estimate the power of opposing forces merely by counting heads, and Ludendorff had factors in his favour which added materially to his strength in battle. For a long time before he opened the campaign of 1918 with his great attack, there had been little or no fighting on the Eastern front, which became for him a vast rest camp and training centre in which his men could be prepared for work elsewhere. Thus, while our men were engaged in desperate and exhausting fighting, large German forces were quietly preparing for their next effort. The collapse of Russia, and the failure of the 1917 campaign to yield any decisive results, had thrown us on the defensive, and given Ludendorff the opportunity of which he skilfully took full advantage, of playing upon the fears of the Allied Commanders by keeping each of them under threat of attack and throwing his whole weight in his own time against some one portion of the front. Further, although early in March the opposing forces in the west were about equal, Ludendorff had large reserves of trained men still in the east ready to come across. Actually between the beginning of March and the end of May, when his strength was at its highest, his forces were increased by sixteen divisions and a large amount of heavy artillery. Therefore, before he joined issue, Ludendorff had at his disposal a large reinforcement ready to be thrown into the battle, while the only corresponding reserve which the Allies possessed consisted in such troops as we could bring from the east and the Americans from the United States. None of these could be ready until long after the German Commander had his men on the spot.

This, then, is the brief history of the preparation for attack and defence. By the middle of February it had become apparent that the Germans were pushing forward the preparations for a great offensive with all possible energy, and there were already indications that they intended to attack the front held by our 5th and 3rd Armies. Ludendorff was, however, much too skilful to expose his hand entirely, and it was by no means certain that the attack on our right might not be a preliminary to a greater blow against our line further north and against the French to the south. The northern portion of our front covered the approaches to Calais and Boulogne ports, which were of vital importance to us, while our front line was little more than forty miles distant from Calais. Therefore in the north every yard of ground was of value to us, and if the Germans had broken through there to a depth of even twenty miles, we should have been in dire straits. In the south we had more elbow room, for our front between St Quentin and the Oise was over ninety miles from the coast, and could, in case of emergency, be more quickly reinforced by the French than could our line in Flanders. Sir Douglas Haig therefore felt bound to keep the greater part of such reserves as he had at his disposal north of the Somme. General Gough's 5th Army held the southernmost portion of our line from our point of junction with the French on the Oise not far from La Fere to Gauzeaucourt, south-west of Cambrai, a distance of about forty-two miles. On this front General Gough had fourteen divisions and three cavalry divisions, eleven of his divisions being in the line and the remainder in reserve, while each of his divisions in the line held on an average 6,750 yards of front. General Byng's 3rd Army on General Gough's left held a front of about twenty-seven miles with fifteen divisions, with eight in line and seven in reserve, the average length of front held by each division in the line being about 4,700 yards. General Gough's liabilities, therefore, were very considerably greater than General Byng's, and the reserves of the 5th Army were much weaker than those of the 3rd, while, as it turned out, the 5th Army had to bear by far the greater weight of the German attack.

Ludendorff's scheme was to drive in the British right and to separate us from the French Army. Throughout the winter he had been planning, with all the method and care of a trained German mind, how to achieve this object, and to solve the problem of breaking through the trench barrier, a problem to which all the generals on the west, on both sides, had hitherto found no answer. All were by this time agreed that the method of attack by means of a great and protracted bombardment, followed by an infantry assault, was a failure; the immense and lengthy preparation which this form of battle involved made surprise impossible, the defender's reserves invariably came up in time, and the battle ended in a slogging match, in which the assailant gained little return for very heavy losses. Ludendorff probably realised that it would be out of the question to keep all his preparations for attack secret. No camouflage could altogether conceal from our air observers that something was afoot. But he conceived that it would be possible to deceive us as to the weight of the blow which he meant to deliver, and to achieve a large measure of surprise by keeping a great part of his artillery and the bulk of his attacking divisions at a distance from the battlefield until the last possible moment. This method had the double advantage of keeping us in uncertainty both as to the weight of the attack and as to whether it would be made in more than one place, for in the weeks preceding the battle he placed his reserves so that they could be moved as readily against our northern front, or even against the French front, as against our right. He decided then to have no long preliminary bombardment, which would have given us a definite indication of his plans, and, as we had found to our cost, would have so destroyed the surface of the ground and broken up the roads and the railways as to make it a matter of great difficulty to get the reserves forward when they were needed. He also decided to bring up his attacking divisions on the eve of the battle by train and by march under cover of darkness. These were the features in which his attack differed most from other attacks which had been tried in the West. In the details of its execution there was also much that was new. Ludendorff studied very carefully all the previous battles fought in the West, and he found that opportunities had often been missed because parts of the attacking line had been checked at strong points held resolutely by the defenders and the remainder had waited until the whole would go forward together. He therefore determined that as a principle he would follow up success wherever it was won, driving in at such weak points as he discovered, and that none of his men who could get forward were to hold because their comrades elsewhere had stopped. In order to develop this method of attack to the utmost, he devoted the winter to selecting from his army the best and bravest of his soldiers and putting them through a special form of training. These men, whom he called storm troops, were to lead his attacks, with orders to press forward as far and as fast as possible, while they were given the assurance that where they were successful they would be immediately supported by the reserve.

By 19 March Sir Douglas Haig's Intelligence Department had discovered that the German preparations for attack on the 3rd and 5th Armies were nearly complete, and it was anticipated that the battle would begin on 20 or 21 March. The attack actually opened shortly before 5 am on the 21st with a bombardment of the greatest intensity against the whole front held by those Armies, while in order to keep us in doubt till the last possible moment as to their intentions, the Germans simultaneously bombarded parts of our northern line, and the French fronts on either side of Rheims. For about five hours a perfect hurricane of shell was hurled against General Gough's and General Byng's defences, and it has been stated by German officers that the rate of fire was so rapid that many of their guns became red hot. Then shortly before 10 am the German infantry advanced. This five-hour bombardment may be compared to our artillery preparation for the first battle of the Somme, which lasted seven days. The battle had not been long in progress before it became clear that Ludendorff was throwing his whole weight against our right, and therefore, though Sir Douglas Haig had guessed accurately both the time and the place at which the attack would be made, Ludendorff had gained a definite advantage in getting all his reserves in motion first. This much was due to his skill, but he was also greatly favoured by fortune. The early months of 1918 had been phenomenally dry, but 19 March had been a day of drizzle sufficient to damp the surface of the hard ground. On the 20th the sky had cleared, and by the following morning the sun had drawn up a dense blanket of fog which enveloped the whole battlefield, with the result that in few places was it possible to see more than fifty yards. We have often during the war created artificial fogs, and screened ourselves successfully from the enemy's deadly machine guns by means of smoke clouds, the preparation of which has cost us much time and trouble. Ludendroff was provided by nature with a more effective screen than we were ever able to produce. Our system of defence depended greatly upon the cross fire of guns and of machine guns, and upon a series of elaborate strong posts so placed that each could help its neighbour with its fire. The fog completely neutralised these preparations, for neither gunners, machine gunners, nor the garrisons of posts could see either the enemy at whom they were to fire or the neighbours with whom they were to co-operate. The German gunners were not so hampered, for their aeroplane observers had noted down the exact sites of our defences, which had been photographed and marked upon the enemy's maps. By deluging the whole area in which our work lay with shells, the Germans were certain of hitting their target, while our artillery, deprived by the fog of help from the air, could only guess vaguely the position of the advancing foe. Nor was the fog the only stroke of fortune which favoured the Germans. General Gough's front ran roughly north and south till it reached the River Oise, and then bent back south-eastwards along the northern bank of that river. In this portion of its course the Oise river runs through a wide and normally marshy valley, such as no great attacking force could cross in an ordinary spring. It had therefore not been expected that the German attack would include this sector, which was lightly held. In fact, one of the arguments which the French put forward in order to induce us to extend our front so far south, was that no large number of troops would be required to defend the Oise, where our line would be naturally so strong as to be impervious to attack. The Oise line had always been regarded by them as a quiet sector. Being very short of troops, General Gough had decided to hold this, apparently the least vulnerable part of his front, with a series of posts, and not to have a continuous line of defence. The dry weather, however, enabled the Germans to cross the marshes without difficulty, while the fog allowed them to penetrate between the posts, often un-observed. The result of this was that the enemy were able to get behind our defences further north and cut off the defenders.

It is not my purpose to describe the struggle in detail. My object is to make clear the causes which led to the defeat of the 5th Army, and to show that they were beyond the control of the brave men of whom that army was composed. From the first day of the battle Ludendorff flung sixty-four divisions against the 3rd and 5th Armies; of these sixty-four, at least forty attacked the fourteen divisions and three cavalry divisions of General Gough's 5th Army, while the remaining twenty-four fell upon General Byng's fifteen divisions. It is therefore in no way surprising that the 5th Army was over-whelmed, but the news that it had been overwhelmed came as a rude shock to the public at home, unaware of the facts. It seemed inconceivable that the Germans should have broken so quickly through elaborate defences, manned by British troops, when we had, despite lavish supplies of guns and munitions and the in-comparable valour of our men, only been able, by continuous effort and at an appalling cost, to achieve much smaller results. Wild stories were flying about of the breakdown of the 5th Army, and it was whispered in the drawing-rooms of London that the men had not fought as they ought to have fought. In the confusion and uncertainty of retreat the true facts could not be discovered and made known, with the result that for long imputations rested upon the 5th Army which were wholly contrary to the truth. Eager to find some silver lining to the cloud, both ministers and public fastened upon the splendid defence of the 3rd Army, and contrasted it with General Gough's apparent collapse. I have no desire to minimise in any way the splendour of the achievements of General Byng's men, but I trust that I have made it clear that the burden which General Gough's troops had to bear was incomparably the greater. In the first stage of the battle very nearly twice as many German divisions attacked General Gough as fell upon General Byng. Each of General Gough's divisions had on the average to hold nearly 50% more front than had General Byng, while the 3rd Army reserves were nearly twice as strong as those of the 5th, yet at the end of the first day of the battle General Gough's left had given less ground than some of General Byng's divisions further north had been compelled to yield. The German storm troops, true to Ludendorff's plan of attack, pressed forward where they found a gap or a weak spot in our defence, but did not attempt to assault the many works, of which the garrisons held out resolutely until ammunition was exhausted. The stream of grey coats trickling through the cracks in the dam spread out sideways and, uniting behind our lines, created a flood which isolated and cut off from all support the brave defenders. Pounded by shell and surrounded by an enemy whom they could not see, these splendid troops fought on long after the crest of the invading wave had swept beyond them. Even more glorious, because their task was more difficult, was the conduct of those troops who escaped the enemy's first onset. Whole divisions endured losses such as never, with perhaps the exception of the famous Seventh Division in the first battle of Ypres, had been suffered by troops in war, and fought on in the front line when reduced to little more than the strength of battalions. We were shocked at the tale of our losses in the battle of Passchendaele, but in three weeks of terrible struggle which began on 21 March, 1918, our casualties were greater than they were in three months of fighting in Flanders of the previous autumn. Hundreds of guns and tanks, thousands of machine guns and vast quantities of military stores, fell into the enemy's hands, yet our weakened line, subjected to an all but intolerable strain, and bent back almost to snapping-point, never broke, and it fell to the gallant remnants of the 5th Army to bar the direct road to Amiens, the immediate goal of Ludendorff's ambition. The retreat of the Old Army is already an epic in our annals; the retreat of the New Army should be to us an equal source of pride, for the odds against which they struggled were greater, the fighting was more incessant, more intense, and more terrible, the stakes at issue no less tremendous. When the worst of the first crisis was past, help came. Real unity of command was established, drafts were hurried out from home, reinforcements were shipped to France from the East. With this aid the New Army made a recovery more complete and more triumphant than that of the Old Army, but that recovery would have been impossible but for the valour in adversity of the Fifth Army.

Published in The European War, July, 1918

Appendices

Appendix I

MINUTES OF THE WAR CABINET MEETING OF 11.30 AM,

7 MAY, 1918

Present:

THE PRIME MINISTER (in the Chair)

The Right Hon the EARL CURZON OF KEDLESTON, KG, GCSI, GCIE

The Right Hon G. N. BARNES, MP

The Right Hon A. BONAR LAW, MP

Lieutenant-General the Right Hon J. C. SMUTS, KC

The Right Hon AUSTEN CHAMBERLAIN, MP

The following were also present:

The Right Hon the VISCOUNT MILNER, GCB, GCMG Secretary of State
for War

General Sir H. H. WILSON, KCB, DSO, Chief of the Imperial General
Staff

Lieutenant-General SIR C. F. N. MACREADY, GCMG, KCB Adjutant-
General to the Forces (for Minute 5)

The Right Hon A. J. BALFOUR, OM, MP, Secretary of State for Foreign
Affairs

Lieutenant-Colonel SIR M. P. A. HANKEY, KCB, *Secretary*

Captain L. F. BURGIS, *Assistant Secretary*

Lieutenant-Colonel LESLIE WILSON, CMG, DSO, MP *Assistant Secretary*

The Prime Minister pointed out that General Maurice directly
challenged three statements which had been made in the House of
Commons: one made by the Chancellor of the Exchequer, and two
by himself.

The first of these statements challenged was one made by Mr
Bonar Law on 23 April, to the effect that the question of the
extension of the line, carried out before the battle commenced on
21 March, was not dealt with at all by the Supreme War Council.

223

It was pointed out that the extension of the line to Barisis had been arranged, before the meeting of the Supreme War Council, between Field-Marshal Haig and General Pétain, and in this connection the following extract from a statement made by Sir Douglas Haig at the Supreme War Council meeting on 2 February was read:

Lastly, during the recent battle in Flanders, he had, at General Pétain's request, agreed to, and had now extended the front first to the Oise and afterwards to Barisis ... etc. (I.C. –42).

The extension of the line, discussed at the Supreme War Council, had been a further extension recommended by the Permanent Military Representatives and this further extension had never been carried out, and had not been alluded to in Parliament on the occasion of Mr Bonar Law's statement. The statement challenged by General Maurice had referred solely to the accomplished extension to Barisis, and had been perfectly correct.

With regard to the second statement, namely, that the army in France was considerably stronger on 1 January, 1918, than on 1 January, 1917, which was stated by General Maurice to be incorrect, Mr Lloyd George said the actual figures were quoted by him from an official War Office document, and were that on 1 January, 1917, the total ration strength of the British armies in France was 1,594,000; whilst on 1 January, 1918, the total ration strength was 1,970,000, which showed a total increase of 376,000 men. It might be argued that there had been during this period a large increase in the number of labour units, but the total strength of such labour units on 1 January, 1918, was 142,000, whilst approximately the strength of these units on 1 January, 1917, was probably 42,000. Consequently, even taking all the labour units out of consideration, the total ration strength of the British army in France at the beginning of 1918 was 276,000 stronger than it was in the beginning of 1917. Labour units, however, might fairly be included in the strength of the army, and at present we were greatly in need of further labour to increase our defensive strength.

With regard to the third statement of General Maurice, in which the Prime Minister has been challenged as regards the correctness of his assertion that there was only one white division in Mesopotamia, and in Palestine only three white divisions, Mr Lloyd George pointed out that he believed that he was entirely correct in stating there was only one white division in Mesopotamia, and that his statement as regards the three white divisions in Egypt had been made on the authority of the report of the Chief of the Imperial General Staff when the War Cabinet was considering the possibility of bringing reinforcements from Palestine to meet the emergency on the Western Front (War Cabinet 371, Minute 5).

It was pointed out that General Maurice had been present when this statement was made.

Mr Lloyd George said that when the Chief of the Imperial General Staff had stated that there were only three British divisions in Egypt, he had asked further questions of General Wilson, and had been told that the other divisions in Egypt were mixed divisions.

Considerable discussion ensued as to the meaning of the charges which General Maurice brought forward in saying that the Prime Minister was incorrect with regard to the number of the British Forces in France on 1 January, 1918, and with regard to his statement that what the Prime Minister said implied that Sir Douglas Haig's fighting strength on the eve of the great battle which began on 21 March had not been diminished.

Lord Milner was of opinion that General Maurice meant that between 1 January, 1918, and the beginning of the battle, a considerable reduction had taken place in the number of the battalions employed, all British divisions having been reduced from 12 to 9 battalions in strength, and that, consequently, the actual front line had been weakened to that extent.

It was pointed out that, if this was General Maurice's contention, he had only taken into account rifle strength, and had paid no regard to the very large increase in artillery, flying corps, tanks, trench mortars, and machine-guns, which had undoubtedly been increased at the expense of the infantry, and should certainly have been included in the fighting strength of the army.

Mr Lloyd George said that one of the most serious considerations was that General Maurice had attended the War Cabinet for the two days following the date of his speech in the House of Commons (9 April), and had never said a word either at the Cabinet or to him privately, challenging the accuracy of the figures which he had given. If General Maurice had considered it was not his duty to do so in the Cabinet, it was at any rate his duty to make representations to the Chief of the Imperial General Staff on this matter.

The Chief of the Imperial General Staff said that he had heard nothing from General Maurice until 30 April, after he had left the post of Director of Military Operations, when he received a letter from him on this subject.

The Prime Minister also pointed out that, while General Maurice might have some answer to the charge, if it could be shown that the reduction of the men in the infantry battalions had not been compensated for by addition to other fighting units, yet this was a matter the responsibility for which did not rest upon the War Cabinet, but on the military authorities, on whom lay the duty of the distribution of our fighting men.

The Chancellor of the Exchequer (A. Bonar Law) stated that this was not an isolated attack on the Government. In the *Morning Post* nearly every day articles had appeared with reference to the strength of our forces in France, more particularly with reference to the reduction in the number of battalions.

Mr Lloyd George informed the War Cabinet that he had received a question which would be put by private notice that afternoon by Mr Asquith. A general discussion ensued as to the reply which should be made and the action which the Government should take in this matter.

Mr Bonar Law said that he held very strong views on this question. The veracity of himself and the Prime Minister had been challenged. He could not agree that this matter could be met only by making statements in the House of Commons, but that, in his opinion, it was essential that a Judicial Enquiry should be held, as this letter reflected on his personal honour.

With reference to the position of General Maurice, the Adjutant-General said that this officer had contravened the Army Act and the Official Secrets Act, both of which were military offences, which could be dealt with under the Army Act without an enquiry being made as to the truth or otherwise of the statements. It would be possible to hold a Court of Enquiry, and if civilians were involved this Court could be held under the Barrett Act; but any Court of Enquiry must necessarily involve obtaining evidence from the French dealing with matters of much secrecy and confidential nature, and Sir Nevil Macready agreed with General Smuts that it would be practically impossible to make public a report of such proceedings.

It would be possible to deal with General Maurice from a purely disciplinary point of view, either by putting him on half-pay or

226

retired pay, or by trying him by court martial, and Lord Milner very strongly urged that whatever course was taken the question of disciplinary action should be kept quite distinct from any other action which the Government might contemplate.

The Adjutant-General stated that he had already written to General Maurice asking him in the usual Service manner for his reasons for having written the letter contrary to regulations.

With regard to the course proposed by Mr Bonar Law as to a Judicial Enquiry being held, the Secretary of State for Foreign Affairs (Arthur Balfour) expressed himself very strongly against any such proposal. He said he was of opinion that the proper course to pursue was for a statement to be made in the House of Commons to the effect that the Ministers adhered to the statements which they had made, bringing forward, if necessary, sufficient facts to prove them, or, if this was not considered sufficient, to hold a Secret Sessions, when the whole subject could be debated.

Mr Bonar Law said that he would be unable to pursue that course, as the charges made against the two Ministers were that they had made misstatements, and if their defence was only to be made in the House of Commons, when General Maurice, who had made the charges, could not be present, it would be considered that an *ex parte* statement only had been made.

It was generally agreed that, whatever course was followed, it would be absolutely necessary to limit the scope of the enquiry to the charges of inaccuracy made in General Maurice's letter, and that it would be most inadvisable to open the door to an enquiry into the many other questions which had been so constantly raised in the Press of late.

Strong objections were taken to any proposal that this question, should go before a Committee of the House of Commons, which was not in any way a judicial tribunal, and equally strong objections were taken to holding a Court of Enquiry under the Army Act, at which two Ministers of the Crown would have to attend if the statements challenged by General Maurice were to be fully examined before such a Court.

The War Cabinet decided:

1. That the Army Council should deal with the military offences which had been committed by Major-General Sir Frederick Maurice.

2. That the Chancellor of the Exchequer, in replying to the

question which was to be put by Mr Asquith in the House of Commons that afternoon, should state that General Maurice's letter raised two questions: one involving military discipline, and the other the veracity of Ministerial statements. The first question would be dealt with by the Army Council in the ordinary way, and, with regard to the second, the Government proposed to ask two of His Majesty's Judges to act as a Court of Honour to enquire into the charge of misstatements alleged to have been made by Ministers. 3. That the Court of Honour, composed as above, should assemble at the earliest possible date and be asked to render a report, if possible within a week.

Appendix II

Mr ASQUITH (by Private Notice) asked the Leader of the House whether the attention of the Government has been called to a letter in the Press from Major-General Maurice, lately Director of Military Operations, in which the correctness is impugned of several statements of fact made by Ministers to this House and what steps the Government propose to take to enable the House to examine these allegations?

Mr BONAR LAW: General Maurice's letter raises two questions—the question of military discipline involved in the writing of such a letter, and the question of the veracity of Ministerial statements.

As regards the first question, that is being dealt with by the Army Council in the ordinary way.

As regards the second question, though it must be obvious to the House that government could not be carried on if an inquiry into the conduct of Ministers should be considered necessary whenever their action is challenged by a servant of the Government who has occupied a position of the highest confidence, yet, inasmuch as these allegations affect the honour of Ministers, the Government propose to invite two of His Majesty's judges to act as a court of honour, to inquire into the charge of misstatements alleged to have been made by Ministers, and to report as quickly as possible.

Mr G. LAMBERT: As this is a question affecting the House of Commons, would not the right hon Gentleman substitute for the two judges, three distinguished Members of the House of Commons, to verify these charges against Ministers?

Mr BONAR LAW: The Government has considered the best method of doing what we consider necessary, and I certainly consider it necessary to satisfy the House that we have not wilfully made misleading statements. In our opinion, that can best be done by the course which I have suggested. I would remind the House that, in order to examine this question, the most secret documents have to be gone into, and it would obviously be a very difficult, and, I think, a very unsuitable tribunal to appoint a Select Committee of the House for that purpose.

Mr ASQUITH: The right Hon Gentleman suggests that this matter should be submitted to two judges. Does he propose to introduce a Bill to enable the judges to take evidence upon oath?

Mr BONAR LAW: We did not consider that necessary, because I am sure everybody involved will be only too ready to place all the information at the disposal of the judges, and, if they are not given anything they want, they will certainly let us know that is so.

Mr ASQUITH: Will the Government bring forward a Motion upon which the matter can be discussed?

Mr BONAR LAW: If my right hon Friend desires that it should be discussed, of course we shall give him an opportunity. Perhaps he might think better to do so after the judges have reported.

Sir E. CARSON: Will the proceedings before His Majesty's judges be public, or held in private, and can Cabinet and ex-Cabinet Ministers be examined upon the subject?

Mr BONAR LAW: It must, I should think, obviously be held in private, for the reason I have given—that it involves examination of the most secret documents. As to who will be examined, I should have thought, if the House has confidence that the judges will properly perform their duty, they should be the best judges as to whom they desire to examine.

Sir E. CARSON: What I desire to ask is, will Cabinet or ex-Cabinet Ministers be allowed to state before the judges what transpired in the Cabinet?

Mr BONAR LAW: I should have thought that was a matter to be decided by the judges themselves, but I cannot for a moment believe that any judge would refuse to take the evidence of any Cabinet or ex-Cabinet Minister who desired to give it.

Admiral of the Fleet Sir H. MEUX: Is the right hon Gentleman aware that the answers given by him will be received with the greatest dissatisfaction by the whole of the Army and Navy? They are sick to death of the way things are going on in the House of Commons.

Mr SPEAKER: I thought the hon and gallant Gentleman rose to ask a question, and not to deliver a Hyde Park oration.

Sir E. CARSON: What I desire to ask my right hon Friend is how will a Cabinet or an Ex-Cabinet Minister be able, unless he be absolved from the position of secrecy which he is bound to observe, without an Act of Parliament to give his testimony before the two judges.

Mr BONAR LAW: There really ought not to be any feeling in the House that we desire to burke examination of this question, and I think the fact that we propose to submit it to two judges—whom I shall be glad to allow my right hon Friend (Mr Asquith) to select if he desire it—is a proof of that. As to the point raised by my right hon Friend (Sir E. Carson), I do not know what steps are necessary, but any steps which are possible will gladly be taken by the Government in that direction.

Mr ASQUITH: It must be clear to my right hon Friend that this is a matter which we ought to have the opportunity of discussing on some form of Motion. Will he give us a day for the purpose?

Mr BONAR LAW: Certainly, should my right hon Friend desire it. Am I to understand that he would prefer that we should not proceed with setting up our Court until that discussion has taken place?

Mr ASQUITH: Certainly!

Mr PRINGLE: Could the right hon Gentleman say that all disciplinary proceedings against General Maurice will be suspended, pending any finding of the Court?

Mr BONAR LAW: I shall certainly say nothing of the kind. Even if every statement were true, discipline in the Army would be impossible if such letters were permitted to be published.

Appendix III

Present:

THE PRIME MINISTER (in the Chair)

The Right Hon the EARL CURZON OF KEDLESTON, KG, GCSI, GCIE

The Right Hon A. BONAR LAW, MP

The Right Hon G. N. BARNES, MP

Lieutenant-General the Right Hon J. C. SMUTS, KC

The Right Hon AUSTEN CHAMBERLAIN, MP

The following were also present:

The Right Hon A. J. BALFOUR, OM, MP, Secretary of State for Foreign
Affairs

The Right Hon the VISCOUNT MILNER, GCB, GCMG, Secretary of
State for War

General SIR H. H. WILSON, KCB, DSO, Chief of the Imperial General
Staff (for Minutes 1 to 7)

The Right Hon W. LONG, MP, Secretary of State for the Colonies

Lieutenant-Colonel SIR M. P. A. HANKEY, KCB, *Secretary*

Paymaster-in-Chief P. H. ROW, RN, *Assistant Secretary*

Mr THOMAS JONES, *Assistant Secretary*

With reference to War Cabinet 406, Minute 5, the Prime Minister
described how, in Parliament on the previous day, the Opposition
had not fallen in very readily with the suggestion of a Judicial
Enquiry, and had put down a motion for a Select Committee. In
his view, a Select Committee would be perfectly useless. It would
be constituted on Party lines, there would merely be a Party wrangle,
and no judicial investigation. This raised the question as to whether
it would not be better to-morrow to state the facts. He understood
that this was the general view of the Government's supporters in the

House of Commons. There was a good deal to be said for it. Even if a Judicial Enquiry were set up, the controversy would not be closed. There was an undoubted desire in all parts of the House of Commons to know the facts. General Maurice, the Prime Minister continued, had made three accusations of false statements made by the Leader of the House and himself. He had examined the matter in some detail, and the least satisfactory of the three issues raised, from the Government's point of view, related to the divisions in Palestine. There now seemed some doubt as to whether on 9 April, when he made his statement, there had not been five British divisions instead of three, as he had stated. The point was not quite clear yet, and was being investigated by the War Office. He believed that one of the divisions had started to leave on 5 April for France, and that another division had been under orders. There had also been in progress a process of the gradual incorporation of Indian divisions in the British divisions. To-day this had been carried so far that he was informed there was only one wholly British division in Palestine. How far this process of dilution had been carried on 9 April, he had not yet been able to ascertain. Whether the facts he had stated had been correct or not, however, they had been made in good faith, and, as he had pointed out on the previous day, the War Cabinet had been informed by the Chief of the Imperial General Staff on 23 March, that there were three British divisions in Egypt; General Maurice had been present; a draft of the Minute had been sent him for correction and he had never returned it. Consequently, if he (the Prime Minister) had made a mistake, it had been made on good authority and in good faith.

Lord Milner said it was a terrible thing to have to announce publicly, so that it would reach the Germans, what our policy was in regard to the divisions in Palestine. This information would be very valuable to them.

The Prime Minister pointed out that this was the danger of statements and accusations made by persons with knowledge of secret matters.

In regard to General Maurice's second accusation, relating to the comparison of the strength of the army on 1 January, 1918, and 1 January, 1917, the Prime Minister stated that he had used the figures in the War Office statistical abstract. General Maurice's contention, however, had not been that the statement was inaccurate, but that it implied that Sir Douglas Haig's fighting strength on the eve of the great battle which began on 21 March, had not been diminished. The Prime Minister informed the War Cabinet that on 18 April, Sir Godfrey Baring had put a question to Mr Macpherson as to whether the fighting strength on 1 January, 1918, was or was not greater than on 1 January, 1917, and Mr Macpherson had replied that the fighting strength was greater on 1 January, 1918. Mr Macpherson's reply had been based on figures supplied by the Director of Military Operations' Department, in fact by General Maurice's own Department. The figures had been as follows:

	Combatant Strength in France	Ration Strength in France
1 January, 1917	1,253,000	1,530,000
1 January, 1918	1,298,000	1,851,000

Of course he could not give the actual figures in Parliament, but this material enabled him effectually to dispose of General Maurice's second contention.

In reply to a question as to why he had quoted the figures for 1 January instead of 1 March, 1918, the Prime Minister said it had been merely to give the same date in succeeding years. As a matter of fact, the figures for March were more favourable than for January, since the fighting strength had increased by 34,000, and the labour strength had been somewhat reduced, owing to the comb-out of labour battalions.

In regard to General Maurice's first point, namely, as to whether the extension of the line as carried out was ever discussed at Versailles, the Prime Minister drew attention to the following statement in General Maurice's letter:

I was at Versailles when the question was decided by the Supreme War Council, to whom it had been referred.

The implication was that General Maurice had been present at the discussion, and several of those present had stated that they had understood it in this sense. As a matter of fact, the Prime Minister said, General Maurice was in the building, but the record showed that he was not in the room when the discussion took place. The extension of the line discussed at Versailles dealt with the French demand that the British line should be extended to Berry-au-Bac, and the recommendations of the Military Representatives that it should extend to the River Ailette, but not with the extension to Barisis, which had already been settled between Field-Marshal Haig and General Pétain. In fact, in the course of the Conference Field-Marshal Haig had informed the Supreme War Council:

That during the recent battle in Flanders he had, at General Pétain's request, agreed to and had now extended the front, first to the Oise and afterwards to Barisis.

The questions and answers in Parliament on 23 April had all referred to the Barisis extension, and not to the further extension discussed by the Supreme War Council, which, in fact, had never been carried out.

The main point on which the Prime Minister wished to consult his colleagues was as to whether he should limit his speech on the following day to answer General Maurice's specific accusations, or whether he should extend it so as to cover the whole history of the extension of the British line.

In favour of the first proposal, it was pointed out that there were great advantages in limiting the statement, in order that fewer persons might become involved; the statement on wider grounds could not be made without involving Field-Marshal Haig and General Robertson.

Mr Balfour said that Mr Asquith would speak first, and he undoubtedly would cover the wide field, so that the Prime Minister should be prepared in that sense.

Mr Bonar Law pointed out that the first paragraph of General Maurice's letter really raised the wider issue. The full summary of the circumstances, which had been circulated by the Secretary, appeared to him to dispose of any suggestion that the Government had acted improperly in the matter.

In the course of the discussion it was generally agreed that the Government had in fact a complete answer to their critics, but that the statement of the Parliamentary answer was difficult, owing to the obligation not to give information to the enemy.

General Smuts laid great stress on this aspect of the question. In replying to General Maurice's second charge, it was, he said, essential not to give figures. Even to give the difference between the numbers in January, 1918, and the numbers in January, 1917, would assist the enemy. It was also most objectionable to give particulars of the numbers of British divisions in Palestine and

Mesopotamia, or to mention the process of diluting them with Indian battalions.

Lord Curzon suggested that on these points a reply might be made that the Prime Minister would have been quite willing to submit his evidence to an Enquiry by Judges if that course had commended itself to the House of Commons, but that, as this had been rejected, he could not take the responsibility of stating openly in Parliament information which would be of value to the enemy.

The Secretary of State for the Colonies (Walter Long) urged that no hint should be said which would seem to impugn the actions of Field-Marshal Sir D. Haig, General Robertson, or other soldiers, as this would only prolong and embitter the controversy.

Great stress was laid on the importance of making the statement in a form which would give satisfaction to Field-Marshal Sir Douglas Haig. It must be made quite clear that Field-Marshal Haig had not wished to take over any additional portion of the line. Undoubtedly Field-Marshal Haig had felt that he was under an obligation to take over some of the line, owing to the decision of the Boulogne Conference on 25 September, 1917, and to the urgent pressure of the French Government and French military authorities, and he had very properly been influenced in his decision by the opinions thus expressed. While this was not denied, it was pointed out that it was clear, in the Secretary's summary, that after 25 September the War Cabinet had at no time put any pressure whatsoever upon Field-Marshal Haig in the matter; that they had resisted all attempts on the part of the French Government to induce them to put such pressure; and that the amount of and precise time for the extension had always been left entirely to Field-Marshal Haig and General Pétain.

Attention was also drawn to the interpretation that General Robertson had placed on the Boulogne Conference, namely, that the matter could not be regarded as decided, and that Field-Marshal Haig had admitted that this presented the conclusion arrived at on 25 September in a different light from the official record.

The Prime Minister invited Lord Milner and Mr Chamberlain to meet him in the afternoon to consider more in detail the character of the statement which he should make in the House of Commons. He hoped by that time to have prepared a rough draft.

Biography

Born January 19, 1871		MAURICE, Major General Sir Frederick, K.C.M.G., C.B.
		Educated at St Paul's School
	1892	Gazetted to Derbyshire Regiment (later the Sherwood Foresters)
	1897–8	Served in Tirah. Medal, 2 clasps
	1899	Captain
		Married Helen Marsh
	1899–1900	Special Service Officer in South African War, despatches, Queen's Medal, 5 clasps
	1900	Brevet Major
	1902	Entered Staff College
		G.S.O.2 at War Office
	1911	Major
	1913	Instructor at Staff College, when Sir William Robertson was Commandant
		Lt Colonel
1914–1918	1914	G.S.O.2 and soon G.S.O.1 in France on Staff of 3rd Division (despatches 7 times)
	1915	Brevet Colonel
	December 1915	Sir W. Robertson selected him to be head of Director of Military Operations, War Office Operations Branch, as Brigadier General, General Staff
	1916	Major General
	May 1918	Retired from Army and became military correspondent for *The Daily Chronicle*
	1920	Helped to found the British Legion
		First and only General Manager of the

237

	Officers' Association at the invitation of Earl Haig
1922–1933	Principal of the Working Men's College
1926	Hon. LL.D. at Cambridge—became a member of Trinity College
1927	Professor of Military Studies, London University
1928	D. Litt of London University
	Trustee of Imperial War Museum
	Member of Senate of University of London
	Hon. Treasurer of British Legion
1933–1944	Principal of East London College which in 1934 became, by Royal Charter, Queen Mary College
1932–1947	President of British Legion
1935–1941	Colonel, The Sherwood Foresters
1944	Honorary Fellow of King's College, Cambridge
1946	Fellow and Governor of Queen Mary College
December 1948	Last visit to London, to Queen Mary College on Charter Day (Prime Minister Clement Attlee presented diplomas)
	Governor of St Paul's School
	Chairman of Routledge
	Chairman of Council of Queen's College, Harley Street
19 May, 1951	Died at Cambridge

Publications

1905	Russo-Turkish War 1877–78
1913	Sir Frederick Maurice, A Record and Essays
1918	Forty Days in 1914
	The Last Four Months
1924	Life of Lord Wolseley (with Sir George Arthur)
1925	Robert E. Lee, the Soldier
1926	Governments and War
1927	An Aide-de-Camp of Lee
1928	The Life of General Lord Rawlinson of Trent
1929	British Strategy

238

1931	The 16th Foot
1934	History of the Scots Guards
1937	Life of Lord Haldane Volume I
1938	Life of Lord Haldane Volume II
	The Armistices 1918 and 1943
1942	Lessons of Allied Military Cooperation
1945	The Adventures of Edward Wogan

Contributor to Cambridge Modern History

Decorations

1914–1918	C.B., K.C.M.G.
	Commander of the Legion of Honour
	Croix de Guerre
	Order of the Crown of Belgium
	1st Class order of St Stanislaus of Russia

Index

Figures in italics refer to the page on which a map can be found.